"Read it again! The second edition improves a classic. Two comparable works for me personally, J. D. Salinger's epic *A Catcher in The Rye* and Stephen King's *Stand By Me*."
~ **Columbia Pictures President, Peter S. Sealey**

THE LONG STEM IS IN THE LOBBY

From Bad Times to Good Times – How I found My Way

By Jerome Mark Antil

Books by
Jerome Mark Antil

Handbook for Weekend Dads—and anytime grandparents
The Pompey Hollow Book Club - AUDIO
The Book of Charlie - AUDIO
The Long Stem is in The Lobby—*From Bad Times to Good Times – How I Found My Way*
Mary Crane – *A Séance with Sherlock*
Return to Tiffany's
Hemingway, Three Angels, and Me
One More Last Dance
Mamma's Moon
Tall Jerry in The Delphi Falls Trilogy - Kindle
Book 1 – Tall Jerry and Summer of Shadows Bodies and Bridges
Book 2 – Tall Jerry and the Sideshow Pickpocket
Book 3 – Tall Jerry and Heaven Sends for Hemingway
The Bayou Moon – a Duet Novel
The Mysteries of Pompey Hollow

THE LONG STEM IS IN THE LOBBY

From Bad Times to Good Times – How I Found My Way

JEROME MARK ANTIL

LITTLE YORK BOOKS

ISBN 978-0-9847187-5-7 Paperback
ISBN 978-1-7353076-1-9 Hardcover

For Mr. V.

Chapter 1

It was snowing the first time she mentioned it. We were slow dancing to *Tears On My Pillow* when she looked into my eyes and told me she was thinking about going into the convent after she graduated from high school. The eleven months to follow were anxious for me, to say the least; we'd talk about being together forever, all while kissing passionately in complete denial. My first real love did me in, truth be told. I was a kid. It was 1959 now, a sweltering summer in Cincinnati, despair gnawing on my gut like a sewer rat. God and I were about to come to blows.

The aches echoed back to the Friday night we first met. It was the beginning of my Freshman year's fall semester at college. My family had moved four times in three states my senior year of high school. When I stepped off a bus in Cincinnati, I was looking forward to four years in the same place. I was a nervous six-foot-ten-inch seventeen-year-old— naïve in matters of the heart and a little insecure being away from home for the first time and with a five-dollar bill that had to last me a week.

She was eighteen, a high school senior, bussed in from across town with a load of Catholic girls, almost like a miracle, for the first weekly dance at our men's Jesuit university. I spotted her eyes sparkling from clear across the room as she walked in the darkened dance hall. It was just as if Donna Reed had come walking out of a movie and into our college dance looking for George Bailey (and I was George Bailey). A narrow, pretty, black velvet headband kept her wavy brunet hair from her face and guided it in soft folds down onto her shoulders. She had inquisitive, twinkling, happy eyes, the smile of a newsstand magazine cover girl.

"C'mon, c'mon," I mumbled to myself, "don't just stand here with your mouth hanging open looking stupid, get over there and ask her for a dance."

One of her smiles up at me was all it took for me to be cooked, and not long after our fourth slow dance we just knew we were about to be grabbing at each other like fool rag dolls and kissing. Complete messes in love and pretty much inseparable we became, for sure contented with it and the feeling it gave us. I would smell her hair in my sleep, her perfumes, powders, and lipsticks in class, on the basketball court, at every turn in my memory. Whether standing on her front stoop, dreaming of a home and white picket fences while her father growled throat clearing hints threateningly from upstairs, or sitting on a park bench waiting for a bus, or just walking and stopping—it was no matter, we'd kiss. Anywhere we found ourselves we'd be kissing, pretending it was Paris. After I got back to my dorm I'd call her, tying up Brockman Hall's only pay phone, when I should have been studying.

We fell in love at first sight in September and here it was, already summer, the summer I was about to lose her to the convent, my longest one ever. The summer I thought I would never get those tastes, those smells, those eyes, that smile out of my memory; never would I get over the emptiness the thought of her leaving me dug in the pit of my stomach.

My college, Xavier University, was the shape of a shallow, wooden salad bowl you'd find at a yard sale—one with a dark, oil-stained crack split right through its middle. The crack: a road named Victory Parkway. On the right side of the parkway, up the sloping hill, looking northeast to the far, V-shaped corner, surrounded by trees, was Dr. Link's white stucco house with Spanish-tile roof. The doc taught business. He rented out rooms. Next to his place, coming this way, was Brockman Hall—a four-story, prison-beige brick dormitory. Freshmen were required to live there. The previous semester I had stayed in room 219 with Gregory Marquis. I wanted to be with her so I lied to my folks about not being able to come home for the summer because of basketball practice. In my impulse I just assumed I could stay at Brockman Hall over the summer, but I was wrong. Proctor Father Dan lived in the dorm year-round and had thrown me a curve. He locked it up tight when the term ended. He didn't want people knocking on his room door, waking him up or interrupting his reading Latin or offering his daily Mass, asking a bunch of damned fool questions about how to get to the armory, or which way was it to downtown Cincinnati and Fountain Square, or did he have any Reds tickets.

I didn't want anyone to get wise to my staying on campus unattended for the summer and maybe calling my mom or dad and telling them, so I didn't bother to knock to get my duffel bag with a change of clothes and underwear, in case asking for my duffel would raise suspicion. Turned out my lack of planning for where I might sleep when college let out rendered me homeless, causing me to have to scrounge for places to lay and sleep nights during the hottest summer on record. I wasn't afraid of grass and trees; I had grown up camping out in the woods. I was an immature six-foot-ten-inch sophomore, only just eighteen, who chose not to go home for the summer; I was deep over my head and in an emotional free-fall.

Back this way was Albers Hall, Edgecliff Hall, and then a modern, tall, glassy science building. Rumor was a Jebbie (Jesuit priest) had discovered the enzymes that ate protein and Proctor and Gamble put them in Tide detergent, to eat grass stains or food stains, which are protein. The campus buzz was that the company had donated the building as a thank-you for the discovery. Then there was Hinkle Hall, a classroom building. At the near end of the right side of the salad bowl was an army green Quonset hut left there since WWII was my guess. It had a halfmoon-shaped tin roof that started on the ground on one side, went up and over the top, and ended down on the ground on the other side. At both ends it had a wooden wall and door with small glass panes. It looked to me like it hadn't been used since it put up soldiers during the war. It had bundled-up cots stacked all through. I slept in it for a while without anyone knowing, just after school let out. It was an oven in the afternoon, and the Cincinnati heat and the hut's hot tin roof kept it a fearful mean through the night in July, so I went outside and lay on the grass with the crickets and croakers. Right across the path was a shanty the university used as a bookstore for students; it looked cooler, but it was locked.

My problem had started about the time basketball players

were told they couldn't go home for Christmas. I played basketball; I was a Xavier Musketeer. We had to double practice most days during the holidays. The varsity needed the freshmen for scrimmage, so I was stuck. My girlfriend stood on her front porch, handing me a Christmas present tied with green crinkly curled-up ribbon. She told me her dad had got her thinking she maybe had "a calling," and now she was giving some serious thought to entering a convent to find out. I'd heard of guys having a calling for the priesthood. A girl having a calling was new to me.

I started looking down into her eyes on that very porch, looking for some sign, for some little confirmation, until I saw in them she was dead serious about considering the convent. Not knowing how much time I had left with her was the reason I decided to lie to my folks about not being able to come home for the summer. I told them I had extra basketball practice. I figured I needed some time and might be able to kiss the whole convent idea out of my girl's mind. I even made up a whopper that I might need my appendix out.

They believed me. No reason not to. I was on a full four-year basketball scholarship, first our family had ever seen—everything paid during the school year, plus seven dollars after every home game and more for away games, what they called meal money. Our freshman team only lost one game all season. We were about the best there was, according to *Sports Illustrated*, and I started. Mom, a mother of eight, was confident my freshman coach—Coach Ruberg—would take good care of her boy in the hospital, so it helped me get away with the lie. Not a word of my yarn was true, at first, but I was so convincing to a doctor examining me that he did eventually remove my appendix at the Good Samaritan Hospital, making that part true. I was doing anything I could dream up to stay close to my girlfriend.

Of all the campus buildings, Albers Hall was the most ivy-covered and college-looking, with its Greek columns and stone carvings, covered walkways and vine-covered brick walls. It had two floors of classrooms and the administrative offices for the university president, Father O'Conner, and for the dean of men,

Father Ratterman. When the basketball season was over, I took a part-time job in the Albers Hall basement, working for a man named Mr. Edward P. VonderHaar, the university's vice president. Mr. V had the calm demeanor of a Cary Grant but with a shorter gray brush cut to his hair. He was also president of the American College Public Relations Association, according to the plaque on his small, windowless corner office wall. It hung next to a picture of Father O'Conner standing with Pope Pius XII, in Rome. The plate on Mr. V's spotless black 1953 Cadillac read XU 1.

It was back about March when I first started working for him part-time. He paid me sixty-five cents an hour for typing the addresses of donors to the university building fund on three-by-five index cards, stuffing envelopes, licking stamps, and mailing invitations to people to give even more money. During work breaks, if he wasn't too busy, I'd sit and listen to his musings about why young men should consider jumping on tramp steamers or cattle boats somewhere and heading off around the world before they grew up and got landlocked. One clumsy morning I dropped a box of paper clips by the door to his office, and they scattered every which way on the linoleum. Down on all fours picking them up, I mumbled and muttered to myself my woes and general disdain, talking and ranting on about how the only girl I ever loved in my whole life was thinking of going in the convent, and now wasn't I the danged fool to go take her to see *The Nun's Story* with Audrey Hepburn, for Pete's sake, that convinced her maybe her daddy was right and she was certain more than ever she had "the true calling" and now I was a twisted knot inside dropping stupid paper clips.

Mr. V, hearing me crawling on the floor grumbling, came close to spitting out his coffee through pursed lips trying to make sense of all he was hearing. He wasn't a snoopy man by nature, but he placed the cup down in the saucer on his credenza and turned his head toward me, swiveling full around in his brown leather chair and swallowing a mouthful of coffee before he choked on it or shot it out through his nose:

"Mrs. Burke! Hold my calls, please!" he shouted. Mr. V

was not one prone to shouting.

"Yes, sir, Mr. VonderHaar!" Mrs. Burke yelled back.

"Pick those up later, Jerry," he said to me. "No time to be wasting on paper clips now."

He sprang up, motioning me toward the doorway with quick flips of his hand, then up the stairs to the main floor of Albers Hall, where he fumbled deep in his pocket for some nickels and bought two bottles of Coca-Cola from the red machine between the bulletin board and the drinking fountain. With the metal bottle opener on the front of the machine he wrenched the caps off each and handed me a bottle. He began pacing a small circle in the hall at first, thinking, arms semi-folded, one hand holding the Coke bottle top against the bottom of his chin, resembling The Thinker's knuckles, propping it up in deep thought as he edged himself into bigger circles and toward the main building entrance and out into a breezeway, walking and now talking to me in a thinking-out-loud, out-of-breath stuttering mumble, just as a coach does in a huddle of a tie game with three seconds to go, all the while trying to introduce me to the concept of "flair." The silver-haired gentleman, in suit and tie, was kind of steering himself through the halls and walkways with a Coke bottle, like it was a periscope. It was a sight.

"Does the girl love you, Jerry."

"I know she does, yes, she loves me."

"Has she expressed why she has decided on the convent over you?"

"It's her dad. He doesn't like me."

"Have you had words?"

"No. That's just it, Mr. V. Her dad thinks I'm a spoiled rich kid – not right for her. Truth is we used to be rich, I guess. We had a big house in upstate New York, but we had to move to a one room apartment in Milwaukee when dad lost all his money. Like a big jerk I never told her dad the truth. I just played something I'm not and let him think I was a rich kid. He didn't think I was right for his daughter."

"A young man in love doesn't need money, Jerry, he needs

6

flair in his dictionary of tools. Look it up, Jerry. Flair is how a person can almost always make another person stop and think. It's the attention-grabber. Done with a proper finesse, flair can leave a very nice, lasting impression on someone, making it most difficult for them not to want to pause and at least consider your message before they forget you. Done well, flair takes a great deal of thought and imagination. It's a primary marketing tool. Flair is that something most ordinary folks wouldn't think of but often wished they had, and they celebrate when you think it up for them, to enjoy and share it with them. Your damsel hasn't entered the convent yet. You have that going for you. This is no time for spilled paper clips. I'm thinking you need some creative flair right now, Jerry."

The faster Mr. V thought, the faster he walked, me following. If he thought any faster, we would have broken into a trot.

He was so convincing, I confessed to him the inclinations I felt I had for it—the flair thing—going all the way back to growing up in the little village of Delphi Falls.

"Mr. V, when I was eight, I thought I was in love with Olivia Dandridge. I saw her three times in *She Wore a Yellow Ribbon*, with John Wayne playing Captain Brittles. It was at a Saturday picture show in a town near where I lived. Why, I thought she was the prettiest girl I'd ever seen, and she wore this yellow ribbon—a mesmerizing yellow ribbon in her hair. Wearing it in those days was supposed to be a signal she liked somebody, see, a particular guy. Well, two of the horse cavalry men both thought it was them and kept throwing up their dukes and fighting over her. I tell ya, I thought it was for me. By the time I got home, I was so in love with Olivia Dandridge I painted my bike with my dad's canary-yellow house-shutter paint that very day. I figured if there ever was a possibility she'd come by the house, she'd see it, don't ya see? Now was that flair, Mr. V, or just being a dumb kid?"

"A wonderful movie. You're a true romantic, Jerry," said Mr. V. He clicked his Coke bottle up against mine in a toast to my childhood chivalry. "That most certainly was flair."

Mr. V paused and turned, looking up at the sky.

"I started here as a freshman in 1927, Jerry, when the world was young. There's not that many of us romantics left in it today. We must bear the standards and wear the colors confidently, proudly, and not let hurt, disappointment, or even so much as a sense of defeat ever dampen our spirits or let us get downtrodden. Flair and its fearlessness is arsenal enough for a vulnerable heart."

I was following him as fast as he walked—I was on scholarship.

"You are down to the final wire, Jerry. It's far too late to try to mend fences with her father. We must be creative."

Pretty much everything Mr. V was saying was going over my head, but I did find it most interesting and something to think about.

Mr. V raised his bottle high in the air, pointing it to the sun in open challenge.

"*En garde*," he barked. "Onward and upward—through the arts, young man."

"You have an idea, Mr. V?"

"Save every nickel you can, Jerry. You may need it in these final hours."

Seeing my plight, that March Mr. V took me under wing during coffee breaks or between classes. Our goal was our bond, to keep my girl from going into the convent. This I did understand. He had an idea a day to help me convince my girl not to leave me in the dust. As the early spring weather warmed into a blistering hot summer, we'd walk between the columns on the walkway of Albers Hall hoping to catch a breeze, conjuring. I would recount things I remembered my dad, "Big Mike," did with flair—for his bakery, back in upstate New York.

"My dad told me marketing was about getting someone's attention. Doing something with such a bang they would stop and take notice and, while you had their attention, asking them for the sale. I used to ride with him all throughout upstate New York watching and listening to him talk to grocers. His stories of sales and marketing, they were adventures to him. 'It's in the numbers,' he would tell me. He would say to try to get people's attention by making a big impression—a good impression, though, so people will talk or think good things about you. Mr. V, is getting people's attention the flair part?" I asked.

"Most definitely," said Mr. V. "Your father is a smart man. It's making a big enough impression to make someone want to stop what they're doing and listen to what you might have to say."

"Dad told me a story about how he learned how simple getting someone's attention could be," I said. "When he was sixteen, in 1918, he had a job driving a telephone company Model A pickup around Minnesota as a telephone lineman. Most people didn't have phones back then, ya know. He'd climb poles and connect phone wires from telephone poles to the homes or businesses in the area. He told me the kids on the hot, dusty summer days near the Indian reservation roads he drove through would run alongside and yell, 'Flat tire, mister; flat tire, mister.' As most would do, in those times, he'd pull over to a stop, get out, and check his tires. That's when the kids would stretch their hands out, grinning at their tomfoolery, and beg, 'Penny, mister? Penny? Penny?'

After a time he'd carry a roll of pennies and stop the truck, get out, and sit on his running board waiting for them, and he'd give each a penny or two so the poor kids with nothing to do or no swimming hole to cool off in could go buy a Popsicle or an icy cold soda pop on a hot summer's day. He always made them tell him what grade they were in, spell a word, and promise they would stay in school. Dad told me it was those kids who taught him the true simple nature of getting someone's attention and then asking for the sale, although he didn't approve of the character in their technique, as effective as it was."

"A nice story," said Mr. V.

There I was, walking almost daily with one of the most important men in all of Cincinnati, maybe one of the most important men in the country, and he was listening to me. I would sip on my Coca-Cola most gentlemanly, rationing every drop, stalling, making it last through the stories.

He had hired me full-time end of term for the summer, but I never let on I was homeless, sleeping under the stars most nights.

With Mr. V taking a break now and then every chance he got and teaching me, I knew I was making a lifelong friend. Between his stories and what my dad had already taught me, I was beginning to understand the power and value of flair, of getting someone's attention in a big way. Knowing since December that my girl was thinking of going into the convent, I forced myself to save most of the money I got after basketball games, the five dollars a week allowance Dad sent me, plus the money I earned from writing English compositions for guys. I was broke so I would help older guys with their English assignments. At the expense of my own homework I was writing hundred-word compositions—earning extra money doing it. I charged for A's ($3), B's ($2), or C's ($1), and nothing for D's or F's.

I knew it was wrong—well, maybe more immoral than wrong—but I knew better than to tell a Jebbie who might recognize my voice in the confessional and put a stop to it. Most of the students at X were a lot older than me, in their twenties, some with families, just back from fighting in Korea and maybe shot at on Pork Chop Hill or someplace. I grew up during World War II and knew a soldier's bravery and what it was like to sacrifice. I looked at my writing their English compositions as doing my part for the boys in uniform. Besides, Hemingway told somebody if it felt good after, it wasn't immoral. Even if I didn't need the money I'd have done it for nothing. It'd been my writer's duty.

I never had the nerve to tell Mr. V how I made my extra money during school. I often wrote the hundred-word English compositions between classes—sometimes while walking and even carrying on a conversation just to show off that I could. One guy asked me how I did it so easy. "I was born a creative, wordy pedantic, I guess; what can I say? It's a talent just comes natural to me, sort of like spitting. I guess it's from being in the woods a lot alone, walking and talking to myself when I was younger," I told him.

I wanted to give her a nice going-away present, maybe a set

of luggage, but when Mr. V started teaching me and opening my mind up about flair and "All's fair in love and war," as he would say, I started thinking bigger than luggage and roses. I figured I had saved up enough writing English compositions and Mr. V's .65 cents an hour to go all out and pay $125 to charter the private airplane with a pilot he told me a senator had used one time. Mr. V was certain nuns would never get a chance to fly in a private chartered airplane. I flew her up to Columbus in June, when school first let out for her graduation from high school, just to impress her and let her get a taste of what life might be like if she stayed out of the convent, and I became a famous writer.

I took her up to meet my brother, the one I call "gourmet Mike," and his family. We caught a bus back to Cincinnati right after supper. The pilot just shook his head but didn't charge me for the hole the heel of her shoe punched in the canvas wing of the plane as she was twisting her hair into a pony tail while trying to step off. He could see I was in love, just shook his head again and said not to worry about it. During the summer I would take her to Moonlight Gardens at Cincinnati's Coney Island and hold her in my arms and gaze into her eyes as we danced under the stars. I took her to the racetrack that was free to get in, where she placed a two-dollar bet and won thirty-eight dollars. On weekends I would sleep in the park on top of the tall hill just behind her house in Price Hill so I could be with her when morning came and we could go for walks or catch a city bus somewhere.

Another time, on a hot Saturday, Mr. V arranged for me to hire a limousine and driver for almost nothing. Hess & Eisenhardt were limousine manufacturers up in Norwood who didn't normally hire them out—they just built them for presidents and big companies—but they did the favor for Mr. V after I hinted at the possibility. I took her fishing and for a picnic in their limousine, just as a president of a country could. Mr. Eisenhardt went to XU years before and was a romantic, too, so I got a good price for the hire. I don't remember any worms or tackle, but she and I sure enough sat in the back seat holding hands and hugging and dreaming with our two tall cane fishing poles and lines stuck out the side window with our bobbers plopping up and down in the Ohio River. The driver sat up the river bank, under a shade tree, gentleman that he was, reading a book. That's when I gave her, between our kisses and our stopping long enough to stare out the back window at the giant Delta Queen Riverboat splashing and paddling on toward Louisville, the three-piece set of light sky-blue Samsonite luggage that had caught my eye in a store window up in Norwood, and that I'd been paying four dollars a week for since April. Nuns would need luggage, this I knew, but I suggested they would be good for a honeymoon—maybe even on that very Delta Queen.

"Their color reminded me of your eyes," I told her.

Her eyes flashed a twinkle as she melted into another kiss.

I took her to the Gourmet Room twice. It was a fancy French restaurant Mr. V had told me about, on top of the Terrace Hilton in downtown Cincinnati. He also mentioned that few people could afford it. It would take more money than I made at the PR Department and more than I had saved up, but I just had to do it, so I'd hitchhike up to Klostermann's bakery every night for a week for each dinner I wanted to take her to, after working with Mr. V all day. Mr. Klostermann knew my dad and he let me ice cupcakes by hand for $1.14 an hour until early morning just before sunrise. After, I would go sleep a couple hours somewhere and go work for Mr. V again. When we went to the Gourmet Room I would take the Maître D aside and tell him how much I had in my pocket and I couldn't go over that or I'd be in trouble.

"Sir, perhaps you will permit me to order for you and your special lady?"

"And you won't go over and you will get a tip too?"

"I will handle everything, sir. Go join your lady, I'll be over shortly."

I kept learning and trying the "flair" stuff Mr. V taught me. I kissed her longer and better each time. We didn't always need a moon. She would raise her hand to my cheek gently, never wanting a kiss to end. I could feel her heartbeat when we danced, but insecure not knowing if she would be going in the convent.

Chapter 2

Fresh off the job one day with Mr. V, giving some thought to where I might lay my head that night, I stepped off the curb onto Victory Parkway to cross the oily crack in the salad bowl to the other side. The smell of road tar melted in my nostrils as I wondered if it could possibly get any hotter. The humidity coming off the Ohio River made it feel more like New Orleans, or so Mr. V would tell me. I'd never been to New Orleans other than in a book, and come to think of it, I don't think Huckleberry Finn did much more than talk about going down there his own self. Once across, I started climbing the steps that reached up the entire height of the very tall hill on the other side of the salad bowl. These stairs were a cement vein that went up the whole side between the armory and Field House, which were built into the hill as its bookends.

The steps were so tall, climbing them gave a body plenty of time to think. I wasn't giving up on the possibility of her choosing me over the convent, but I was starting to think perhaps Mr. V had a point about tramp steamers and cattle boats. Thinking about them could get the threat of the convent out of my head; maybe I could become a famous writer after all, using the flair he and my dad were teaching me by just traveling around the world from port to port on steam freighters. My dad had already taught me how to bake. "Everybody has to eat," he would say. Big Mike would agree with Mr. V about jumping tramp steamers, although if Mr. V knew the truth about me sleeping homeless every night around campus this summer, he would most definitely be on the phone telling my dad I was barely surviving—and then dad would be disappointed with my tall tales—even if I was a heartsick-in-love, broken-spirited, plain-not-thinking-straight, temporarily-crazy-in-the-head eighteen-year-old. Lying to my dad was wrong, I knew better than anybody, and I had to carry that. So was writing compositions for money, for that matter. I tried other enterprises: shaving guys' necks and around their ears for a quarter, after they got homemade haircuts. I even ironed their shirt collars and cuffs for a quarter so they'd look nice under V-neck sweaters. Xavier men had to wear ties to class. Truth was, quarters didn't stack up quite as tall or spend as well as a bunch of folding dollar bills from A's, B's, or C's for compositions that took me five minutes to write and always earned me more in dollars than they cost me in inconvenience or contrition.

About a third of the way up the stairs, at the first landing, just before they got steep again, I caught a bold, rank smell. Maybe from my armpits, I was thinking. It seemed to be an odor I wasn't all that familiar with, one I felt worthy of my attention. It was offered up as a sign to a boy in that stage of still growing, never being quite sure of what surprises to expect from his body—especially in the motionless, blazing hot air of a concrete alcove oven. It was from me, the smell, I was certain, not a smell coming from the armory or the field house where I practiced and played basketball.

I knew I had basic washing, shaving, and tooth brushing down as any young man out in the world had ought to—and always felt I was fairly near Sunday presentable in that regard when I went out in public—but the baking air lingering this rank in my nostrils got me thinking I was maybe in need of some help getting my clothes properly washed. A boy whose only home is about to become his wits doesn't think of packing a bag. I was thinking maybe it was my shirt and not me. Each night I'd find a sink and dip my undershorts in the basin of cold tap water and use them as a wash cloth for a stand-up sink bath. I'd rinse and wring them out best I could and pull them on damp to help me stay cool through the heat of the night until I fell asleep. Maybe two months was too long to wear the same shirt. I made a mental note that tonight I'd ask my friend Carlo Mastropaolo where I could get clothes washed without anyone knowing the details of why I was even on campus during the summer. He'd know.

Carlo was a nice, short Italian man with a gentle smile, wavy hair and a mustache, a quiet demeanor and pleasant disposition. He owned a small Italian restaurant, Chico's, on Montgomery Avenue—back up the hill in Norwood, behind the right side of the salad bowl, about a ten-block walk past the tracks. Carlo once played violin for the Cincinnati Symphony Orchestra and now gave lessons when he wasn't pulling up a chair and talking with customers or pouring coffee at his restaurant. Carlo would always tell me not to bump my head on the door as I walked in. He understood what I was going through, what with my girl about to leave for the convent. His mother took him into the kitchen for a talk the night she heard me tell him that if my girlfriend really went into the convent I would feel like I was being tossed out like a squeezed lemon.

"I know a breaking heart when I see one," she told Carlo. "A growing boy with a breaking heart still needs his greens. You be good to that boy. Don't let people tease him. He's a good boy."

He would let me sign the tab and pay when I could. Romantics had to stick together. I didn't eat much more than mostaccioli and meatballs ever and maybe a glass of water so I could keep ahead of the tab and his hospitality without wearing out my welcome. His mother was the cook and she always sent me a salad—on the house.

I made it to the top of the stairs and headed the four blocks beyond the other side of the salad bowl, looking for a "turn of the century" three-story gray-stone and green-shingled house set back a bit off the street and surrounded by big trees like it had been grand and important in another time past. I stepped off the campus and started the walk to what might hopefully be my secret new summer digs. Some upperclassmen had rented the house last year and named it the Sodality House. It was meant for young men who were very religious, maybe even thinking of the priesthood, who helped younger students in need. I wasn't thinking of the priesthood, I liked kissing too much, but I was in need. I still prayed regularly for my old friend Charlie Pitts and for my Aunt Kate, who have since passed, and I kept praying to God; He'd let my girlfriend stay out of the convent.

I'd never been inside the Sodality House, but I had just seen a notice for it with a picture tacked on a bulletin board and thought maybe the place was empty for the summer. The thought was, if I could get in, I could open windows on the west side of the house and not get seen. An ample breeze two stories up could surely keep a body cool enough to fall asleep in this summer heat. As I walked I could hear music in the distance; it seemed like it was coming from a radio through an opened window. Maybe from the Sodality House. The closer I walked, the better I could see two windows on its second floor pulled open and a young man, maybe my age, shorter, with neatly combed, pitch-black hair, sitting on the sill, back to one side, legs stretched across the window ledge, in a short-sleeved shirt, reading a book.

"Hey," I shouted up, stopping and wiping sweat from my forehead.

"Hello," said the young man, looking down timidly.

"I'm second year," I said back up. "I was figuring on maybe staying here tonight—for a while even, maybe—if it's okay."

"Okay," said the boy. "There're many beds."

"Do they charge to stay there?" I asked. "I'm a little short, ya see."

"I've been here a week," he said. "Nobody else has been here. I don't think they charge, but I don't know. The door is open. You want to come up?"

I detected an accent. I thought Spanish, but decided to mind my manners and not ask. I stepped up the six stone steps, opened the front door, and walked in through a main entrance hall and then up the wide wooden staircase to the second floor. There were four tall doors in the hallway, two on each side. I guessed at the room the young man might be in, peered in, saw him, and walked in. The room had six beds in it with bare mattresses on them; one bunk bed was turned sideways in front of the opened windows. I extended my hand. The lad earmarked a page in the book in his hand, *The Old Man and the Sea*, closed it, and shook my hand.

"I'm Jerry," I said.

"Tomas," said the young man. "Tomas Vargas."

I took the book from his hand and looked at the front cover, the spine, then the back cover.

"Is this good? I think I would like Hemingway, from what I hear. You going to X?" I asked.

"I don't know—about going to Xavier University, I mean. I'm from Cuba. There are many problems in my country. My father sent me here; he told me to wait for his telephone call."

I handed the book back to Tomas and stepped around the room, looking at beds.

"It's a very good book. It's about a nice old man, a fisherman, and a young boy. My father met Mr. Hemingway in Havana," said Tomas.

I started in the heat.

"Excuse me. Where did you say you were from?"

"Cuba," Tomas said. "It's a country ..."

"I know Cuba. Holy Cobako. Why of course I know Cuba," I shouted.

For the first time in my life I felt I was a part of international intrigue, just as in the movies.

"I mean about your dad, for real? What you said—your dad met Hemingway?"

I grabbed the book from his hand and pointed at Hemingway's picture on the back cover.

"This Ernest Hemingway here? Where, when?" I asked.

"He did. They had drinks together at a gambling casino in Havana."

I lifted the book up, examined Hemingway's picture carefully, imagining what it would be like to meet him at a bar. I handed the book back.

"Well, I'll be," I said. "Someday I'm going to be a famous writer."

I looked around the room again.

"What problems?" I asked.

"What?" asked Tomas.

"In Cuba. You said there were problems. What problems in Cuba? Jack Paar—he's a late-night TV show host—he went down there, said Fidel Castro was good and winning the revolution and problems would be over. Why, he said everybody liked Fidel

Castro because he was beating hell out of the dictator, Batista. I can't think of that fella's name—Batista right?"

"Batista; he is a bad man, this is true. Dictator, as you say. But now Fidel is no good," he said.

"Well, did he win or lose?" I asked.

"Fidel drove Batista out, but now he's changed; he's already taken my father's land and our hunting guns. He left us with a few acres to feed our family, my father, my mother, my brother, and me, like dirt farmers. The sugar plantation had been in our family for many generations," said Tomas, now staring blankly at the floor.

I liked his frankness, his honesty. It crossed my mind that had I been as honest with my girlfriend's dad about our moving to a one room apartment in Milwaukee when dad went broke, I wouldn't be in the mess I'm in now.

"Well that sure stinks," I said. "He sounds like those Hitler or Mussolini bastards," I added.

I edged around the room feeling mattresses with the palm of my hand, trying to calculate the directional flow of breezes through the opened windows.

"Fidel went to high school with my brother. They were even friends. Now he is my brother's enemy and the enemy of people who have businesses. He's a communist. His brother is, too. Communists take everything away. They say they are Robin Hoods but they are just crooks. If anyone argues with the revolution for any reason, they go to jail. Father put me on an airplane to get me out of the country while I still could get out. He knows a priest here at the university, Father Holland, who said I could come and stay until my father could decide what to do with me," said Tomas.

"Father Holland—teaches theology," I said. "He's nice; only gave me a C. Good talker, though, can stir ya up, make you think."

"I don't know him," he said. "They gave me the address and told me the door would be unlocked and to stay here."

"Unlocked all this time, eh? Well isn't that my dumb luck," I mumbled to myself.

I settled from my tour of beds on the bunk bed that straddled two opened windows.

"You use the top or the bottom?" I asked.

"Top, please, if you don't mind," he said. "I like to watch the stars and think of my family watching the stars."

"Ya know, I'm not totally convinced about that North Star stuff pointing north," I said. "Takes me forever to find the Dipper, never know which one I'm looking at. Why do they have to have two Dippers anyway? I've studied it from four different states now; tops of cliffs in New York, riding trolleys in Milwaukee, laying on the grass here. I still can't tell heads from tails without a compass. I'm just not convinced."

I grabbed a pillow from a bed nearby and threw it on the bottom bunk—claiming it. The lower bunk was windowsill high and certain to catch breezes throughout the night. I pointed toward the bathroom.

"Is that way north?" I asked.

"I think so, but I don't know," said Tomas.

I'd sleep with my head facing north, I decided. I moved my pillow to the other end of the bunk.

"I'm getting hungry. You hungry?" I asked.

"I'm hungry," said Tomas.

"You like spaghetti?"

"I've had two apples today. I didn't want to leave the telephone in case my father called for me," said Tomas.

Tomas pulled a suitcase and a canvas bag off the lower bunk while I walked to the bathroom to splash my face with cold water, rubbing the wetness over my head. It was a learned afternoon ritual that offered temporary relief from the sweltering heat. I lifted my arm and smelled my armpits to see if the rankness of the shirt was following me too badly. I wondered if my girlfriend could smell it when we danced.

"Let's go," I said.

We walked down the stairs and out of the house. Tomas burst into talk, like he had been holding it in out of loneliness and fear. There seemed to be such a relief in his meeting someone closer to his own age. All down the sidewalk toward the armory and field house stairs he never stopped talking about missing his family and how he worried about his *madre y abuela* (mother and grandmother) back at home worrying about him. Down the street and then starting down the hot concrete steps on the left side of the salad bowl, Tomas rambled on and on about the look in his father's eyes when Fidel took his land; how his father had told him since he was a little boy that he would someday manage the family's sugar plantation; how he had taught him how to care for the crop and watch for the weather, what to do when the winds blew, how to get the cane to market, and how to bargain and wait for a good price.

"So is the sugarcane business considered farming, or ranching? I only know about dairy farms," I muttered to myself.

"When it would rain, and they couldn't work outside, Father told me many stories of how hard his *abuela y abuelo* (grandmother and grandfather) worked, always saving their money so they could buy more land to build a proud heritage for their families," said Tomas.

Tomas told me how the villagers loved his father, respected him, and would come back year after year for harvest; how sad it was, not knowing if those people were out of work or if they now worked for Fidel Castro and his brother. I could see the pride welting up in his face when he spoke so lovingly of his father and of the others in his family. I could see the despair in his brown eyes from not knowing what the future had in store for him alone in a country away from his family. I stopped and turned.

"There's something I have to tell you, Tomas," I said.

"What's that, my friend?"

"My dad used to be a big deal, but he lost everything too, like your dad is losing everything. I just don't like talking about it. I feel like I'm disrespecting him, like I'm betraying him when I talk about it."

We crossed Victory Parkway and started up the other hill on Dana Avenue to Chico's. Listening to Tomas made me homesick and melancholy.

"My father's a baker," I said. "In the 1940s and early1950s,

I would ride with him for endless miles and hours through central New York State while he checked stores that sold his bread. We'd spend all day and drive from Binghamton, New York, down near Pennsylvania coal country, way up to Watertown close to Canada and our Mississippi River—the St. Lawrence Seaway—then back on down around the famous, quiet Finger Lakes stretched out like an old-timey, five-fingered Yankee baseball glove. I'm sorry; those are parts of our country," I said.

"I know New York and Pennsylvania," Tomas said. "New York Yankees, Pennsylvania Pirates." He laughed.

"Pittsburgh," I said. "Pittsburgh Pirates."

"My father's sugarcane went all over the world. Large ships would carry it from Havana," he said.

Halfway up the hill on Dana Avenue, I stopped talking, paused, and turned around just to gaze back at the other side of the salad bowl and reflect—the armory steps, the football stadium, the trail we had just come down from and back up this other side.

"My dad could drive for hours," I said.

I pointed down the hill over at the expanse of the football stadium across the salad bowl.

"My dad designed a sign, Tomas, they built so high up on the side of a great hill between the city of Cortland and the town called Tully, back in New York, why, you could see it for twenty, thirty miles. People sure talked about it and even drove for hours on Sunday afternoons just to show it to the kids and look at it up close as a wonder of the world, like a Niagara Falls. That's a big waterfall between New York and Canada. That was 1935, I think, and to this day no one knows how he built it without walkie-talkies or any other way of talking almost a mile up the hill to help him from down below. The whole sign stretched out a couple of football fields in width," I bragged. "Why, the 'D' alone on the sign stretched up the hill more than three hundred fifty feet tall. Can you imagine?"

I was missing my dad, feeling guilty about my lies about not being able to come home, and just muttering away all yackety-yackety-yack with someone I'd just met and hardly knew.

Tomas said, "You miss your father, I can tell. That's okay, I miss mine, too."

We turned back and continued our walk to Chico's. I buckled up, straight and tall, masking my guilt, my loneliness. I started spewing thoughts aloud just as though I was dictating a composition for an A, just to impress my audience of one.

"On rides in the country with my dad," I began, "each sound in the car seemed iambic ..." I interrupted myself. "Is iambic the best word here? Iambic, like pentameter—a poetic beat," I thought out loud. "I'm just not sure; I'll have to look that one up."

I rattled on.

"Iambic to the particular moment, like the roar in a crowded baseball park. With all four windows opened and the two wing vents turned back to help cool us off at sixty or seventy miles an hour on country roads—every air sound would compete to be heard over the already raucous, pounding, ear-whapping of air breeze's flopping sounds coming in from all sides. But, magically, just as in a crowded baseball park, regardless of the pitch of the crowd noise, the boos and the whistles, I could still hear the distinct sound of my dad's voice above the other noises. It was just like you'd always hear that crack of the bat, for a home run or triple. It's magic, you can hear that crack above the other noise."

"My father would take us to see baseball in Havana. I remember the crack of the bat for certain," said Tomas.

"On our drives, Tomas, we'd always be looking around every next curve in the road for another adventure or maybe a fishing hole; could be a domesticated buffalo we'd stop and stare at through a fence and dream of Buffalo Bill, or just a pair of donkeys we could pet and think of Mary and Joseph on their way to Bethlehem. After we moved to the country was when my dad and I became best friends for life. I was seven. I never got to work in the bakery as you got to work on your plantation, but lucky for me, I heard and learned how to market a product, from every word he ever said. I knew I wanted to be a storyteller, you know, a writer just from listening to him tell them. His stories were always the crack of the bat, to me … the home run. I'm sorry you can't be with your family," I told Tomas. "It's just not right."

"My father gave me a world globe *para Navidad*," said Tomas. "He carefully showed me your wonderful St. Lawrence Seaway on it, where ships would take our sugarcane from Cuba to Montreal, Canada. Someday he was going to get me a ride on a ship."

"Navidad?" I asked.

"It means Christmas. *Feliz Navidad* means Happy Christmas," he said.

"Well, I'll be. Imagine me learning that walking to Norwood," I said.

Tomas and I walked quietly now. I started thinking of lying to my dad and mom, and of my girlfriend about to leave me any day now, maybe forever. Neither of us said another word until we got to the distraction of the train tracks.

"Follow me," I said. "We'll go this way."

We stepped on a rail of the track, raised our arms straight out for balance, and walked it a good hundred and seventy feet to the next street crossing while we cleared our heads. It took our minds off homesickness for a spell and only cost us a block or two out of our way on our trail to spaghetti dinner at Chico's.

"We are just alike," said Tomas. "Two young men out of the nest, one tall and one short—missing something or someone but just the same, even though we are from two different countries."

Stepping off the rail I halted, turned, and made a bold observation.

"Just imagine, your father met Ernest Hemingway, in person," I observed.

"He did," Tomas said.

"And now you, my new friend, Mr. Tomas Vargas from Cuba, a world traveler, have met the one and only Jerome Mark Antil—in person."

We laughed at my arrogance, and I pulled Chico's door open.

"Don't bump your head," chided Carlo, standing by the cash register.

Tomas and I walked in confidently and headed toward a booth over by the corner.

For several hours we talked about our fathers and what they had taught us and how we missed them. I told him about Mr. V. I chose not to tell Tomas about my girlfriend's maybe leaving me for the convent. I didn't want to diminish our mutual pain of homesickness by sharing my personal problem. I asked him about Cuba. Tomas told me of the gambling casinos in Havana, although he had not been to one. I told him about the gambling and prostitution there was in Newport and Covington, cities right across the Ohio River, in Kentucky.

"Have you been to them?" asked Tomas.

"Well, there's this time when I was a Freshman," I began. "A guy named Tito Carinci, see, a real nice fellow—it turns out who went to Xavier one time, played football. Heard he was pretty good at football. Tito has a place down there, Covington. Everybody says he's mafia, but I don't know that. Some of the basketball team I play on borrowed a car and went to his restaurant in Covington one time. When we went inside, Billy Kirvin, being our team captain, asked for Tito, and he told the lady we came from Xavier to meet him."

"Did you see prostitutes?" asked Tomas.

"Not sure. At least I don't think so. I'm not sure what a prostitute looks like," I said. "She walked us over to a coat closet with one of them Dutch-door things, you know, the bottom half of the door with a shelf on top—a counter on it. The hat-check girl stepped out of the coat closet and told us to step in. She closed the top and the bottom of the door and the whole closet just started to move up, it was an elevator. It was the dandiest thing. When it stopped and the door opened, there was Tito standing there smiling, waiting, at the entrance to a whole smoke-filled floor of gambling, roulette wheels and blackjack tables, men wearing green shades over their eyes and stacking chips and counting money. It went on forever. Tito pushed a basket in our guts and told us to empty our pockets. Then he handed us each fifty dollars' worth of gambling chips. He gave us each ten chips; they had five dollars stamped right on them, in gold.

"He set the rules quick: 'These chips are yours.' He said, 'Yours to win from or to lose from, or to cash in and keep the money. Win what you can and keep it—but if you lose, it will have been my chips you lost, not your money. Understood?'"

"Caramba," said Tomas. "Exciting. Such an adventure. Did you go back?"

"Nah. Never could get a car. Other than going to the Latonia horse races with my girlfriend, it was the most fun I've had, other than maybe sitting behind home plate at a Cincinnati Reds game with my basketball team. We got to see Hank Aaron play, some others," I rattled.

"Orlando Peña plays for Cincinnati," Tomas said. "He's from Cuba. Perhaps we can go see him play. I wonder if he knows about what Fidel is doing."

Summer was ending long before the heat. In a gentle rustling, like a rambling brook carrying that one leaf downstream, an occasional student would walk through campus. Tomas and I eventually lost connection, going our separate paths just as I'd become accustomed to athletes doing after games of battle—like ships passing in the night. The respect you gained in your opponent's eyes through the course of a basketball game or even a game of chess was always a fleeting memory. The doctor registered me into Good Samaritan on Labor Day weekend for my appendix operation, just before school was to start up. From my hospital bed I glanced and could see my girlfriend stepping into the doorway of my room, to say goodbye.

I began to shake; I could see the glistening of tears welling in her eyes; I could tell, from her sad, turned mouth, that the tears had been there for some time and now she wanted me to raise my arm, motion her over to my bedside, take her in my arms, hold her tightly, and kiss her, to wake her from this nightmare we were both in. I saw the silhouette of her father coldly leaning against a corridor wall in the distance behind her, waiting for her in the hallway. I wondered if it was too late to tell him the truth, that I wasn't a spoiled rich kid. I looked away, concentrating my eyes on the light cracking through the lowered venetian blinds. I didn't ask her over to my bedside. I didn't beg her not to go. I didn't kiss her or hold her or smell her hair.

"Bye," I said.

She was gone from my life. It was real now.

My appendix and my heart came out the very same day.

Xavier University came to life again. I walked to the Sodality House after work one day to jump in the shower and noticed Tomas's things were gone. An upperclassman, dropping a box on a bed and walking down the stairs for another, asked me if I belonged there.

"Yeah, I sleep here. Well, no, I guess I don't technically—that is, belong here. But I'd like to. Who are you?"

Chapter 3

Bob Hock stepped back into the room carrying another carton box with a frayed rope-strand holding it together. He looked over.

"You registered yet? They opened registration yet?" he asked. Then he looked at me again, recognizing my face. "Aren't you Antil, on the basketball team?"

"Yeah, I am. Can I stay here this year?"

"Don't see why not. Tell them at registration. It's called Sodality House, case they ask."

Bob was from Portsmouth, the first to walk into the house at the beginning of fall term. I jumped in the shower when he started carrying up more boxes from the trunk of a car, where someone sat in the driver's seat, waiting to leave again.

Tim Boylan was next, having just driven from Elyria in a black convertible. He was carrying in suitcases. I scrambled into my clothes, walked over, and picked my things up from the bunk.

Tim shook my hand. "Seen all your home games last year. You're Jerry. You guys were great. Kirvin, Thobe, Enright, Pinchback, wow! You can room with me, if you want. You can have the bottom bunk, because you're so tall. Give me a hand, will you? We need to carry the bed over to a room on the other side. It has north light, better for reading and study."

"Tell me, is there any place closer than Brockman Hall where I can wash my clothes?" I asked. "Been doing 'em up in Norwood. Most of my stuff is still over there. I need to go get it later, if it's unlocked."

"Use the machine in the cellar," he said. "Make sure it's plugged in."

"There's a washer here?" I asked, feeling foolish. "Well wouldn't you just know?"

"Throw a nickel or a dime a load in the soup can on the shelf for the Tide. Whoever empties the Tide goes and gets more."

Life was getting better by the minute. Boylan and I took the bunk apart with pliers, lifted the sections, and carried it and the mattresses in four loads across the hall to our new digs, a small room on the north side of the house. There was a nice air coming over the Sodality House. It felt like more of a home than Brockman Hall. There everyone knew everyone else was a freshman. Here a guy didn't know who was in what year or what they were studying unless it came up. Here a guy felt like he belonged.

I walked down to the armory for early registration and stood in a line for an hour or more, selecting my classes. I picked thirteen hours. Papers in hand, I went down the back stairs two levels to the athletic department on the ground floor and around the halls to the coaches' offices. Scholarship players were required to leave a list of their classes and where they were staying for the team manager. Someone in the athletic department took care of paying the rent for housing and food vouchers and would go buy the books and deliver them to our rooms. I interrupted the varsity coach standing by the window of an office conference room looking through papers. He was a tall, stocky man in a shiny black tailored suit and heavily starched blue shirt and loosely knotted silk tie. He had short, slicked-back hair and a small cowlick in early sprout on the back right side of his head. His face was as red as rouge, like a ceramic French painted doll.

"You know where Coach Ruberg is?" I asked.

He sneered up at me and I soon had a feeling asking for *Coach* Ruberg was my first mistake. *Coach* Ruberg was my freshman coach last year. Now, for the varsity, he was only Assistant Coach Ruberg.

Head Coach turned and looked up at me with a glare that said, "Don't you remember who I am, boy?"—as though I had interrupted him.

"You're Antil, aren't you?"

"Yes, sir."

"You're with the big boys now, son," he said. "You'll have to tuck your own self in this year. Welcome to varsity. Put your things in the box on that wall, like the sign says." He turned back toward the window, like I wasn't even there.

He knew damn well who I was. My junior year in high school, in New York, we were 17–2 in season games. My senior year in high school, in Milwaukee, we were 17-2 in season games. All County, All Star, All City, All Catholic. Last year the Xavier freshman team went 15-1 a lot better than his varsity team's losing year.

I didn't much care if he coached the NIT championship win two years prior. I didn't like him already. I gave his vanity a cheap smile, threw the list of my classes in the bin on the wall, and walked out. My last semester and summer were already miserable with my girlfriend drama. If Coach Ruberg wasn't going to be around this term, it'd be worse. Why they didn't just make Coach Ruberg varsity coach, I'd never understand. Last year our freshman team would scrimmage varsity every Wednesday afternoon, open practice to students, and we'd go even or beat them nearly every time. The varsity had won the NIT before we came to school, but not much since.

Walking back up to the Sodality House, I now had two chips on my shoulder: God, for keeping my girlfriend in the convent, and the varsity head coach. He knew who I was, all right, the self-absorbed dandy. I may not have been the best on the freshman team, but I started and we went 15-1. I think our winning with Ruberg and without him pissed Head Coach off. Jack Thobe was our freshman forward. No one could get near enough to stop his soft hook shot. Our starting team was him, Billy Kirvin, who was fast and deadly out deep and on the foul line—he led the nation on the line—Frank Pinchback, who could jump-shoot like Oscar Robertson, Jimmy Enright with his good hands, good eye, and speed—and me. I was the tallest starter, but too light. I was like a stick: six-foot-ten and 190 pounds, but I could move like a little man, rebound well, and was strong defensively.

Chapter 4

It was just before Christmas my Sophomore year. On the team's roster, I was sitting varsity bench, considered an eighth man. I was on the bench until January because of my appendix surgery, losing interest in the game and didn't much care. I was getting out of shape. I always started every morning with five minutes in the Bellarmine Chapel praying to God to send my girl back to me. I found it interesting that the more I wasn't playing, without the pressures of being on court in a game, the more observant I was, the more aware I was becoming of the world outside basketball. I was getting bigger hints of racism in the area, although I couldn't quite put my finger on some. My best friend on court was Ducky Castille, a black from Schenectady, not terribly far from where I grew up in New York. At five-eleven, Ducky could jump from a standing position and dunk the ball with both hands, dribble between and behind his legs at full speed and in turns, and, with his bursts of speed, get around any guy on the court no matter his size. He was a pleasant sort, a nice-looking young man who sported a trimmed hairline mustache. He had played on the NIT-winning team in '58 and was popular with the crowd in Madison Square Garden. The game reel film show him being fouled, bounced and sliding on the floor by a couple of giants, and him sitting up and resting his arms on his knees, shaking his head, and the crowd from over the world cheering him on like a brave hero, his shy smile beaming.

Ducky spent a few nights with me early in the summer, sleeping in the Quonset hut. I never asked him why he was sleeping there. I was later to learn he wasn't confident he could get a hotel room in Cincinnati, being black. Naively I'd guessed he was just waiting for a ride back home for the summer.

It was starting to grate on me that the black guys on the team—Ducky, Frank Pinchback, and those guys from over at the University of Cincinnati, like Oscar Robertson and Paul Hogue, all of them, the best players in college basketball—couldn't any of them go to downtown Cincinnati and sit at a Woolworth's lunch counter and eat a meal. *"We reserve the right to refuse service to anyone"* was what the sign said. "No Negroes" was what it meant. It wasn't much talked about, but it bothered my very nature wondering exactly why it was that someone would even care who came and spent money to sit, eat, and talk. I remember the previous year watching the XU varsity play UC, our friendly crosstown rival. After a fast break where Oscar stole the ball, faked out three guys, and scored, a voice bellowed from the stands, "You may be good, Oscar, but you still can't eat at Woolworth's."

I remember when it happened suddenly feeling older, more grown up. I felt certain it wasn't a student from either school, but I couldn't begin to imagine the hurt in a young man's heart having to hear it and being treated that way. I couldn't imagine what it must have been like to be black. Looking around at the crowd from the bench, I had to blame the presidents of the universities and the coaches themselves for not having the balls to go take Woolworth's and places like them to task. I even blamed the president of the United States for letting this sort of thing go on. I had heard black players quite often couldn't stay in the same hotels as their teams in the South.

The more I dwelled on it, the more cynical I became. What was this "Xavier Musketeer—all for one and one for all" hoopla, anyway? What a joke. At practice I would hit the water jug to cool down, drink and splash my head. I seemed more on edge with each practice—still upset with my girlfriend being gone. I was scraping money together to send a dozen roses to her in the convent.

I tried not to show it or dwell on it but thinking of her all day and night got me so my stomach was wrenched and started burning up and I couldn't sleep most nights. I kept playing over in my memory how I'd just stared blankly out through the venetian blinds at Clifton Avenue from my hospital bed when she left my life forever. I knew I was too young for being a sophomore and was still aching for her like I had lost my first puppy dog. Many young men in those days, during and following World War II, were like geese or swans, mating for life. When they knew they had found the right one, they would not let go. It's just the way it was then. I even carried a strand of her hair in my pocket, even though I pretty much had given up on going to chapel each morning and begging God to let her come out of the convent. I still wanted her out but knew it was up to Him now, and only Him. My last hope was in thinking if He could call her in, He could damn well send her home.

Then it all fell in on me. One afternoon, during a basketball practice, I had a particular edge about me, as a person gets when he has too much weighing on his mind with no end in sight. The kind of an edge that wins games. I was looking good, going through the moves on court, pretty much in a routine I had learned from a few years of playing on nothing but winning teams, not having to pay any particular attention– I was letting my instincts make my moves. Nothing off court was making too much sense to me. This practice I found myself working up a blind pushing and wild shoving, grabbing out, getting my hands on the ball with aggressive slaps and snaps at every opportunity. I was getting myself in a zone I'd been in before in key games. I was jumping and steaming up and over the rim, almost in a rage, not the more methodical, slow-motion pace of a typical practice.

Seemed I could see Ducky from my keen peripheral vision, and we were playing smooth, at our own speed, smooth as silk, handing the ball back and forth between us and around others, making points and assists like the pros. I trusted Ducky. He trusted me. That's the day Assistant Coach Ruberg walked over to me at a break in the play, leaned in, and whispered, "Where's this coming from, ya big dummy? I knew it was in you. You keep this up and you'll be starting again, for sure, like you did for me. Now keep it up!"

We went on to scrimmage for another twenty minutes, more laps, more fast-break drills. Then I was put at the foul line for two free throws, a special free-throw defensive-positioning drill. I took my first shot. The ball hit the front of the rim with a thud and bounced down to the floor.

Head Coach, with his painted red face, stuck a rolled-up piece of paper to his mouth like a megaphone and cracked wise

from the sidelines: "Antil, get your damn head out of the convent!"
I jolted. I couldn't believe my ears. I felt humiliated. I could immediately see nervousness for me in the eyes of the teammates around me. I sensed their vibe—their disappointment in Head Coach's insensitivity. If I'd been older and more experienced, maybe it would have been different. But I wasn't; they knew I was just a kid.

I stared down at the foul line, pretending I was in control, my emotions trembling. I faked a cool bouncing of the ball one time. I bounced it again. I straightened up, palmed the ball in one hand, leaned down as I would to touch my toes, set the ball on the foul line, stood tall again, and brushed by three teammates as I walked out of the gym, the armory, the field house, my scholarship, and the university in one pass. I hopped two steps at a time, skipping down the back stairs to the ground-floor locker room. My mind raced with images I knew I could do nothing about. The time I was four, in our back yard in Cortland, and the sky had turned black with the rumbling of low-flying Army Air Force bombers on practice missions, as if they were bombing Cortland. I remember shaking in tears, waiting for the bombs I'd seen in the newsreels at the Saturday morning picture show. My mind was rattling then as now with what seemed like images of black puffs of flak, exploding everywhere on all sides of me. A coach was supposed to be a player's best friend, like a big brother, a father figure. It was inconceivable to me that he could think, much less say, what he had said. I pulled my pants and shirt on over my body sweat. I thought of Ducky and Pinchback and of Oscar and of Woolworth's and now my coach. What had I gotten myself into even coming to this place? What could I possibly learn from an institution, I wondered, that just sat back and did nothing, said nothing—and only played the game while they posed pretty for pictures with the Pope?

I grew up in dairy farm country where there weren't these prejudices. No one ever told me that some people in control wouldn't have the balls to speak out, up, or even give a damn in this world. My dad would have. I grew up thinking we'd fought the war because everyone cared. Everybody here seemed to just stand by and watch. I was already pissed at God. At this particular moment I was pissed at man as well. Head Coach? Hell, he didn't even count the second he said what he said. He didn't matter anymore.

I let the bottom floor's athletic room door slam behind me; still sweating from no shower, I started pounding my feet up the vein of cement steps beside the field house. At the first level up, I could hear the muffled whistles and basketballs bouncing from the team practice behind the fire door exit as I passed by. I read the sounds as indifference to my walking out. No matter, I thought to myself. I kept climbing the hill to the Sodality House.

I lay on my bunk thinking what to do. I rolled over three or four times. I wasn't going back, that was for damn sure, but I wasn't certain what my options were. I was shaking with doubt and determination on the one hand, but still a kid on the other. I didn't have experience enough to have earned any confidence, so I needed clues as to what to do next. Should I call my dad and tell him what I did? What would he and my mom say? That I was a quitter? I rolled off the bed, stood up, and headed down the stairs and back over across the salad bowl to see Mr. V. I knew I could trust him. In making the decision to go see him, I convinced myself that, along the way somewhere, I would work up the nerve to tell him the truth.

As I reached the bottom step to the basement offices, he caught my eye.

"Mrs. Burke, please hold my calls. Come in, Jerry, take a seat."

I was never to learn who, but someone called him after I walked out of the gym, knowing he was a good friend of mine. My guess has always been it was a Jebbie watching practice from the top of the stands; maybe Father Holland.

"Jerry, the man dishonored himself, brought shame and embarrassment to me personally and others I know who work at the university and know what happened," said Mr. V.

"You know what he said?" I asked.

"At the very least I feel he owes you an apology," said Mr. V. "I can and will insist on one, if you wish."

"I don't even like him."

"Jerry, what do you want to do?"

"I don't know."

"You still have your scholarship."

"I quit."

"I could demand an apology from the head coach. I would go through Father O'Conner if I have to. What do you want?"

"I don't know, Mr. V. But I sure won't play for him again. Ruberg, I would. Not him."

"You're certain about not playing basketball? Why don't you take some time to think about it. Take a few days, perhaps. I will be honored to drive to your home and explain to your parents just what happened today and how dreadfully sorry I am on behalf of the university."

"I won't play for him, I tell ya—and I don't want my dad and mom finding out this way."

"How can I help you, my friend?" he asked.

It was time to be a man. For a full year I had been on a treadmill of sorrow and looking under rocks for hope.

"I only want to be a writer someday," I said. "Is there anything you need written, Mr. V? You don't have to pay me so much as a nickel if you don't like it."

Mr. V sat back in his chair, relaxed his face, and smiled. I could tell he saw an opportunity to calm me down, maybe change the subject.

"A writer? Interesting. Not surprising. You have a good vocabulary. How did you come upon that? Were you a reader growing up?"

"Only a couple of books, I guess, *Tom Sawyer*, part of *Huckleberry Finn*. Two of the Hardy Boys stories, a couple of Sherlock Holmes stories. Oh yeah, *African Queen*. Well, most of it," I said. "I read *Of Mice and Men* last year. Liked that one."

"I read *The Saint* mysteries," said Mr. V. "If you like mysteries, you'd enjoy reading about the saint. He's a crafty rascal,

36

that one."

"My brother Fred, all the time he was at Cornell, he would mail me a word every week to look up and learn. I got so I was pretty good at knowing what words to use and where. Sometimes I can think of the best word to use but can't spell it and have a time trying to look it up in the dictionary," I said.

"Will you miss basketball? I heard you're talented."

"I'll play somewhere, maybe the Y; I could even try out for the Royals. Dolphe Schayes could get me a tryout."

"Jerry, about wanting to become a writer one day. If you choose not to play basketball and give up your scholarship, I have an idea you might consider. But I do want you to give a lot of thought to not giving up your scholarship. Want to take the weekend and think about it? Talk to some of your friends?"

"I won't play for him, ever."

"Would you like to hear my idea?"

"Sure."

"I think you might consider auditing classes—further your education as much as you can. Any classes you wish, audit them, for as long as you like, but I would do it at our night school."

"What's audit?" I asked.

"You just attend any classes you wish. There'll be no cost. Take an empty seat, anywhere in the class. Let the professor know you're auditing. You'll have to buy your own books, that's true, but your exams won't be graded and you won't earn credit for the courses you take," he said. "If you do audit, and if anyone ever says anything, ask them to call me."

"Not day school?" I asked.

"You'll need money to live, so I have an idea for daytime work, one that might just give you a solid understanding of words."

"Words?" I asked.

"Words are going to become your world if you are to be a writer. A writer can always use some good basic training in the use of words. Learn the secrets to their flexibility, their potential, and their power when each is lined up as a brush stroke on a canvas."

He was selling me. Mr. V was actually selling me. I smiled, but wasn't sure quite what he meant. He pulled a piece of paper from a little box on his credenza, lifted a pen from its holder, and scribbled a note.

"I'm giving you a man's name and number, Jerry; he's a gentleman by the name of Myron Jones. I'm going to call him on your behalf. You'll find him most interesting. Mr. Jones is a senior vice president of the Union Central Life Insurance Company, downtown, at Fourth and Vine. He's in charge of their advertising and public relations. You've seen the building; it's the tall white one on the corner on Fourth Street, downtown. If you choose not to play basketball, go meet him and see if he has a job for you. Try my idea of night school. Give it a year or so, and see. Work your days with words, and go to night school with books; you won't be skipping a beat, and I do believe you will have a job that will help your craft all your life."

Mr. V stood and extended his hand. "Stay in touch and keep me posted on your decision, my friend. Come visit. Cokes are on me."

"When I audit courses and they don't grade my exams, do I get a degree that way?" I asked.

"Will you need a piece of paper to tell you what you've learned, Jerry?"

"No."

"I didn't think so. A degree does not make a man. Go get paid for the privilege of learning the wonderful world of words during the day, study the textbooks and attend the classes at night. It's almost as good as catching a steam freighter or cattle boat around the world. No time to lose, my friend. Be off."

"Should I tell him you sent me?" I asked.

"He'll know you're coming. I'll have called him already." Mr. V smiled. He turned and picked up his phone receiver.

I stepped out of his office. "Good luck, Jerry," said Mrs. Burke with a smile.

Up the steps, out of Albers Hall, down the drive maybe one last time, turning right on Dana Avenue, crossing Victory Parkway and heading up the hill. My adrenalin was pumping so hard I caught my second wind and sprung into a run. I ran full out to the Sodality House. I was in a hurry to ask Bob Hock if I could continue living there. The house was empty when I climbed the front steps and the stairs to the second floor. No cars, no people. I paced about, going from room to room. I walked over to the telephone in the television room, picked up the receiver, and slowly dialed the numbers, one digit at a time, that Mr. V had written on the piece of paper. I was connected.

"Mike Jones."

"Mr. Jones, my name is Jerry Antil—a Mr. VonderHaar told me to call you."

"Well hello, Jerry. Good to hear your voice. I just hung up from a talk with Ed. My sports fan friends still talk about the nail-biter your freshman team played against Dayton last year. They were fast-break artists—what a team—but you boys sure came through and held your own like champs."

I grinned into the phone. "Mr. Jones, may I make an appointment to come see you?"

"Call me Mike, and I've already had a nice talk with Ed. He says some pretty good things about you. Xavier needs you on court, Jerry, but you can start here Monday morning, if you want the job. You'll be assistant to the director of production in our sales promotion department. Interested?"

"Yes. I'll take it. Absolutely, I'll take it," I said. "Thanks a million."

"Not quite a million, Jerry." He laughed. "Be here at eight-thirty on Monday. Sixty-five dollars a week will have to do for now. You know our building?"

"Yes, sir, the tall white one on the corner of Fourth and Vine, right?"

"That's the one. You'll find my name on the directory— Myron Rhett—with an 'H'—Jones. Look for it in the lobby and come on up the elevator. I'll take you to personnel and we'll get you situated."

My world started over with that one phone call. After the

summer and fall I had gone through, I felt as if I was closing the curtain on a smudged window of my life. I felt like I had a clean slate. I was as excited with the new turns in my life as I had been when Sister John Domenici dropped eighteen scholarship letters, including the one from Xavier, on my desk during my senior year in high school. I was even ready to try to put my girlfriend behind me. Now I had to call my mom and dad. I looked at the clock in the hall and guessed my dad would still be in his office. I dialed his office number.

"Hello?"

"Hi, Dad—Jerry."

"Why hello, Jerry, me boy. Are you in town? Want me to make some spaghetti?"

"I'm in Cincinnati, Dad, but I quit college today."

There was a long pause.

"I wanted to call and tell you personally."

I could hear my dad closing his office door.

"Want to catch a bus home and talk about it, son?"

"I already have a job, Dad. Sixty-five dollars a week to start."

"But why, son?"

"Hard to explain, Dad. On the telephone."

"You have a scholarship. A full boat? Everything paid; pretty nice."

"I know."

"Your mother tells me your grades are decent, she's so pleased. Want to come home and talk about it? Want me to come down?"

"My grades stink, Dad. Well, maybe not English," I said.

He paused, and waited, but hearing silence, he continued, "I can't understand why you want to drop out, son."

"I didn't want to drop out, Dad. I wanted to quit."

Dad knew me well enough and understood the difference between my metaphors and my statements. I could tell in his tone. He saw I was becoming a man. I didn't want to relive the ten months of agony I'd gone through losing my girlfriend and decided to spare him my summer and fall miseries, my lies to him and Mom, and how I'd felt plowed under like a stripped cornfield with my disappointments in a world away from a simple, uncomplicated Delphi Falls. I knew Dad had faced his own crisis at twelve, when his father died from a fall off the barn roof. Mom told us the story when Dad went to the sanitarium with tuberculosis a few years back. He still didn't know I knew: how he had to quit school in the ninth grade when his dad died and he went off to the Dakotas to work the wheat fields and send money home to his mother, a mother of seven. My dad was no stranger to a young man's need to chart his own course through a storm.

"What do you want to do with your life, son?"

"I want to be a writer, Dad, a good one. I got a job with this insurance company downtown where I can work with words and learn."

Dad didn't lecture. His only talk about careers to his sons and daughters was that it didn't mean a flip what any of us chose to do in life, "just do it better than anyone else forty, fifty hours a week and you will always make a good living," he would say.

"Can you write, son?"

"I think so."

"It's not an easy living. May take a long time," said Dad.

"Dad, you sent me five dollars a week all the time I was here. I made another twenty dollars a week writing compositions for guys. I'd get three dollars for an A, two dollars for a B, a buck for a C, and no charge for a D or F."

Dad chuckled at the hint of integrity in my unethical larceny. "Well that certainly was resourceful."

"I got so I could write hundred-word compositions walking between classes. I want to be a writer, Dad."

"I'd give it some thought, son."

"This is a good job—the insurance company—and I will learn a lot so someday I can write. I don't need the five dollars anymore."

I wasn't budging. I could tell Dad sensed it was deeper, my reason for quitting. But he also knew his fishing buddy was a thinker and not one for small talk or glib conversation. His friendship wouldn't let him challenge my emotion with debate. As my dad, he just opened small windows of thought for me to peer through.

"Won't you miss your teammates, son?"

"Dad, I played basketball because I'm tall, because it got me places. Basketball and tall is such a cliché. I want to show I can write."

Dad knew there was more to it, which he told me later. He knew me; he knew I wasn't a quitter. He had seen me carrying garbage cans and burning garbage all summer when I was twelve, in the basement of the Hotel Syracuse, and never complaining.

He stayed silent, waited for me to speak first. I unraveled like a spool of thread.

"I started at seventeen. Nearly everyone here at X was just back from fighting in Korea, some even married with families, in their twenties. For my whole first year, Dad, guys would pass me on the school path, on the way to class, and yell, 'Hey, Stretch, ya getting any?' And I'd answer back, 'Sure am, every week,' thinking they meant money from home."

Dad snorted into the phone.

"Dad, I'm going to be a writer. That's all there is to it. I won't get that from taking science or math."

"You're going to have to tell your mother, son. Write a letter would be best, at first. Tell her you're taking a break to figure things out. I'll try to square it with her. If you want to be a writer, I'll help you get started. Let me know when you're ready. Think about taking a bus up so we can talk. We love you, son."

"Thanks, Dad."

"Good luck with the job. Stay in touch, Jerry me boy. If you ever get hungry, come home. I'll make spaghetti. We'll go fishing."

I hung the phone on the receiver, feeling much better. I went downstairs and out of the house and plopped down on the front stoop, waiting for Bob Hock to come walking in.

It wasn't long when a brand-new sparkling little white Fiat

sedan turned in the drive, started tooting its horn obnoxiously, and drove up to the steps within a foot of where I was sitting. It looked like a small toy box. The horn tooted again.

"Jump in," yelled Hock with a big grin on his puss. "Let's go for a ride in my brand-new car."

It took a few minutes; learning how to get my six-foot-ten-inch frame into a small Fiat sedan shoe box. It was an art. Folding me in was like turning a new chapter of a whole new book. Bob's eyes beamed as he shifted the gears of his first automobile. He turned corners with the grace and confidence of an Indy driver. I hardly fit in the thing but had plenty of room to enjoy his happiness, share his pride. Bob was from a poor family in Portsmouth, on the Ohio River. His mother worked at a shoe factory for minimum wage. He'd put himself through school and was about to deliver a message that, to me, was a miracle, a message that would give me cause to lighten up on God somewhat, and to see things a little bit clearer.

"I'm going for my master's, starting next semester at night school," said Bob. "I got a job downtown in the meantime. A friend of my mom won this in a raffle, gave it to me for nine hundred dollars. He didn't want me taking a year off to work the steel mill just to get a car."

I held back my news, for the time being.

"That's great. Where's your job? What doing?"

"Western Southern, it's an insurance company down on Fourth Street," he said.

I blurted my news from walking out on the coach to starting at the Union Central Life Insurance Company on Fourth Street on Monday morning; how I was going to attend night school, too. Bob soaked it in, listening like a brother, unjudgementally being there as a friend.

"You can ride down and back with me. It'll be perfect."

We scooted like a roller skate up Vine Street to a White Castle hamburger house, for a treat of some nine-cent hamburgers. We got a buck's worth each, plus milk shakes, and sat in celebration and talked for an hour or so. Bob told me about his someday wanting to become a probation officer working with troubled kids. I told him my dream of becoming a writer.

"Where're you going to live?" I asked.

"At the house," he said. "For now, anyway."

"Can I stay, even if I'm off scholarship?" I asked.

"Sure. The university doesn't control us. I think your rent is paid up through next June, anyway, if I'm not mistaken. Check with Boylan."

We talked of how those little burgers kept many students alive and fed.

"Who would have thought you could ever be able to walk in and eat for a dime?" asked Hock.

A month later someone told the newspaper that I had been declared ineligible because of my grades, and the paper printed it that way. It wasn't true. I withdrew with passing grades. It was a goddamned lie coming from the left side of the salad bowl.

Chapter 5

Working with Mike (as he insisted I call him) Jones and my boss, Virginia Hicks (Ginny), I had one of the most quality-filled years of my entire life. The sales promotion department of the Union Central Life Insurance Company was incredible. There wasn't a detail of writing and printing the written word that I wouldn't experience and learn. There were four full-time writers churning out pages of interesting and readable advice daily for families on budgeting and building for the future. Large insurance companies were trustworthy in the day for estate planning. People relied on them as a source of financial and health information. The bigger and better ones didn't let them down.

We published a monthly flier called *Dollars and Sense*, a semimonthly two-hundred-page policyholder magazine, and an endless supply of brochures on every type of insurance available from one of the most respected and reputable life insurance companies in the country. Every word of every page had to be proofread by four eyes, out loud, without distraction—one person reading to another reader. The company had the largest privately owned printing plant in the city, aside from the newspaper, nestled in the basement of the building. Huge letterset presses and typesetting equipment would take the words written by the writers and proofreaders on the fourth floor, proofed and laid out in our department, and turn them daily into glossy magazines with stapled spines, folded brochures, fliers, and pamphlets.

Mike was a man who took an interest in everything he did and liked when people did the same. He'd walk proudly up to your desk and ask how it was going and if he could help in any way. He'd take his middle finger and push his glasses up on his nose and greet you with a big, wide—but genuine—smoker smile, his eyes grinning through happy squints. He was a graduate of DePauw University.

Mike loved music, especially jazz. As a jazz trumpeter, he'd had occasion to know Rosemary Clooney and other singers and musicians; he'd had drinks and dinner once with Bing Crosby, and played backup trumpet a time or two at the WLW radio station—once for the famous singer and actress Doris Day, also from Cincinnati. He was as fascinated by the detail of running words, almost like music notes, through the department as he was about enjoying life and music. He would grin and wave a salute as he walked with long, confident strides through the department to his corner office, tucking a fresh pack of cigarettes into the breast pocket of his shirt, saying hi if he caught your eye.

He flipped out when I told him Stan Kenton had played for my senior prom in high school. (The Catholic schools in Milwaukee banded together for economic reasons and put on one large collective senior prom in a hotel ballroom.) Mike didn't micromanage, he just made it clear what level of quality and attention to detail he expected. He was a great man, and he was a trumpet player. He loved jazz, and anyone who listened to jazz with him at Stan's Blue Note or down in the Coal Hole in the basement of the hotel across the street would know there were no ethnic or color barriers in jazz.

"When you touch the words that go through our word factory," he said, "take an ownership in them—just as though you were the author of them or the end reader. Speak up if you see something you don't like or don't understand. We have readers out in the real world counting on you. If you don't understand something, they won't. It'll make sense one day, Jerry, the writer in you will just come out one day, but first things first."

Mike affectionately called Ginny Hicks "the Indian princess," her tight, curly hair tied back for work in two tight ponytails, mainly keeping it out of her face. Ginny was a joy to work with and to learn from. She was patient in her delivery and let me take on any of the challenges I wanted to try—including layout and pasteup. She made me the official liaison between our department on the fourth floor and the printing plant in the basement—which made me feel important. If there was ever a place where I could learn every single little detail of words and their journey onto pages to be read, I was in the thick of it. Three people in the department handled the proofreading, design, and production management. Mike later signed off. I was one of the three. I learned the styles of four writers. I saw their different approaches. I learned grammar. I learned how to take their words into a design, and I was a student of every aspect of the printing process.

Bob Hock drove me downtown every day. I'd walk from his parking garage on Fourth Street over to the Union Central Life building at Fourth and Vine. I remember it was my first day of work learning that dress hats weren't for me. I had stepped out of Bob's car and started walking down Fourth Street when a pigeon shit on my hat. From the splash it looked like it was from twenty stories up. From that day on, no hat, and I hugged the curb side of the sidewalk. Every weeknight I would walk back and he'd drive me to the Sodality House for a change of clothes and a walk to class if it was a school night, or over to Chico's for some mostaccioli and meatballs if it wasn't. There was a big round table with an assortment of people—about eight—who would grace the supper table as they came in.

It was like a family meal, and we talked into the dark. Larry McDermott, for example, a kind, gently spoken, affable redheaded gentleman; the president of a large printing ink company; and Joe, the quiet librarian for Xavier University. Various assorted others in all shapes and temperaments would come by and join us. Every time I was inspired and spent countless hours trying to write a short story for submission to *Reader's Digest*, I would pass it around the table for feedback. Everyone seemed to like my stories. Everyone except for *Reader's Digest*, that is.

Late fall, a friend of Hock's from his job at Western Southern fixed me up with a girl he'd met at the Busy Bee Lounge one Friday night and thought I would like. She invited me to a UC football game the following day, a Saturday. I loved her southern drawl. She was from Lexington, and we seemed to hit it off. It was the last football game before the Christmas holiday break for both campuses. My thoughts still hovered around the convent and that waning hope my girlfriend would appear on my doorstep, but Debbie and I went to the game in the UC stadium and had fun. The day after the game she invited me to a movie on her campus. During the movie, she slipped a folded piece of paper with her home telephone number into my shirt pocket, to call her during Christmas, if I cared to.

Worked out I cared to.

Just before ten one evening, I dropped my economics book to the floor, crawled off my bunk, stepped into the darkened TV room barefoot, fumbled around in the dark, and picked up the telephone to call her. I would wish her a merry Christmas. I'd get her on the phone first and then sit in the overstuffed easy chair by the television and talk for a spell. As I heard the phone ringing, I started to feel around in the dark for the chair. A male voice answered.

"Hello."

"Hi, is Debbie there?"

"Who's calling?"

"This is Jerry."

"Jerry who?"

"Jerry Antil."

"Where're you calling from?"

"I'm at Xavier, in Cincinnati."

"Debbie ain't going to be talking to no goddamned Yankee Jew."

Click.

My first thought was defensive— I wasn't Jewish. Then I froze in the shame that I had that thought. I stood speechless and began to shake in the dark. The hatred in his voice was for anyone he thought was a Yankee. He hated us all. The receiver fell from my hand, bounced off the top edge of the television, and dropped to the floor with a thud. I could feel the blood rushing from my face. I was right scared; this seemed like a death threat to me. It was like I had just talked to the Klu Klux Klan I'd heard about.

I was a young boy from Delphi Falls in some strange world of hatred I'd never seen in real life before. The phone call made it come back to me. Woolworth's in downtown Cincinnati, where blacks couldn't sit and eat at the lunch counter, and anyone who worked at Woolworth's or anyone who sold goods to them and let them get away with it. Every one of them gave people like this idiot an absolute power—over his own daughter or sister (I wasn't sure which) and probably entire families, maybe even entire neighborhoods. Being away from school full-time, and not playing basketball anymore, I had forgotten. I started remembering the war years I'd grown up in, with the Hitlers and Mussolinis and their hatred and atrocities. I sat on my bunk, feet on the floor, and shook for an hour.

Driving in the next morning, Hock told me this was the South, tried to console me by reminding me we were sitting in the middle of the Mason-Dixon Line and it was going to take some time before things changed.

I didn't want to wait. The phone call last night was like a time bomb set off in my brain. I stepped off the elevator and caught Mike's eye standing by his office door.

"Mike, something happened last night, and, well, I just got to tell somebody or I'll bust. I need your advice," I said.

"Just marry the girl, or leave town," he bellowed out in laughter, walking into his office, inviting me in with an arm motion. "What's up?" he asked, sitting down, motioning me to sit. He saw the look on my face and knew it might be serious.

"Push the door," he said.

I told what had happened with my phone call the evening before. Mike had a sense of my naïvetés and stepped slowly in careful, responsible steps, as a mentor and friend. After I told him my story, he slid his coffee cup closer to him on his glass desktop and placed it on a sheet of paper.

"Jerry, a new country, like America, is kind of like a runaway kid," he started. "More than one country tried to adopt this kid (us), most by force, and this kid kicked the crap out of them, every one of 'em. A runaway kid like us can't grow up without having some blemishes or some pimples. Doesn't make blemishes or pimples right, doesn't make them good—just makes them facts of life sometimes. What a kid nation like us needs are good writers to tell the truth and good artists to show the truth and good musicians who play harmony, each setting examples for the nation of what's possible. Jazz tells the blues, and it came from New Orleans."

Mike pointed his finger toward his window, at the old, retired steamboat that was moored as a restaurant way over on the Kentucky shore of the Ohio River.

"See over there?"

"Where?"

"That riverboat across the river. See that boat?"

"I see it."

"Wasn't too awful long ago that'd be carrying slaves somewhere on it," he said, "but that pimple's cleared up."

"I wonder if she knows I called and he said that," I said.

"Hell, he was probably a dead-drunk nobody or an old jealous high school boyfriend who she told about you—ever think of that? Who knows? My guess: a jealous prank. Put it in your book—you know, for that song you'll write someday, Jerry."

"Song?" I asked.

"You know ole Hank?" he asked.

"Hank Williams? Sure."

"Got a favorite?"

"Same as my dad's, 'I'm So Lonesome I Could Cry,'" I said.

Mike picked up his coffee cup and held it in both hands for warmth, looked up at me over it, and whispered in a raspy, perfect pitch through the words and melody:

Hear the lonesome whip-poor-will
He sounds too blue to fly
The midnight train is whining low
I'm so lonesome I could cry.

"Nice," I said.

"You know what ole Hank said about songwriting, don't you?" asked Mike.

"What'd he say?"

"Ole Hank said a body had to survey a lot of farmland looking over the backside of a mule to be a good country singer. Something like that." Mike slurped some coffee.

"That's nice," I said.

"It's a metaphor, Jerry. That phone call last night is just another notch in your life belt; it just got you looking at some asshole from Lexington—but hell, he could have been from anywhere. Lexington doesn't have the corner on assholes. There's plenty to go around, about everywhere. If you're going to be a writer, you'll have to get a lot dirtier than from ducking some jealous drunkard's punch."

"Thanks, Mike."

On weekends sometimes, Mike would join us at the Coal Hole lounge or some other dark smoky place where we could talk and listen to good live music. He would close his eyes and hear the tones of the trumpet or sax talking to him. He would encourage me daily to fill my book, as he would call "my memory files," with observations and experiences of life so one day I could write about them from experience.

"Take it all in, Jerry, every second, every hour of every passerby; watch everything and study it all, every smell, every detail," he would say.

Chapter 6

It was a Wednesday night, just before Spring Break. Some of the guys at the Sodality House were sitting around on the sofa and floor watching the eleven o'clock news. Some were stuffing their duffels with laundry to take home to their moms over the break, others with swimming trunks and sweatshirts for their treks to the Fort Lauderdale beaches and fun. Most lent an ear to the television, catching up on the news of the day. The sports news came on, and the television camera focused in on a sneery-eyed short man, hair blowing in the wind, with knife-sharp articulation and a slow, deep southern drawl, like he was dragging a trotline with his tonsils. It was Governor George Wallace of Alabama, the announcer said. Governor Wallace came on the television and was talking cold, fearless, and straight to the camera:

"I, for one," he started, "wouldn't like to see our boys play basketball with the coloreds of Loyola University in any playoffs up north in Chicago. The boys of Alabama don't have to be playing a team of coloreds just to show how good they already are," he said to the willing microphone. "Our boys are winners, and they don't have to prove anything by going to Chicago."

Every person sitting around the television gasped. I stood, frozen, and watched for more. There was no more. This was the first time I felt I was a part of the bigger picture. I was seeing it from the outside as it affected a world I once knew: college basketball. I looked around the room at my mates watching the news; they sat there listening to the governor in disdain—yes, I could see it in their eyes—but they were also watching in helplessness, a fear, knowing this was the world we lived in. It was then I remembered the basketball game I'd attended at the Garden as a freshman, where I watched an empty bourbon bottle heaved from the stands bounce on court just behind Oscar during a time-out. It dawned on me that it now appeared that no one at the real top was doing anything about it. If state governors, who were at the top like Governor Wallace was, talked that kind of hatred and trash and got away with it, God help us. God help America, and I still wasn't all that happy with God Himself at the time.

This was the first time I felt inspired, that doing nothing was only an option and that no one had to just stand there if they didn't choose to. I walked up to the television set, pushed the off button, picked up the telephone receiver resting on top of the television, and dialed "O."

Some of the guys stopped their packing to watch and listen.

A couple of clicks and pops on the phone and a voice came on: "Operator, how may I assist you?"

"Operator, I want the governor's mansion in the state of Alabama on the wire." I didn't say please.

Bob Hock raised his brow at my nerve. I put my hand over the mouthpiece.

"I've seen my dad get people on the phone a million times," I said. "I'll just mimic him."

I was learning my second lesson in marketing—positioning. People only take you or your product or service as important or as serious as you present it to them in their first impression of it. If I thought like my dad, I could be my dad, to some extent. "That's why the New York Yankees have a dress code" my dad would say. "They come to the ballpark looking like winners."

"One moment please," said the operator.

I was a nineteen-year-old boy whose knees were shaking. For all the operator knew, I was another governor. The guys mingled closer, gathering on the floor to listen.

Someone at the other end picked up the phone.

"Governor's residence," the voice said.

"Governor Wallace, please."

"Who may I say is calling?"

"I'm Jerry Antil at Xavier University in Cincinnati."

"One moment, sir."

I was about to faint.

"This is Governor Wallace, how can I be of service?"

I trembled. Visions of his sneer looking at the television camera slapped me in the face. Will he get me? Can he kill me?

"Governor Wallace, I play basketball at Xavier University, and I don't think it's fair, you're not letting your team play Loyola University—just because of the color of some of the players on their team. It's not fair. I don't think it's right."

I felt my chest pounding like a kettle drum.

"Young man, I hope our boys play them and I hope we beat them handily. Thank you for calling, son. Goodbye."

Click.

I was amazed he told me they might actually play now.

Four guys sitting around, watching and listening, dropped their jaws and stared into space as I hung up the phone, turned, and walked to my room, my knees wobbling. What was the boldest thing I'd ever done in my early life turned out, in retrospect, to be the one thing I did that I'm proudest of.

The next morning Mike yelled at Ginny and his four writers to come into his office. "Quick, folks, we don't have all day." They scrambled in. With Mike's grin, they sensed a party. "Gather round, gather round." He shuffled them in like cattle in a pen. "Close the door, Wagner," he said to one of the writers, and he plopped down in his chair with a major grin on his face, ready to take it all in again, like a big kid. "Tell it again, Jerry. Start over. Go slow—don't miss a detail. Tell them about your phone call last night. You've got to hear this, gang." He grinned.

I told the story again, not missing a thing. I told about Spring Break coming up at Xavier and half my friends at the Sodality House packing to go to Fort Lauderdale and the basketball finals being scheduled and about us watching the eleven o'clock news, about Governor Wallace coming on television and what he said about Alabama playing Loyola. I recounted my telephone call in every syllable, word for word, everything I said, what the operator and his house staff said, and every word the governor said.

"And you just picked up the phone asked the operator for the governor of Alabama?" Mike bellowed in glee.

"I told her I wanted the governor's mansion in Alabama," I said. "I didn't say please, to make it sound more important. Like they do it in the movies. I thought I heard someone saying governors lived in mansions, so I tried it—asking for the governor's mansion. I remember listening to my dad outright asking to be connected to people like that on the telephone. He'd just say, 'Get so and so on the wire for me, operator.'"

"Whatever possessed you to do it, Jerry?" asked Ginny.

"When I saw what he was saying about not wanting his team to play colored guys, I thought about Oscar Robertson and Ducky and Frank Pinchback—guys I know or played with not being able to eat at Woolworth's," I said. "One of my good friends, Ducky Castille—I thought of him not being allowed to play basketball in Alabama just because he's black. About calling the governor—my dad always taught me telephone operators knew everything and how to find just about anybody. Myrtie, our operator back home in New Woodstock, sure did."

The writers clapped their hands, celebrating my daring.

"This young man has a passion smoldering inside him, I can smell it," said Mike. "He wants to write. I don't have to tell anyone in this room, eagles take wing, and he's an eagle. I've watched him fly on the basketball court, and believe you me, the kid has grit, he's got a burning need to fulfill a talent that's about to bust out. We'll lose him, sure, but let's give him a break he can remember us by so we can say we knew him once. It's been better than a year now; any ideas on a writing assignment he can cut his teeth on before he takes off? What can any of you spare?"

Bud Wagner said, "Mike, the Lester Rosen story. Lester was our biggest million-dollar insurance sales producer last year, and we were about to do a feature in the magazine on him and his Million Dollar Roundtable award. How about letting Jerry interview him and write the piece?"

"Good one," said Mike. He then looked at Ginny and winked. "Princess, you see to the travel arrangements, and see he has expense money."

Ginny winked back and smiled.

To the best of my understanding, that was the first and only time the Union Central Life Insurance Company ever sent a writer on a trip to gather and write a story. Mike Jones was that kind of a friend, one who cared about my future and getting me off on the right foot.

Everyone shook my hand as they stepped out, congratulating me for my call to the governor and wishing me all the luck in the world. It was almost like they were saying goodbye. I started out the door. I lagged back.

"Travel?" I asked Mike.

"Lester's in Memphis, Jerry. How're you going to learn what makes a southern million-dollar-producer gentleman tick if you haven't stomped a 'boll weevil' under foot along the way? Go work it out with Ginny. I'll meet with you before you go. Fill you in. Get out of here. I'm behind a whole hour already because of a goddamned Governor Wallace." Mike beamed at me.

I started toward my desk, stopped, turned back, and stuck my head into Mike's office again.

"Mike, I just remembered, my sister teaches at the University of Tennessee, in Memphis. She lives there somewhere close. If I can stay with her and save on a hotel bill, can I stay over another day and visit with her and the family?"

Mike reached behind him, picked up his phone, and pressed a buzzer on it, for his secretary.

"Helen, tell the Princess to make Jerry's plane reservations to Memphis going in on a Friday afternoon. He'll spend Monday with Lester, and have him fly back that evening." He hung up the phone. "Work for you?" he asked. "You've got a couple days to catch up with your big sister."

"Thanks, Mike, I won't let you down."

"Jerry, soak it all in, the good, the bad—see it first, observe it, then you decide how you want to write about it one day. Keep your mind's eye open and alert at all times, my friend. You'll only let me down if you don't get to Beale Street and listen to some blues. Call Lester and make an appointment. Tell him you're coming to him."

Chapter 7

There was something inspiring about holding back the curtain and peering out through a small portal window of the DC-7 at the two large propeller engines on the wing on my side of the plane. It added a sense of adventure to my imagination. They each belched a blue and then a white smoke puff as the blades began to slice the air. I thought of the stories my oldest sister's husband, Don, told of being eighteen in the early 1940s, a year younger than me now, sitting behind the wheel of his B-17, lifting off with two, three thousand other planes in darkness for another bombing raid on Hitler, some planes and crews lucky, some not so lucky.

In the air, I watched below and saw the lush stretches of America, the emerald green hills and pastures of Kentucky and the rich, multicolored Virginia mountains rolling by under me like cupcakes on the conveyer belt at Klosterman's bakery, waiting to be grabbed up and iced. The hills and mountains melted into flat, beige cotton fields with endless rows of dirt, dusty brown roads, and lines of empty hopper cars resting on the rail and stretching as long as the wet, whiskery rice fields, their mouths open like baby robins waiting to be fed. The plane banked left and circled the airport once, then left again, leveling out and settling in for a landing. Coming down, watching the runway lifting to meet the belly of the plane, I thought back to the time I was seven and my dad put me on that DC-3 all alone to Syracuse, just for the adventure. I thought of the magic of his waiting for me when I landed.

Clunk.

The thud of the wheels touching down broke my trance. Looking out, I noticed light reflecting on the otherwise unseen turning of the long propellers. They belched a great gasp of air and then seemed to exhale, the sound like a barn fan I remembered from growing up. My hands clenched armrests as the sudden slowing jerked me forward from my seatback and snug into my seatbelt.

In my turn, I stepped up to the opening of the plane and

leaned down, as careful in not bumping my head as I was determined not to miss a thing on this new adventure.

Memphis hot was not the muggy Cincinnati hot, which was more like a hot wet barber's towel. This heat snapped at my face like a hot plastic hardware-store flyswatter. It reminded me to stay awake. The thought ran through my mind that there would be no dad to meet me here, as I stepped into adulthood. I was on my own now. I was a writer on assignment; it was official and for real, my inner self mused. Even in the heat, the thought of being a writer gave me a chill, a sheepish, hair-on-the-back-of-the-neck tickle; I gritted my teeth and grinned.

Walking from the plane to the sidewalk that led to the airport building, I saw an impressive bale of cotton as tall as I was, it seemed—fluffy puffs of white, raw cotton hemorrhaging at both ends of a tight wrapping of coarse white cotton cloth. It was like a cheap cigar, bigger than life, on display for visitors' and newcomers' viewing pleasure. It was West Memphis's way of saying "welcome," and that the cotton we wore every day was pretty much their industry. I walked past the bale. I didn't yet appreciate the "pick that cotton, tote that bale" element of the human sweat and toil it represented.

My imagination stirred and played an overture, like I was in a movie, as I pulled the West Memphis airport door open for the first time in my life. Noticing reflections behind me, through the turning glass, I held the door and stood aside, letting a lady and her young son just three steps behind walk through first. Flashbacks of my dad removing his hat in elevators, never turning his back when there were ladies present, came to mind. I turned, gently tipped my head down to an even six feet as they walked by. She smiled at the courtesy. I walked in slowly, deliberately, not wanting to miss a single detail, taking everything in.

Skycaps rushed about pushing two-wheel carts, some loaded with luggage, others empty, on the hunt for treasures of their own. Fine southern ladies with tight combed hair, wearing sunglasses with ivory rims and long, tufted crinoline dresses, stood as though pedestaled beside stacks of matching luggage. In the air the scent of crisp crackling seared bacon from the counter sandwich grille blended with black boot wax being slapped on the leather of the Bostonian dress shoes of a man perched high on the throne, reading a meticulous, creased, and folded *Wall Street Journal*. The heat inside the airport was about the same as it was out by the cotton bale, without the impertinence of the gusts that mussed a lady's quaff or set a gentleman's silk tie in a recalcitrant slapping up at face or shoulder.

Off in the distance, the full length of the great hall, through sun-beamed hazes in an intermittent glowing down through tall windows, like leaning Greek columns, my eye caught the image of a shadow-darkened silhouette of a man. He appeared to be a lone man standing at the far end of the busy terminal, a straw dress hat in one hand pressed to his breast, as any southern gentleman might in someone's home. He wore a wrinkled seersucker suit and a striped tie, his other arm stretched high, patiently sweeping the air long and slow like a ship's lone flag semaphore. While walking in his direction, my eyes darted about the hall, respecting the advantages of peripheral vision, as they had been trained to do on very busy basketball courts during game crunches where every detail captured could count to your advantage. My curiosity vacuumed the Tennessee airport, missing not so much as a speck of dust, taking in all the faces and expressions, observing the habits of another place.

I could make it out now, the face of the man waving the arm. It belonged to my brother-in-law.

Norman Bjourne Bredesen was a tanned, balding man with an inquisitive look in his eye. He was athletic, trim, and a healthy early to midforties. Of Nordic heritage, son and brother of Lutheran ministers, he had served most of his adult life at sea, as a merchant mariner—and served in that capacity throughout the war. Norman was part fish, we were convinced. When Dorothy first brought him home to Delphi Falls to meet the folks, he climbed our seventy-foot waterfall like a salmon before even saying hello to my mom. He was the first to have climbed it. When we drove to neighboring Cazenovia for a Sunday picnic on its lakeshore, he swam the full distance of the lake and back while we had sandwiches and potato salad and wondered if he was charming or touched in the head.

It was charm, we soon agreed. He was a decorated hero in World War II, having saved the lives of many sailors—diving through burning oil at sea to bring them aboard another vessel while his own, torpedo-gutted, was beginning to sink. He swam to their listing ship to look for more men, and when he swam back to the rescue vessel after a long delay, the ship's captain asked him what had taken him so long.

"There was no one else on board, so I found the galley and made a sandwich before I jumped ship to swim back," was his explanation.

He would tell the story of how the survivors watched as their faltering supply ship relented in burning oil and lifted its bow, turning like the eye of a water buffalo with a lion's jaw lodged in its neck staring off in final submission, giving in with dignity. The ship bow paused as if to salute one last time, then began to sink back down, quiet, efficient, with all the sailors' pictures from home, into the ocean's darkness, to her grave.

During the war, Norm was shot through the jowl by a Nazi officer who boarded his ship for an inspection at a neutral port and thought he was reaching in his wall safe for a pistol, not his papers. He sewed his own stitches in his neck with needle and thread.

After the war, he lost his ship and source of income, and every penny he had, after a storm lodged it on a coral reef and ripped its hull apart, rendering it and its contents unsalvageable. He removed the ship's clock from the wall of the wheelhouse with a screwdriver, dove off the deep side, and swam with his friend, the ship's clock to shore. He would say that on many stormy days at sea alone in the wheelhouse, the ship's clock would be the only voice he would hear.

Norman's smile turned as big as his wave when I caught his eye. He gave me a big embrace, kissing me on the cheek and welcoming me aboard—welcoming me to Memphis. He was landlocked now, but he welcomed me like he was welcoming me into a port somewhere around the world.

"Dottie's at the hospital," he said. "She had a baby boy, Eric Bjourne, born late Wednesday night—big healthy baby. We called your mom and dad. Has word gotten to you yet?"

"Not yet. I heard she was pregnant, wasn't sure when the baby was due, though. There'll be a family letter coming around soon telling us the baby news."

"You're just in time," he said. "We'll let her sleep today, see her later. Bring her home tomorrow. Right now I have to get back to the clinic for a meeting. If you don't mind, I'll drop you at the house; Karen will love to see her Uncle Jerry. We'll have wine and cheese later, maybe go to Beale Street. We know this great bistro, reminds me of a port in Haiti ... better music, though."

Norm worked for the Public Health Department of Civil Defense. My other brother-in-law, Don (the ex B-17 Pilot), got him the job after Norm lost his ship and floundered a spell. Norman never lost his passion for the sea, but he managed as well as he could on dry land.

"Do you work in Memphis?" I asked.

"Forrest City; it's across the river, in Arkansas. That's where we live, for now," said Norman. "Across the mighty Mississippi; the federal government's Health Education and Welfare Department is trying to eradicate syphilis one neighborhood and village at a time."

He tried to make it sound as if he was as fulfilled as he had been as a merchant marine, but I saw through it.

"Tell me about you. What are you up to?" he asked.

"I'm a writer, doing an assignment, my first one. What hospital is she in?"

"Memphis."

"No hospitals in Forrest City?"

"She's in Memphis."

"Isn't there one closer than Memphis? Is it a long drive?"

"Fifty miles.

How come Dorothy's in Memphis if you live in Arkansas?"

"Oh, we have a hospital, but you know Dottie. She refused to have her child born in a state where Eugene Faubus was governor and his name may appear on the birth certificate. The man blocked the Negro schoolgirls from entering the elementary school and she's never forgiven him. Christ's sake, she's stubborn. You know your sister when she gets her head set. She was not about to give Governor Faubus the privilege of increasing his state's population or tax revenue at her baby's expense. She wouldn't make sense even when her water broke. I had to drive ninety, ninety-five—damned near flew over an embankment into the rice field, barely missing a farm wagon without taillights, just trying to get her to the bridge, across it, and into the hospital in Memphis without getting killed or arrested. That was her final word, even after about the third time she screamed into labor over the Mississippi. God, I love that woman!"

Listening about the governor of Arkansas not allowing black children into schools reminded me of my phone call with Governor Wallace just a few weeks before with his cold, heartless denial of the black basketball players at Loyola.

I didn't have to write one word down of this adventure into Arkansas and Memphis; I would never forget a depressing moment of it.

Norm turned the car west and we headed into a late afternoon sun.

Chapter 8

The old Volvo coughed onto the bridge, still wheezing from its midnight run across the border to the Memphis hospital a couple nights before.

Crossing over the Mississippi River bridge from Tennessee to Arkansas felt like picking a book from a shelf of the past and paging back in time of another world. Every ripple or wave of the massive mud-embrowned river legend was a page, stirring my memory's index, whispering a different thought with every steel girder flashing past and blocking the sun. I strained my neck back hoping to see a steamboat, maybe a raft, maybe the kindly old storyteller himself in white hat and moustache, waving.

As we drove into the village, he shifted the Volvo down slow to a crawl, like a ship entering a harbor. I could tell right off, Forrest City was like no other place I'd seen. It was a low-income cookie-cutter white suburban neighborhood, like a harmless big old spider, filled with white folks working the power plant or the factory or two, surrounded by a stringy cobweb of poor black families with their modest homes, shacks, and shanties, their fix-it shops with one light bulb hanging down on a wire in the middle, vegetable and fruit stands, ironing boards on porches, and medicine shops with church fliers glued to the windows. Each with opened front doors for air, quiet testimony there'd be nothing worth stealing or even snooping around inside for. Two broad-busted black ladies with scarves tied flat over their heads stood in starched white dresses, one on each side of a large laundry basket that took them both to carry. They were hanging white sheets and pillow cases on a tight rope clothesline strung twice between two shotgun row houses with an empty baby crib in between. Two small, barefooted Negro boys were kicking at a patched-up soccer ball.

"Scat on out of here," the ladies told them, "kickin' that ball—before you raise some dust and our dander for sure, ya here? You both git and go play on the other side. Not goin' to be tellin' you agin, now. Git."

Then they put big broad grins on, laughing and smiling, their bosoms bouncing, telling each other what wonderful boys they both had and how much they loved those boys, rascals that they were sometimes.

After Norman came home from his meeting, he invited me to go for a walk. He picked up an old television from the floor of the garage and carried it while we walked. I talked with Norman the few blocks from their small, comfortable home into town, into the black section of town, taking it all in, trying not to stare. Norm told me the interstate highway would come through soon and it would change everything for the town, like the railroads and rivers of old had for other places. We were heading to the local TV repair man to see if he could get the foggy wriggle out of it. Norman had run out of coat hangers to rig up an antenna long enough to pull in all three channels from Memphis. He could almost get one. Dorothy had run out of patience. She'd be happy with the one channel if she could see it.

"I teach speech therapy," she would declare. "I'm not all that inspired by listening to evening news on a television that sounds like the newscasters need speech therapy. Either get it so we can see and hear it, or get a radio for our bedroom."

Norm wanted to surprise her with a good picture by the time she got home from the hospital tomorrow.

"This part of town is wonderful," he said. "It's like a port in the South Pacific I tied up to once. I needed a compass. I'd broken the lens out of the one I had, setting a bottle of brandy on it without watching what I was doing. You can find just about anything you want in town, here, like Singapore, if you hunt for it. The locals aren't big on advertising, you just have to find it yourself, ask around for it. If they are in the mood, and they like you, you can buy it."

"Mr. Norman," said the silvery-gray-haired black man in suspenders and blue Sears Roebuck work shirt as he lifted the television from his arms and turned, carrying it into his one-room shop to set it on the work table for what could very well have been the twentieth time.

"I think I pretty near did all I can do for this here particular television," the man said. "I'll look at it again for you, because you carried it all this way, but I think it's seen its last days. You sure it ain't never been dropped, Mr. Norman? Now you know you and Miss Dorothy been moving about some, don't ya see, you sure it never been dropped? I 'spect it has."

Norman would give it one more hope.

"Mr. Washington, I had an engine mate once, picked him up in the Philippines, not near as smart or as talented as you are. He kept my ship running on fumes and baling wire through a two-day storm in the middle of the Triangle one time," he said. "Now I know there is just some secret to this television's problems, and bringing it back to you enough times will show it someday, and I know you're just the man to find it. Why, I see it fine. It's my wife who has the difficulty with it."

Television parts don't wear out like pistons and gears, was Norman's logic.

Norm turned to me. "It's a process of elimination, at a dollar fifty a visit." He winked. Then he asked me in a whisper, as though I'd been away at sea, "You have any idea what these things cost new?"

"Mr. Norman, I got to go to gospel tomorrow, but come by Monday and I'll have her ready for you best I can do," said the television man. "I swear, Mr. Norman, I'll surely do my best, but I think it's been dropped a time or two."

We walked through the town square, Norm buying two oranges here, a small can of lighter fluid there. He'd ask a man just how long the used garden hose was and were both ends good. He told a lady in a rocker on her front stoop that her quilt should sure enough be in the Smithsonian, turning her face into a big, near toothless smile. "Oh, go on out of here," she said. "But thank ye kindly, Mr. Norm."

I took it all in. I felt the sense of the poverty of Arkansas, but I could see and feel the graciousness in the faces, good people dealing with the bad hand they'd been dealt. This seemed a long many miles different from the stature and pride at my Memphis airport greeting, just across the river. I didn't see sadness here, but I saw melancholy, resolve, which didn't make me feel any better. The townspeople I met and watched trusted Norman and Dorothy. Norman had been a ship's captain at sea long enough to know that ship hands were reliable and trustworthy or they weren't. It was a simple matter of character and makeup, not color and ethnicity. He was color-blind, and his wife, more than a decade junior to him, adored him for it.

When she came home on Saturday afternoon, we celebrated the new baby boy.

"Dorothy, the bedroom television will be as good as new by Monday," Norm promised his wife.

He plunked a block of cheese on a sheet of newspaper in the middle of the table, a bottle of wine for them, a tall bottle of Canada Dry ginger ale for little Karen and me, and some glasses and knives. At my Catholic Confirmation, when I was twelve, I had taken an oath not to drink any alcohol until I was twenty-one. Norman respected that. Dorothy rested on a stack of pillows spread out on the floor with the new baby boy in a port-a-crib nearby; Karen gently petted the baby's tiny hands with her finger. We had everything we needed to take us far into the night with conversation, laughter, stories of adventure, and sharp cheddar.

I told about my call to Governor Wallace. Norman pounded his fist bottom proud and firm down on the table in approval again and again, shouting, "Here, here!"

Dorothy said, "You're just like Dad. You are so much his spitting image."

She told the story about the time in the early fifties when she suggested to Mom that she was going to work on her master's and wanted very much to do a dissertation about General Douglas MacArthur.

"And?" I asked.

"Dad was walking by the table when I was saying all this to Mom, and he interrupted us and said, 'Give him a call.'"

"Give who a call?" I asked.

"MacArthur."

"*The* General MacArthur?"

"Exactly, *the* General MacArthur."

"Dad told you to just—give him a call. Wasn't he like Eisenhower or Patton, something, high up, important?"

"General Douglas MacArthur ran the whole Pacific during the war and ran the Japan occupation after the war," Dorothy said.

"Well, did you?"

"I did. The operator took a while but found him at the Waldorf Astoria in New York City and got his wife on the telephone first. After I told her what I wanted to do, Mrs. MacArthur invited me down and I was their guest for almost a week. I got to interview General Douglas MacArthur right in their hotel salon and at high tea every day at three o'clock in the Waldorf Astoria lobby cafe. Oh, it was wonderful. We kids were so lucky to grow up with our mom and dad always telling us anything was possible—some more than others, with Dad's traits. You're so much like Dad."

I beamed at the compliment.

Later, I stretched out on the sofa in the dark, smelling the wines and cheese and lingering over memories and stories. I smiled, staring through the window up at a full moon. Off somewhere I could hear gospel voices and piano—hymns starting and stopping, then starting again, rehearsing over the stirs of scratching katydids and locusts. It lulled me to sleep.

I opened my eyes and got up with the sun on Sunday. I closed the screen door behind me and went for a walk, alone, leaving everyone else to sleep in. It was sometime after dawn, but I wasn't certain of the time. This would be my last day to visit, to soak Arkansas in; tomorrow I would be in Memphis with Lester Rosen all day, interviewing him, flying out that night. I walked down the neighborhood sidewalk to the same main street of the village we had walked to the day before, and then along its sidewalk. The shops and stores were buttoned up in quiet rest. A few old men sat alone on stoops or the top steps savoring a new day, listening to a rooster off on the outskirts of town. One man with a pipe, another rubbing a cloth over a shoe he held in his left hand, the other shoe resting on the step beside him.

I walked through town, eyes down, best as possible, letting people have their privacy. Between the dry-goods store and the small pharmacy with the Coca-Cola image painted on its brick wall, the paint peeling, I noticed a large silhouette of what seemed to be a two-, maybe three-story white stucco building way off in the distance. I walked to the end of the sidewalk, turned, and looked again, this time with a better vantage. It was a hospital, according to the painted sign on the road. It was set back a fair distance from the road, on what looked like brown baked dirt and crabgrass; I had the impression lawns never "took" later than spring in the hot Arkansas sun. I decided to go see the hospital. Take a look at the place Dorothy refused to have her baby in on account of Governor Faubus.

I looked both ways and crossed the highway, walking toward the building. I could see dried topsoil settle on my shoes the closer I walked to the building. I watched nurses in white uniforms being dropped off by people in cars and old pickup trucks.

I walked up the steps, pulled the door open, and entered a large front hallway, ceiling fans every eight or ten feet throwing shadows along with their helpful breezes. I walked in maybe ten feet more and studied the tall wall in front of me. There were two drinking fountains in the center, about five feet apart, dividing the wall. In the center of the wall to the right of the drinking fountains was a sign that read, WHITE WING, with a painted arrow pointing to the right. In the center of the wall to the left of the drinking fountains was a sign that read, COLORED WING, with a painted arrow pointing to the left.

I stood frozen. Its dehumanizing arrogance didn't register, at first. Then it did. A sense of fear came over me. I didn't feel shame. I didn't feel dishonor. I felt fear. As my peripheral vision took everything in, I looked down at the drinking fountains again. The one on the left was marked COLORED and the one on the right was marked WHITE. I stood there blank, stupid.

I turned and walked out.

I tried to make sense of what I had seen as I retreated across the large lawn. Let me get this right, I thought, was that a WHITE drinking fountain and hospital wing that blacks, like my black basketball buddies, couldn't go in, even if I was in the hospital there? And the same for me: I couldn't visit them if they were in there, in the wing for COLORED, or drink from that fountain?

I walked back to Norm and Dorothy's. I wasn't feeling anything yet. It wasn't processing in my young, inexperienced mind. As I passed by the alley next to the pharmacy, I saw a hand painted sign and an eight-inch by ten-inch trap door on the side of the small pharmacy building. The sign red, "COLORED PICKUP ONLY". Not eating at Woolworth's, I could process. I just thought that was rude and stupid. Not wanting a team to play another, I could process. It was a free country, wasn't it?

But this experience, people not being able to go inside a pharmacy because of their skin color was as monumentally pivotal for me as seeing the films of the death camps, the poison gas showers and cremation furnaces Hitler had built and marched millions and millions of Jews into throughout the war, shoveling their ashes into pits.

This sight was no different; COLORED WING could have said JEW WING. The hospital even had a restricted WHITE WING. Who decides these things? Who lets people get away with deciding these things? This experience jolted me, the images stuck in my brain as if they had been branded there. I'd heard about things like this, but I'd never believed it happened. There was little or no "national" news during that period. I kept remembering the fear I felt at the moment. I felt like no one was free in America if presidents and governors could decide these things. I'm ashamed now at my selfish fear, almost cowardice, at the time. I remember thinking as I walked back to Norm and Dorothy's that it was this very ground I was walking on, pretty much right under my every footstep, where more than half a million American fathers, sons, and brothers had killed each other for reasons akin to the shallow feeling I had in my soul. I thought of the Jews under Hitler in

Germany and the Negro slaves in America before Emancipation on my long walk back to the spider. I was just a bug in the scheme of importance that Sunday morning. It seemed to me that Emancipation in this country still had some final chapters to write if we were to be a free America. This fellow Jim Crow needed to be hung.

I had a great time with Lester Rosen. Lester was one of the very top in insurance sales for Union Central. He sold more than a million dollars a year—meaning he wrote so much insurance that he generated a million dollars a year in premiums paid to the company. He was such a gentleman and gave me all the time I needed to ask away. He'd point me into some questions he thought might be of interest. He never bragged or carried on as being rich or important. He was a regular guy who liked just about everyone he met, and he would take the time to learn more about each one every time they met up. He brought out pictures and albums from drawers to show me and framed newspaper articles from walls. We even crawled through the window of his tenth-floor office onto a wide ledge on the outside of the building. From there he pointed out the spot where the three states of Tennessee, Mississippi, and Arkansas came together. He obliged me with a stunt photo. He pulled his phone and its long cord out onto the ledge and posed for me as though he was on an important business call in the hot noonday sun, ten stories up.

The article was printed almost as written and was well received. The company eventually sold their tall white building down on Fourth Street and was moving its headquarters to a new building north of the city. As Mike had predicted earlier, it was getting to be that time, so I said my goodbyes and left Mike, Ginny, and the gang.

In a way, we all said our goodbyes to a lot of fun and many memories in the department and the downtown pubs, Coal Hole and the Blue Note.

After work, Bob Hock and I rode in his Fiat to White Castle.

"You should see what it's like down in the South, for

Negroes—places like Forrest City, Arkansas. It's pretty sad," I said.

"I'm sure we only see the tip of the iceberg up here," he said.

"I remember playing Kentucky and they played Dixie before the game," I said. "I thought it was all a joke, you know, like the Kentucky Colonel."

"Kentucky have any blacks on their team?" Bob asked, knowing the answer.

"You know, I never counted blacks—whether a team had them playing or not. I never thought of people as 'black' or any different."

I told him about the hospital experience in Arkansas. I told him what my sister said about how, in Little Rock, the black kids were only allowed in the balconies in theatres or in courthouses.

"Today is my last day at Union Central," I said. "Can you take me to the bus depot? I want to go see my mom and dad."

"Sure," Bob said.

brown leather.

Guys celebrated their cars in those days. Owning a new car was an accomplishment for a young man. Their choice of car model and brand was their statement to the world. It was a step toward their independence. No cars were made during World War II, when we were growing up, so we'd hurry to the car shows since and buy car magazines to celebrate the new models. It wasn't uncommon for a guy to let another guy take his car for a spin around the block or just sit behind the wheel in admiration. Bob Hock had offered, but I couldn't get behind the wheel of his Fiat. It was a festive occasion to have both good weather and a convertible, and to be invited for a ride with the top down. In the early 1960s, in small-town America, intown "cruising" was the rage. For guys, it meant cruising to see and be seen by girls—and the opposite was true for the girls. Cruising in an open convertible was the ultimate—like being in a tickertape parade. Most town curfews for teens was ten o'clock. Cruising was a sport and could go for hours after a visit to and early drive-in movie first, for a dinner of popcorn and hotdogs and flirting.

The guy holding the brush on the shutter paused and peered down at me like a sniper.

"This yours?" I asked, looking up.

"Yeah."

"Nice."

"Chicks like it," he said.

He continued again with the painting strokes as I stepped away from the car and into the house. I said my hellos to Mom, and plopped on the far end of the sofa from her. The middle cushion was stacked with books and papers near two feet high. Mom had papers in her lap, making notes into a three-ring binder, but was always ready to stop what she was reading or doing to visit with any of her brood that took the time to come by. She was so happy to see us that each of the eight of us thought we were her favorite.

"Why Jerome, I prayed for help putting the books from those two cartons on the piano bench up onto those three top shelves, and here you are. Heaven sent!"

I lifted a chair out of the way, set it in the small dining room, and began stacking the books from the cartons so I could reach them up one at a time into their new home, the top shelves I had built when I was in college.

"Dorothy's baby—Eric—was like over ten pounds, Mom, but he and Dorothy are doing well. Norm and little Karen are too; I had a nice time with them. I think Dorothy is back at work now. She drives into Memphis to work. I saw Elvis Presley's house. People were riding horses there, not him I don't think, couldn't tell, we drove by too fast."

"Did you take pictures of Dorothy, Norm, and the babies, dear?" Mom asked.

"Yes, but I bet I forgot them. I've been looking at a rooming house I can get for ten dollars a week. They clean and change the sheets every week, so that's good. I get to use a shelf in a refrigerator in the hall, only share a bath with one other roomer. I'll look through the boxes when I get back, okay? I'll mail them, I promise."

I stepped into the small kitchen to pour a glass of water. The back door was open. I could see the painter through the screen, walking toward the door.

"Top-down kind of night," he said, catching my eye. "Want to go cruising later, maybe start at the drive-in?" He was finished cleaning his brushes, setting things on the steps.

"Whatcha got in mind?" I asked.

"Girls love convertibles. Lots of girls at the drive-in," he said with a wry smile. "Then we can check out the scene downtown. Everybody will be cruising."

"What time?" I asked.

"About dark, maybe in an hour, hour and a half," he said.

"Okay, sure," I said. "I have to talk with my mom awhile, eat. Pick me up later. I'll go."

Mom was as incredible as my dad. There I was, changing another boat in midstream, and here she was, at age sixty-one, now a sophomore at St. Francis University, studying psychology. She had raised eight and now figured it was her turn to pick up where she left off in 1920, when she fell in love with and married my dad and started having kids. Mom listened to my stories, hearing every word, but would always come back, lovingly, thinking of the grander picture, a different way to look at things.

"Mom, are you disappointed I quit college and the scholarship?" I asked. "I'm still in night school."

"Jerry, when birds fly from the nests a parent only has to worry the first time they jump. After that you just watch how far they fly. They all can fly— every one of them. Some higher, some lower. The farther they go the more confidence a mother has in them, the better the job we feel we've done as parents."

"Yeah, but I was messed up because of a girl. My girl went into the convent and it messed me up," I said.

"That's nature's way. You'll meet someone someday," she said.

"You want the books lined up by height, Mom?"

"Yes, dear. You've traveled the furthest from the nest for your age, Jerry. We're so very proud of you. The world seems at peace for a time. I pray this Vietnam stops soon."

"I'm 1-Y, Mom. They could draft me, but I'm too tall for some stuff, I think."

"Whatever you decide to do, I know you will do it well and be happy. You have so much of your father in you. Think everything through. Patience and planning are virtues. You've been reared properly, with values. I hope one day you can settle down, but until you do, trust your instincts and character, son. Impulses can be a distraction."

I took a shower and got ready to go to the drive-in. When I left the house, Mom was reading.

Chapter 10

Even with the slight chill in the air, the weather was dry—perfect for cruising with the top down. It was a clear night, dusk was settling in. The seats were soft brown leather, plush, and it felt good riding through town, not missing any of the sights. At a stoplight we pulled up next to a Greyhound bus smelling of diesel. I looked up at it, thinking of my ride up from Cincinnati. Through a darkened open window I watched a girl's face while she lit a cigarette, using her hand to shield the wind from blowing out the match. Her eyes smiled down at me in the glow. She raised and lowered her eyebrows in a friendly wave as the bus engine roared and whined, pulling away on its journey, carrying more secrets into the dark. As we approached the drive-in movie, Red began to scheme.

"I'll back in the exit with the lights off. Why pay?" He laughed. "They never watch the exits." Red grinned at me as he was about to pull something over on the drive-in movie people.

I stared over at him, studying his features for the first time. I didn't know anyone like him. He had a sneaky look about him, as if he'd been abandoned in the world, orphaned from people or friendships or relationships. His short-sleeved shirt had a rip in the bottom of its pocket and his fingernails were dirty.

No mom, I thought.

"I have money, let's just go in normal," I said, wondering if this was a good idea, being with him at all.

Red didn't want to burn a possible friend quite so fast. He turned the wheel sharp, pulled up to the drive-in ticket window, and braked. I handed him a ten. The girl in the cage made change, handed it out to Red, and he passed it over to me.

"I'll get the popcorn," he said.

"None for me," I said. I wasn't feeling comfortable with him for some reason.

Red pulled into the theater and rolled the car down several of the gravel alleys between the fronts of cars on the one side, slanted up on mounds to best view the outdoor movie screen, and the tails of cars on the other side. The movie screen was still blank with floodlights glaring, circled by dancing, flying moths playing tag with their heat and glare, waiting for the show to start. Driving at a crawl, on prowl, he was looking for girls alone in cars, without dates. His convertible was his lure. Each car we passed had a speaker attached to the driver-side window. Kids were yelling and talking between cars, some hanging out windows, some sitting on their hoods and leaning back against their windshield, some making out in the back seats. Red turned the wheel left, pulling up into an empty slot, and turned the engine off.

"I'm going to scope things out before the movie starts," he said, opening his door and stepping out of the car. "I'll be back."

"Put the top up," I said. A feeling came over me: I didn't want to be seen with him.

"You kidding, man?" Red asked.

"Put it up," I insisted.

Red gave me a look, unsnapped the boot covering the top, folded it, and dropped it on the back seat floor. He pulled the lever raising the top, and as it came down over the windshield, he latched it on the driver side. I latched it on mine. I watched him turn and walk away. My mind began replaying the past month or so; my instincts were telling me to just go with it all and be cool. Xavier and my life at the university and at the Union Central Life Insurance were just a few hours down the road; but as with any transition in my life, it seemed it was a million miles and a long time ago. I thought about Forrest City. I felt alone, just as I did the time we moved from Cortland to Delphi Falls— from Delphi Falls to a one room apartment in Milwaukee.

Red opened the car door and climbed in just as one of the flood lamps on top of the movie screen exploded, causing everyone to honk their horns and cheer. The lights soon went dark and the picture screen came to life with cartoon images of dancing hotdogs and soda pops and music scratching through small speakers. People scattered to their cars with armloads of popcorn, some crawling feet-first through open car windows and laughing, some adjusting the volumes on the speakers clinging to their windows and settling in for the show.

Red reached across the front seat and poked at my arm, grunting.

"Hey, man. Check the tits—look at those tits."

He was motioning with a wave of his hand below the dashboard toward a well-endowed girl in a form-fitting sweater walking in front of our row of cars, looking for her own.

"Them are some set of melons. Hot damn," he said.

I was sinking into another place, as they did on *The Twilight Zone*. I was certain she could hear him with our open windows. The deeper I sank, the more I could feel I was leaving the world I had known for the past year or two. Red was an anomaly. He wasn't bright, but he didn't seem the type to stop anyone from eating at a Woolworth's counter if they wanted to. He'd probably sneak them in. There was a simple honesty to his raw, unattached nature.

He reached under the front seat and pulled out a paper bag. He tore the top down, exposing a fifth of bourbon, yanked the cork top off with a pop, and handed it over to me. I stared at it. He held it in front of me until I took it from him.

I held the bottle by the neck, lifting it up from the bag just long enough to read its label. J.T.S. Brown. I thought of the pledge I had made to the bishop at my Confirmation when I was twelve— not to ever take a drink until I was twenty-one. I smelled the open neck of the bottle. I thought of the varsity coach wisecracking about the convent. I thought about the recruitment billboard I saw coming into town; maybe joining the Marines was a better way out of my melancholy. I put the bottle to my lips and cranked it back for a full mouthful, a swallow and then a coughing, choking, and wheezing, trying to catch my breath from the alcohol fumes that filled my lungs and nostrils and broke my pledge. I looked over at Red staring at me. He guessed it was my first.

I stared back with a "So? What are you looking at?" I tipped it back for another swig, then another, then one more. I handed the bottle and sack back to Red. He held the bottle and bag in front of him, studying it for a spell. Then he popped the cork back in, tightened the sack around the bottle, and put it on the floor, under his seat.

"Let's get outta here," he said. "I got an idea. You know how to drive?"

Red took the speaker off the window and hung it back on its rack. He started the car with a rumble and backed it off the ramp and pulled forward down the gravel alley looking for the exit. My head was spinning a bit.

"Where ya going?"

"Gas, first—I got this place."

Red drove through the night and the back streets of a Fort Wayne I didn't know, looking into the quiet of empty alleys or businesses. The Mercury slowed like a cat and edged up onto and over a curb, pulling to the side of a tall, three-story stack of two-by-fours at some lumber yard. Red pushed the lights off as the car came to a stop. He reached under the seat, pulled the bottle out again, this time handing it over to me with the cork still in while he checked out the surroundings in rear and side mirrors.

"Wait here, I'll only be a sec," he said.

I pulled the cork out of the bottle and waited for the door to close behind him. I sat there watching the light bulb and green porcelain shade that stretched down on the long wire just to the side of an empty train car on the warehouse railroad siding. I took another swig. It wasn't long before Red got back in the car, started her up, and drove out and onto the street, pulling his lights on.

"That's my secret gas-stash," burbled Red. "If'n they ain't smart enough to lock their pumps up, they just inviting me to their gas. Fair is fair enough."

I turned around in my seat, trying to see the pump that he had apparently just stolen gasoline from, but my sight was now as blurred as my concern seemed to be.

With the score of a free tank of gasoline, Red was giddy. His simple world seemed to revolve around small victories and measurable pleasures. Nothing more complicated than just not getting caught. He felt he had a cohort in me. He blabbered:

"If we had couple-a tires, I'd show you some real fun, we

could roll them down the quarries. Ever see a tire splash in a quarry? They sound like atom bombs with the quarry echoing the splash. No shit. No tires, though. Shit. How 'bout them knockers on that bitch? Oh my, oh my, oh my!"

"Tires shar easy," I slurred.

"Huh?" queried Red.

"Fifty—hic—fifty-five Chevy. Wagons." I could hardly form my words.

"What?" asked Red.

"Fifty-five Chevy wagons—hic," I repeated. "They got a handle ... on the outside of their rear gate. Hic. Tire's just lying there in the open, on a shelf."

I took one more swig and put the cork back in the bottle, punched it down with the palm of my hand. The car drove through the night out from the downtown area, past the midtown residential area, and out toward the country. Red stepped on the brakes, pulling the car over to the side of the road. He pushed the lights out.

He looked over at me with a grin. "I gotta piss. You drive. I'll be right back." He opened the driver door and motioned for me to slide over before he closed it behind him.

I remember hearing the clunk in the trunk of the car and Red getting in the passenger side and telling me to take off, but it was then I couldn't remember much more than the state trooper's flashing lights behind us, almost on our bumper. I stopped the car, turned it off, and just sat there. A trooper came up on Red's side of the car and one came up on my side. Each had his right hand on his gun handle.

"Get out of the car," said the trooper by my side of the car. "Now! And keep your hands in the air. Now! Move!"

Had they seen Red take the gas? Did they know I was drinking and not twenty-one? My mind was a slur ... but I got out of the car and raised my arms.

"Turn around and put your hands on the top of the car."

I did. The officer frisked my legs and butt, then he patted my sides and chest.

"Hands behind you."

I put my hands behind me and the officer clicked on handcuffs. I could hear the metal snip, snip, snip as he tightened them on my wrists. It was sobering.

"Sit there on the curb. No talking. Right here. Sit."

I was in serious trouble. I wasn't sure exactly why. Red had stolen the gas, not me, I rationed to myself. I remembered the safety net of Xavier and my life there and at Union Central. I thought of my friends at Chico's. Then I remembered talking with Bob Hock about his becoming a probation officer working with youth. I remembered going with my algebra-professor Jebbie down to city hall in Cincinnati one time and his showing me how he worked with kids in trouble and his showing me the jail.

"I'm going to be a probation officer," I offered, in a disingenuous shot to get some sympathy.

"Not anymore, you aren't," the trooper answered as he walked to the other trooper to talk. "No talking." It was about then a paddy wagon came, turned around on the highway, and backed into where I was sitting on the curb. The officer helped me up off the curb and walked me over to the paddy wagon.

"Climb in here, sit on that side. No talking," he said.

It wasn't long before Red was climbing in, handcuffed. They sat him on the bench on the other side of me.

"No talking, not a word, either of you," the officer said.

I smelled like bourbon. The handcuffs cut into my wrists. Red looked down at the floor. I thought of my girlfriend in the convent and how disappointed she would be in me. I thought of my innocence as a little boy fishing on Little York Lake with my dad and how disappointed he would be in me. I thought of the people I had let down, Mr. V, Mike Jones, Bob Hock, my roommate Tim Boylan, so many who thought they could count on me. I thought again of the billboard I had seen downtown about joining the Marines. They probably wouldn't take me now.

The wagon slowed to a stop and backed into the downtown city courthouse and jail. They took Red in one direction and me in another. That's the last time I ever saw Red. They took me into a room where two detectives sat, took my handcuffs off, and asked me a lot of questions. I told them the truth, that I was drinking for the first time, that I was pretty sure we had stolen gasoline. I told them I would try to show them where we went. I remembered a tall stack of lumber and an empty train car and the light hanging down. Then they asked me about tires.

"What tires?" I said.

"The tires you stole."

I slumped in defeat.

I told them I had given Red an idea about '55 Chevy station wagons, but that was all I remembered. I only remembered him getting out to pee before we were pulled over.

"If that was the clunk I heard, he only took one. Maybe I can show you where we were."

"If you only took one, why were there four tires in his trunk?"

"Four?!"

The investigator leaned in. "What about '55 Chevy station wagons?" he asked.

"They have a handle on the outside back. Just open it and the tire is sitting there," I said. "But I promise I only heard him put one in the trunk."

"How would you know that Jerry – the handles? You've done this before?"

"No. Never. I swear. My mom had a '55 Chevy station wagon is all. That's how I knew. I was just talking, drinking."

"How long you know Red, son?"

"Just met him today, when I got home from Cincinnati and my dad brought me from the bus depot. He was painting shutters on my dad's house. He asked me to go to a drive-in with him is all. I figured no harm. I liked his convertible."

"We'll check your story out," said the investigator. He stood up, had me stand, and turned me over to a uniformed officer. There were no lights on in the hall we stepped into. The officer pulled the first darkened cell door open, moved me to its opening, nudged me through, and closed the door behind me with an iron clunk. I sat down on the bed and stared at the lock on the cell door. All I could think of was that that lock would never be opened again for the rest of my life, maybe. I knew I was in trouble now, of my own doing. People in trouble didn't matter.

In time, a man in uniform came.

"Get up, slim. On your feet."

He unlocked the door and, holding my arm, led me out to the main hall, where policemen were walking around talking, some drinking coffee, some smoking. One asked me how tall I was. He stood me up against a wall and then stood me sideways for mug shots. Another man in uniform walked me over to a tabletop, and taking my hand in his, he made fingerprints and palm prints using a greasy, black-inked roller. Then he pointed the direction he wanted me to walk. It was a cell in the far corner, within sight of people and the front desk.

"Here you go, till we hear from the judge," he said as he unlocked the cell. There were two bunks on one wall and two on the other, and a toilet with no seat attached on the back wall between them.

"This here's our holding tank. Welcome home. Grab any bunk."

"Will I be here long?" I asked.

"Long?" asked the officer. He sneered dispassionately. "I'm figuring petty larceny is good for one to eleven. Might as well get comfortable, you ain't going nowhere, boy."

He clunked the door closed and rattled it with a grin to illustrate it was locked for good. I stood and watched him walk away and over to the front desk area. My heart sank, I felt numb, and my mind was a blank. I didn't even know who I was. I had gotten into a fix I could never have imagined myself in. I had no idea what to expect next. In what seemed forever, another officer came to the door and told me to stand back while he unlocked it.

"Time for your phone call, bub."

Firmly holding my arm, he walked me down to the desk area next to the table where they had fingerprinted me. He picked up the receiver and shoved it at me.

"Make it good, kid. You only get one."

I thought through the telephone numbers I had in my brain and remembered Mom and Dad's home phone and dialed it. Dad answered on the first ring.

"I'm in jail, Dad."

"I know you are, son."

"Can you come get me?"

"I can't help you."

"What?"

"You'll have to trust me, Jerry. If I got you out now, it wouldn't go good for you at all. I can't tell you why; you'll just have to trust me."

"Please get me out of here, Dad."

"I'm sorry, son. I'll see you soon, though. Goodbye."

I held the receiver to my ear, pretending, so no one would see that my own dad had hung up on me. I mumbled some words and a "goodbye" and placed the receiver back down on its cradle.

"Can I call again?" I asked the officer.

"You had your call. Only one call, kid. Let's move it," he snorted.

The officer returned me to the holding tank. I crawled up on the top bunk, lay down, turned my head to the wall, and wept, thinking what had I done and what everyone must think of me now. They never turned the light out in the holding tank, so I could never tell what time or even what day it was. All I could do was count the meals, usually elbow macaroni and ground beef served in tin pie plates. I would sit up, eat, sitting on the edge of my bunk with my legs hanging down, and then jump off and set the pie tin and spoon next to the door and crawl back up and cry again.

At one point I was startled by the metal sounds of the door being clanked opened. Four uniformed state troopers stood there while two others walked down the hall, holding like they were crutches the arms of an enormous black man shuffling because of the shackles on his legs and ankles. He had handcuffs behind his back. He weighed at least three hundred pounds and was easily six-foot-two. They laid him down on his stomach on the lowest bunk across from me. They left the shackles and handcuffs on him.

I lay there and stared down at his seemingly lifeless body. He had blood marks on every rip of his shirt in several places around his back. They looked like stab wounds. I was too scared to sleep. I peered over the edge of my upper bunk mattress and stared down at him endlessly. At one point, several hours after they had brought him in, I was sobbing from despair.

"Hey keed," came a muttered voice.

I froze. My eyes got as big as turnips. I muffled my breath and wiped my tears, trying to listen.

"Hey keed," came the voice again.

It was the man on the lower bunk talking into his mattress, trying to get my attention.

"What?" I asked.

"C'mere, keed—cigarettes," he said.

"I don't have any," I said in a meek, cracking voice.

"Nah, c'mere, keed—cigarettes," he said again.

I got the idea the man wanted a cigarette and couldn't get to them because of his handcuffs. I climbed down and asked, "Where are they?"

"Shirt pocket," he groaned, lifting a shoulder.

Watching the blood on his back, I reached under him and took a full pack of Pall Mall cigarettes and a book of matches from his shirt pocket. I sat on the toilet rim and opened the pack, took one out, and started to put it toward his mouth. He squinted an eye open:

"Naw, keed—they for you."

"For me? I don't smoke."

"I need my sleep. Take 'em and smoke 'em. No more crying, keed. I need my sleep." He closed his eye and lowered his head to the mattress.

I crawled back up on my bunk, stared at the cigarette in my one hand and the pack in the other, set the pack down next to me, and lit up for my first cigarette smoke. I spent the next few hours learning how to smoke, but I had no more tears.

Sometime before the pie tins of food and tablespoons were

to come, I bolted up from a sleep, sensing voices I knew. I sat up straight and looked through the cell door, out by the front desk in the lobby. I could see and hear my dad. I looked down at the pack of Pall Malls on the mattress beside me. There were six left in it. I got down from the bunk and put the remaining pack and matches in the man's shirt pocket.

"Thanks, mister," I said.

The man raised his head off the pillow. "Good luck, keed," he muffled.

I was later to learn he was one of the ten most wanted men in the country. To this day, I've always thought of the man with the stab wounds on his back, the man I didn't know the name of, as my friend.

An officer came to the cell door— unlocked and opened it. "You're out, Antil. Let's go."

He pointed at my dad. Dad wasn't smiling. He waited for me to walk the long hall and around to where he was standing. He put his arms on my shoulders in a comforting hug. "You okay, son?"

"I'm okay."

"Let's go have coffee."

My eyes squinted in the sun as we stepped outside and down the steps. To the right, the paddy wagon was backing in with another load of criminals. We walked across the street to a smoke-filled diner and sat in a booth facing each other.

"What did you learn from this, son?"

"That I can't call you."

That was the only moment in my entire life I expressed disrespect for my dad.

Dad would have normally laughed, but he didn't. He would have normally smiled, but he didn't. Depending on the judge, I was potentially facing eleven years in prison. That wasn't funny. He wasn't offended. He didn't offer me an ounce of sympathy. I did what I did, and no one else made me do it—that was the sense I was feeling from him.

"Red is trouble, Jerry. They told me all about it when they

91

called to tell me you had been locked up. That's why I couldn't talk to you. He was on parole and they've been following him. Had I bailed you out, as a prominent parent, it wouldn't have looked good for you. You would have had to go to court with him, maybe get sentenced with him. I wasn't taking that chance. They wanted him, not you, but being you were with him, you're just as guilty, according to the law. They had seen him steal gas several times. He's already been taken to county for violating parole. He'll be serving a lot of time. When we go to court tomorrow, I want you to plead no contest, and take your medicine, understand?"

"Yes, sir."

"Let me tell you what you've learned, Jerry. People will bring you down to their level before you will ever bring them up to yours, so be careful who you make as friends."

"Yes, sir." I was beginning to see how right he was.

In the hallway of the courthouse, my brother Dick walked up to Dad with a concerned grimace. He pulled out a roll from his pocket—a thousand dollars—and handed it to Dad. "In case Jerry needs it in court," he said. "I'll sit in the back."

The district attorney stood up.

"Your Honor, this is a petty larceny case against two individuals. One is a matter of a parole violation, which has been turned over to county. The other, here, is a first offense, and the city would like to go on record: he was fully cooperative with the investigation. All affected parties for the events leading to his incarceration have been contacted. None are pressing charges, Your Honor."

The district attorney then sat down. The judge looked over at me and told me to rise.

"Young man, you're charged with petty larceny," he said. "How do you plead?"

"I plead no contest, Your Honor."

"Thirty days, suspended. You may go, son." He slammed his gavel down on his desk and set it down.

Outside the courthouse, Dad reached over and handed Dick the thousand dollars, turned to me, and said, "Let's go home. You make this right with your mother, and then I'm taking you back to Cincinnati, today." He started down the courthouse steps ahead of me.

I walked over to Dick and shook his hand. I looked in his eyes and knew he understood what I had just been through. I knew he was there for me.

"Thanks," I said.

"Bourbon will do it," he quipped. "Stay off the booze." He smiled a big brother smile.

"I was thinking of getting a room at a rooming house, Dad," I said.

Dad paused and turned. "You want to be a writer, son. I'll get you started. We're going to Cincinnati where you have roots and friends. Cincinnati is where you can get a fresh start. You need to be with your friends right now. Hop in the car."

The ride home to see Mom was a somber, quiet ride. I knew Dad knew I was a good kid, but I made bad decisions and had to deal with them in my own way. Growing up when he did, in the teens, twenties, and thirties, he had seen everything. I jumped out of the car, ran in, took a shower, packed my duffel quickly before I came out, and hugged Mom good-bye.

"Jerry, I want to show you something," she said.

I walked over to her. Mom showed me several pictures of me playing in the back yard at our house in Cortland when I was in first grade.

"Jerry, did you know you were born on a Wednesday morning?"

"No."

"At seven-thirty in the morning it was. Did you know you were my only baby who stayed awake smiling all day and slept through the night, every night?"

"Really?"

"It's true. Jerry, you were born grown up, inquisitive, thoughtful—a good boy. You always let me get a good night's sleep every night."

"Thanks, Mom."

"It's not the bumps in the road that we have to fear. Remember breaking your nose in basketball?"

"Twice, Mom," I said.

"It's how we land after the bump and what we learn along the way that's important. You went right back into the game and finished playing. Do well, Jerry. You're my Jerome Mark, you know. Be yourself. This was just a bump. Learn from it. Write me letters."

Dad was waiting in the back with his car idling. I stepped off the steps, walked over to the burning trash barrel, and tossed in the pants, shirt, and underwear I had been wearing all the time I was in jail.

Chapter 11

The car rolled through Fort Wayne's downtown. I couldn't believe I was out of jail, free to leave the city. I rested my elbow on the open window to feel the brush of the air that I'd missed for the past three days. Small stores with people sweeping the sidewalk and shops with clerks in the windows, I wondered if everyone who caught my eye could tell I was just let out of jail. Did I look like an ex-convict? Would a policeman know I was a jailbird just by looking at me?

"Jerry me boy, when we get to Cincinnati, I want you to find the Yellow Pages. Write down the name and address of every advertising or public relations agency in Cincinnati. Look under the headings. We'll see what you have as a writer."

"Okay."

My mind wandered and I remembered driving all throughout central New York with him when I was seven, eight, and nine, and his going on and on talking sales and marketing and how it was all about doing the numbers. "If you want to sell anything, you have to do the numbers," he would say.

"It's in the numbers, right, Dad?" I asked, smiling. "you're going to make me do the numbers, right, Dad?"

"It's in the numbers, son," he answered with a smile, impressed that I remembered; happy that I was beginning to put the past few days behind me.

"Life is best with simple rules," he started. "First rule: never do anything just for the money. If you only do things for money, you will miss out on opportunities just sitting there waiting for you to discover them. Second rule: no matter what you choose to do in life, if you do it a solid forty, fifty hours a week, and try to do it better than anyone else, you'll always make a respectable living and never know failure."

"I know. You told me that."

"If you want to be a writer, then it's best you learn now: sales and marketing have got to become your Mississippi, son."

"Huh?" I queried.

"Your middle name, Mark, came from the writer, Mark Twain; he had thirty years up and down on the Mississippi to learn from. Your mother has always said you were going to be her writer. Your given name St. Jerome was a man of letters. But even Mr. Clemens had to step out and knock on some doors and sell his books one at a time. The first books didn't just pop off the store shelves like people think they did."

"I didn't know that," I said.

"For you to earn a living as a writer, you first have to sell someone on the idea of letting you write for them. It's a lot bigger than writing the compositions like you told me. Use the marketing I taught you driving through central New York all those years, son. Mark Twain gathered his wonderful stories while steaming down the Mississippi. Let my old Buick be your steamboat and what I taught you about marketing be your Mississippi."

I was comforted by Dad's confidence in me and the enthusiasm of his plan to get me started. Knowing he still trusted I was a good kid, I fell asleep while he drove from Indiana into Ohio and through the farm and hog country, the two of us traveling together just as we had done when I was a little boy. When he nudged me gently to wake me, we were on Fourth Street in downtown Cincinnati. Just two blocks from the old Union Central Life Insurance building, which was now a bank.

"Let me find a parking spot and we'll get you fixed up," he said.

"What do you mean, fixed up, Dad?"

"You're in the real world now, Jerry. You'll have to dress the part. Let's go get you some clothes."

In 1960 there was no place where someone six-foot-ten could buy a suit or dress shirt to fit. They just didn't exist. The longest sleeves would still be more than five or six inches above my wrists. The team's blazers at XU had to be custom made, we were all so tall. In one downtown shop on Fourth Street a man fitted me for two suits like an artist. In another shop I was measured and fitted for five custom-made shirts. We got two pairs of wingtip shoes and some socks, underwear, a belt, and ties. As the tailor measured me and pinned cloth around me like a sculpture, Dad would entertain the staff and reminisce about his youth growing up in Minnesota.

"I was six-foot-six at fifteen—in 1917—and there was no way I could ever find a suit or coat to fit," he said. "I saved my pennies from working the wheat fields, driving thrashers—teams of six horses—through the Dakotas, from age twelve to fifteen. I had a couple of suits and a topcoat hand-tailored in Minneapolis. I got so many compliments, and my appearance opened so many doors, I could never understand why every young man didn't get tailor-made suits and coats."

"Exactly," said the tailor, looking up with pins in his mouth. "Clothes always make the man."

"People think they can't afford them," Dad interjected. "I couldn't afford them, either; I sent half my money home to my mom. But I had no other choice if I wanted to be a success. They were worth the sacrifice, every penny. Just because you're a ninth-grade dropout, there's no need to advertise it."

The suit tailor and salesman loved his stories. Dad was beaming, knowing he was about to launch his tallest son into the marketing world—his world. Dad stood back and pointed at me standing on the stool, being pinned and tucked, and said, "Folks, meet Jerry me boy. He's the seventh child of a seventh son of a seventh son."

The tailor made a quick sign of the cross, kissed his thumb, and went back to pinning.

By now Dad had me convinced that any art, even writing and drawing, was no different than any other occupation in the discipline required for success. They all took time and hard work.

The handmade suits and shirts from the other store would be ready in nine days. Dad turned, tipped his hat adieu, bowed with grace, and told the shop owners we would return.

Walking to the car, he said, "Show me how to get to the Sodality House."

I flinched at the thought of going back so soon after being in jail, but because of my on-court basketball training, a learned "team" instinct, I just followed Dad's lead, his confidence, and pointed the way up Victory Parkway then left on Dana Avenue up the hill. Dad convinced me it would be best to stay among friends for a while. Bob Hock was outside, hosing off his car and giving it a sponge bath. He was happy to see me. I introduced him to Dad.

"Where can I find a car for Jerry?" asked Dad.

Bob pointed at a bronze-colored 1950 Pontiac under a tree. "Finley's selling that one for fifty. Runs like a top. Straight-eight—push-button starter on the dash."

Dad counted out a hundred and handed it to me as my stake.

"Jerry me boy, you get the Yellow Pages, do your homework like we talked about. I'll be back in ten days to take you downtown to pick up the clothes. If you have all the lists done by then, I'll get you started off on the right foot."

Dad shook my hand and smiled. He reached over and shook Bob's hand, thanking him for his caring and generosity. He got in his car, pulled the door closed, and drove down the drive, waving from the window.

I went upstairs to my room and said hello to Tim. I put fifty dollars in an envelope and put it on Finley's pillow, with a note for him to leave the signed pink slip for the Pontiac on mine.

"I'll get the pink slip and keys later," I told Tim. "Have him leave them with Hock, if you see him."

I set my duffel on my bunk and walked over to see Mr. V and tell him about everything. He offered me his complete confidence and said he knew our friendship was genuine because I had told him the truth.

"Most young men," he quipped, "including me, can't even remember their first good drunk. At least you'll have something to tell your grandkids."

In all our years of friendship, my spell in the pokey was never so much as hinted at after that. Mr. V considered it a nonissue.

Dad came back as promised. He parked his car at the Sodality House, and we took the Pontiac for my first drive downtown in my new wheels. The suits (one a charcoal gray, the other a navy-blue sharkskin) and the dress shirts fit perfectly. The shopkeepers folded their craft in tissue paper and boxed it all up.

"Press the pants every week or so, young man. Have them dry-cleaned every three or four weeks," said the suit tailor. "Always hang them nice."

We put the boxes in the trunk of my Pontiac and drove to Chico's in Norwood for lunch, coffee, and to talk before Dad left town.

"Watch your head," said Carlo as I walked through the door of the restaurant. "Oh my," he added as he saw Dad, "I see where the boy gets his height. You must be Mr. Antil." He shook Dad's hand and introduced himself. We saw an empty corner booth, sat down, and talked.

With my new clothes tucked away in the trunk and my list of advertising and public relations agencies on my desk back in my room, Dad rehearsed my moves and carefully began his training of how I should make my entrance to the agencies.

"I want you to call on four agencies a day," he said. "No less. More, if you're not getting in to all four. Write down the four agency names and addresses the night before, so you're organized and ready first thing in the morning. First thing in the morning is important. Owners of businesses get to work early. Only talk to owners. Only owners can make arbitrary decisions. Owners don't have to follow the rules. Every day, call on four of them, and when you've called the entire list over time, start at the beginning again. Do your numbers, son. When you get writing jobs, do the writing only after you have made all four calls that day, or write late into the night if you don't have a class that night. Keep your mornings for sales and marketing."

"How much do I charge?" I asked.

"You don't charge, son; that is, you don't quote a price at first. Agencies that handle advertising and public relations will have budgets in mind for the worth and value of the services they need. Sell them on you first. Then, always let them tell you their budget. If they talk about a writing project, when the time is right, ask them what their budget is. Whatever they say it is, that will be your writing fee, at first. When you build a name and a demand for your services, you can negotiate for more."

"Don't you mean 'if,' Dad?"

"Jerry, me boy, no such word as 'if' in marketing. 'When,' always. 'If' means you can give up and walk away. 'When' means you get it done, no matter what it takes."

Dad went on and on, like a sitting professor, repeating important points, scratching reminder notes on paper napkins, having fun preparing his seventh child for a world he knew all too well: marketing—a world he'd stepped into at eighteen. I was very proud, looking and listening to him. I knew how important he was in business and in the community, but I'd never heard it from him. If someone asked him what he did, he would say, "I'm a baker." He was a modest man. His contemporaries knew better; they thought of him as a kind, generous, gregarious soul, but often considered him a marketing and sales genius in the baking industry. They knew my dad created the Duncan Hines baking brand and created Donald Duck bread for Walt Disney.

"You're six-foot-ten, Jerry me boy. You very well could be the tallest person in the state. Always be proud of your height, stand straight and tall. We'll use it to your advantage."

Dad let me in on his plan.

Every day, until I got established, I was to carry a big white box of long-stemmed roses with a fancy blue satin ribbon tied around it in a bow. He repeated again and again to spend my days going to every agency in the area—plowing the field, as he called it—and spending my nights planting the seeds writing—going to night school.

My first day out went like this:

I walked into an advertising agency reception area in my new suit, dress shirt, and tie, carrying a box of long-stemmed roses. I handed the box to the receptionist, stood tall, and announced with great urgency: "These are for the president of the agency."

The receptionist got up from her desk, took the box from

my hands, and hurried back to the president's office. I learned later that the president paused what was going on in his office, stood up, and, looking at the box ... opened it. At one end he saw a curious snipped-off rosebud, and in the middle a fancy envelope with a card inside. Going along with the riddle, the president pulled the card from the envelope and read it aloud:

"The long stem is in the lobby."

He stepped out of his office, carrying the card, walked the long hall into the reception area, saw me standing there, caught my smiling eye—stared up at me, amazed at my six-foot-ten height—and busted into laughter, while inviting me back with generous hand motions to join him in his office for a chat, coffee, and, as it turned out, some writing assignments. I repeated this introduction for several weeks. The opening worked so well that, even if the president wasn't there, someone would open it thinking, "VIP," and come out to the lobby and invite me back, even if it was only to talk basketball.

Mr. V had tears of laughter welling up in his eyes when I told him how I got my first $250 worth of writing assignments my first week alone. ($2,200 in 2020 value) He called Mrs. Burke, his secretary, and Jack Moser, the university's development director, to come to his office and hear the story about the rosebuds and the "long stem in the lobby."

"That most certainly was 'flair,'" he chortled. "My goodness," he added, "Cincinnati has no idea what it's in for. Go get them, young man. Show them how it's done. What a fascinating man your father must be."

From my first start, late in the winter of 1960, to just before my twentieth birthday in April of 1961, I billed $3,800 for writing projects. $33,000 in 2020 value in less than five months. A new Cadillac cost $4,000 in the day. I loved my $50 Pontiac and kept driving it for two years, even though the heater wasn't working. By that spring in 1960 my long-stemmed roses were the talk of Cincinnati's advertising and public relations circles. I left the Sodality House and moved into a $10 a week rooming house up in Hyde Park.

Then one day a gentleman by the name of Don Gaffney, the president of Adams, Gaffney & Grant, the largest public relations agency in the Midwest, telephoned Mr. V to inquire about me. He asked Mr. V if he had heard about this Jerry Antil fella, or if he knew how to reach me. Mr. Gaffney was in charge of anything creative (writing, art, and design) produced for his agency and wanted to talk with me. He figured Mr. V, as president of the Public Relations Society of America, would have heard about me, and my rosebuds, by this time.

Little did he know Mr. V was already my best Cincinnati friend, and like a big brother; he was my mentor.

Chapter 12

Mr. Gaffney introduced me to his partners, Russ Adams and Doug Grant. He took me into his office and we sat and talked about their agency, the public relations business, and Cincinnati.

"PR doesn't have the budgets advertising does," he said. "They can't measure PR value because they think it's easy. Boy are they wrong. Nearly everyone believes what they read in the newspaper or hear on the news."

"For real? Is that the truth, Mr. Gaffney?" I asked, eager to learn and soak up information like a sponge.

"Absolutely," said Mr. Gaffney. "Call me Don. What most people don't know is that almost seventy-five percent of what they read in the newspaper is planted there through different companies' press releases. That's what PR is."

Don asked about some of the writing assignments I had and how I handled them. He said there was a bigger picture to PR than writing.

"Creative and communicative writing is good, and necessary. It's the kind of writing that someone will want to pick up and use in their newspaper or on their radio station as is," he said. "But getting the press to write about you, on the other hand, is huge; if you can get a newspaper or radio station or television station to want to do the writing, to report your story as news, you've done something, by golly. Then you've really done something. You've made a story newsworthy."

"It all sounds great," I said. "You got anything for me to write?"

"Tell you what, Jerry. What if I say, here's an assignment, and let's see how you do with it? Then we can see if we fit together, and if it works out we can talk other things. How does that sound?"

"What's the assignment you have in mind, and what's your budget?" I asked.

"How about two hundred and fifty dollars? The building we're in is owned by the Norwood Improved Building and Loan.

They're also a client. We'll pay you two hundred and fifty dollars to get some press for them. Think you want to give it a try?"

"When or on what terms would I get paid?" I asked.

"What say we think it would take a few weeks," said Don. "Let's give you a third advance on it every week for three weeks. Make something happen and we can talk about more assignments, more opportunity. If nothing happens, we'll talk about that, too. Russ and I think it will be worth the risk. How about it?"

"I'll give it a shot."

Don and I shook hands. He walked me downstairs and gave me a complete tour of the Norwood Improved Building and Loan, introducing me to everyone there. I turned and shook Don's hand again and told him I would study up on the building and loan business over the weekend and come by on Monday. It was late in the day. I drove down to Xavier to see Mr. V. As I drove in he was walking to his car. We waved.

"Where you headed?" I asked.

"Home for a quick bite, and to get my tux. I have an important university meeting with Father O'Conner, some others at seven," he said. "What's up?"

"I took an assignment I wanted to ask you about," I said.

"Follow me, we'll have a hotdog and a soda and we can talk," he said. "I want you to meet my sister."

Mr. V was renovating an old house on Ashland Avenue. It had three stories and turrets. He had it divided into three one-floor apartments. His sister lived on the top floor; he lived on the second floor. The first floor was empty, being painted.

"I call this my straw room," he said, walking me into a room off his hallway and turning on a light. It had a straw area rug in the middle and a Polynesian-like bar at one end. "Listen to some music while I boil a couple of hotdogs and get ready. I'll only be a few minutes." He clicked a knob of the floor-model radio/phonograph and tuned in some music. "This is a local FM radio station I like. Most people don't know about FM." He left the room and headed for the kitchen and bedroom. He came out wearing his tuxedo, tying his bowtie.

While we ate hotdogs and drank our red crème soda, I asked Mr. V about the FM radio station and why not a lot of people knew about it. "It's relatively new," he said.

"I have a radio in my car," I said.

"That'd be AM radio, Jerry. FM radio takes an FM receiver most old radios don't have. Actually the sound quality is much better than AM, but they're having a devil of a time trying to convince advertisers and selling time."

"Mr. V, can you guess and tell me the top five things people who would buy homes and finance them through a building and loan would have in common?"

"Why do you ask?"

"I need to know the building and loan business by Monday," I said.

"Is this for an assignment you have?"

"Yes, sir. You just gave me an idea with the FM radio thing, so I need to know. What five things would a lot of them do to, say, pass the time or entertain themselves? Any ideas?"

"Interesting question," he said. "Let me think."

Mr. V picked up his crème soda bottle, pressed the top of it to the bottom of his chin, stood up, and walked over to the window and looked out.

"I've got it," he said, turning to me. "Well, besides watching television, I would say going on picnics, playing bridge or canasta, going to dances at their church or social clubs, and maybe attending weddings." He looked pleased. "Oh they'll do other things, depending on the budget and the times, like bowling, movies, Reds baseball and such, but I'm comfortable with my list. Simple things people can always count on to entertain themselves and share the fun with other people at the same time."

I thanked Mr. V, ate my hotdog and left. On the way to my car I managed to convince myself my idea I had was so good I was going to become a rich writer so I drove to an Oldsmobile dealer and asked them what they would give me for my Pontiac towards a new Oldsmobile Cutlass. They gave me $50 and the keys to my new car after we signed the papers.

"We'll mail you the payment coupon book," the salesman said.

That weekend I spread the daily newspapers on my bed and turned page after page looking for ideas. On Monday I called Don Gaffney and asked for a few more days. I drove to an FM radio station in Cincinnati and visited with the general manager. I told him about my idea— to have a bridge 'card game' tournament on a Saturday morning soon. I wasn't sure when yet and asked him if his station would consider covering it live.

"That's called a remote. We don't have the technology for a remote," he said. "We don't have the announcing staff, either. Our engineer in the control booth usually just reads from sheets handed him. We're a pretty simple operation."

"What if I get an announcer, somebody like the guy who writes the bridge column in the *Cincinnati Enquirer*? Could you do it then?" I asked.

The general manager tweaked his chin. "Tell you what I can do. If we can record it on a Wollensak"—a reel-to-reel tape recorder—"we can broadcast it later on radio, like it's a live performance."

"What will that cost?" I asked.

"You find an announcer, try to get some listeners, and I'll run up to three hours, no charge," he answered.

Next I contacted the bridge editor at the *Cincinnati Enquirer*. After I bought him a cup of coffee and told him about the fun he could have on a Saturday morning, letting his fans hear him on radio, he announced the NIBBRIDGE Tournament (The Norwood Improved Building and Loan Bridge Tournament) in his column. He was delighted at the potential recognition and agreed to be our tournament radio emcee. He asked for a copy of the tape as payment for his time. The tournament contestant roster quickly filled up with 120 entries—thirty tables—and was a wonderful success. Not only had the event been written up several times a week over a two-week period, the building and loan name was repeated often throughout the bridge tournament show as well. It took place in the middle of the building and loan's lobby.

"Respectable," said Don. "You have a knack for it. With some training on press release writing, you could be quite a PR guy."

"It was fun," I admitted.

"Here's the deal," said Don. "I've talked with Russ and Doug. We can't afford large fees on an ongoing basis like agencies can, but we'd like to offer you a full-time job. How does sixty dollars a week sound?"

My first thought was I made more than that at Union Central Life not much more than a year ago— and I was more than tripling that now. My second thought was Dad's rule number one of never doing anything for money. I remembered that Mr. V was a PR man; this would be the same field he was nationally known for. What a wonderful opportunity to learn—and still write. In the euphoria of the moment, it hadn't dawned on me that I was about to have regular car payments that might give a stretch to sixty dollars a week.

"I'll do it," I said. I shook Don's hand. He stood and walked me around the office, making the announcement. Standing in Russ's office, I offered the guys an idea.

"Have you guys ever heard of a teletype machine?" I asked.

"You being a wise-ass?" quipped Russ. "Everyone knows what a teletype machine is. It's how the press gets news from the wires."

"Exactly," I said. "I love the noise they make starting up, the paper chattering through it line by line, letters punching and clacking and stacking one letter at a time and the bell ringing and clanging, making a helluva noise."

"They always show that *teletype* scene in the movies," said Russ.

"Well, guys, the times I was down at the *Enquirer* and then over at the FM station working on the NIBBRIDGE tournament, you know what I observed?"

"Their teletypes?" asked Don.

"Those, but more than that; I saw that every time the teletype started up with the bells and the banging, people stood up and flocked to it—actually gathering around it, reading it as the news came through. I bet they don't do that when the mailman comes in bringing press releases you send them in the morning mail. Why don't we get a teletype machine and send press releases to the news media like they already like to read them, hot off the press?"

"Jesus," said Russ. He chewed his cigar to the other side of his jaw.

"You can rent them just like a telephone. I already asked. They come and hook them up and everything. Not only can you receive teletype messages, you can send them. Every station or newspaper has a teletype phone number. So does AP and UPI."

"Who told you all this— that we could rent a teletype?" Russ asked.

"I saw a repair truck for one and talked with the driver a long time."

"Jesus," said Russ.

"What?" asked Don.

"It's been standing right in front of our noses all this time and we never even thought about it," said Russ, rolling his cigar in amazement. "Jesus."

"My dad used to tell me that listening was an art," I said. "He used to say that most people listen while they're trying to think of something to say. They can never hear or learn that way. He said just listen and don't talk and you can soak in more, learn more, and come up with ideas easier."

"Order a goddam teletype, Don," said Russ. "Good on you, Jerry."

Three or four months flew by. I earned my wings passing out snow cones to kids at softball games for Gold Medal— a snow cone and popcorn machine manufacturer client. I wrote press releases for Buick's new import car, the Opal. I remember it was on a weekend when my phone rang. As I fumbled to answer, I saw it was four in the morning.

"Hello?" I mumbled.

"Jerry, Don here," Don said.

"What time is it?" I asked.

"How soon can you get to the office?"

"Why? What's up?"

"There was a tragic nursing home fire—many people were killed, and all hell is breaking loose with the new governor, Rhodes. The Ohio Nursing Home Association is our client. The state is threatening to demand sprinkler systems in nursing homes instantly or he'll close them all down with no warning. Come to the office as soon as you can. We'll need to write a press release. We need to get ahead of this before the morning news comes out."

The Ohio Nursing Home Association had already been working on self-governing, requiring sprinkler systems; they had predicted something like this if the state didn't support their proposed legislation. The state had been dragging its feet, and now, in the wake of a tragedy, they were completely overreacting and wanting it done—now.

I got to the office in jeans and T-shirt. My first four attempts at writing the release— Don would look at them and crumble them up.

"Press releases are upside down from advertising copy," he lectured patiently. "Try again, but this time say everything in the first sentence, like it's a headline—who, what, where, when—and why? That's all people read anyway."

Because of the tragic fire and the deaths—this one was overwhelming for me. I was almost writing it in tears, thinking of the people who died. I tried one more time and handed it to Don. He tapped his fingernails on the desk like a snare-drum roll at a military execution as he read it carefully. He then set it down, turned to his typewriter, rolled a piece of paper into its carriage, cracked his knuckles, and began typing on the keys like it was a machine gun.

Ratatattattattattattat … then a *ding* at the end of a line— and he would slap the arm and send the carriage slamming back to the beginning of a line … *Ratatattattattattattat.*

About thirty dings later, he was done. He ripped the sheet of paper out from the typewriter and handed it to me.

"Here's how it should read," he said. "You'll get the hang of writing releases."

The page began with a quote from a J. Mark Antil, executive secretary of the Ohio Nursing Home Association, attacking the state fire marshal for overreacting—for talking out of both sides of his mouth—and using a public scare tactic of threatening to close nursing homes that didn't have built-in fire extinguishers, which would force most of them to close. We agreed that nursing homes should have fire extinguishers, just that they should be given a reasonable amount of time to comply.

"Who's this J. Mark Antil?" I asked, looking up.

"That's you, Jerry. Until further notice, you're the executive secretary of the Ohio Nursing Home Association, for a spell, anyway. We're just learning this new Governor Rhodes guy. There's a meeting at the capital in Columbus at eleven. I can't be there, you go instead. Here's the address."

I pointed to the -30- at the bottom of the release.

"Don, what's this -30- for?" I asked.

"The -30- means end of story," said Don. "A -30- tells the editor or typesetter that it's the end of the story."

"I'll be," I said.

Go home, put a suit on, and drive to Columbus. Just listen and take notes. If anyone asks why Russ or I didn't come, tell them we're getting with the past governor, Michael DiSalle, to get some pointers on getting this under control."

"Do you know how to type this into the teletype machine and send it, Don?"

"I'll have it sent out by the time you get home to change. Take off. You need gas money?" asked Don.

"I'm okay," I said.

I left the offices, jumping down two stairs at a time, and drove back to shower and put my suit on. My adrenalin was pumping like a teletype machine.

I was on time for the meeting at the statehouse in Columbus and everyone welcomed me and passed around a pot of coffee, and we got down to business. I listened and took many notes as things were said. I was learning the insides of politics and of association management. Several hours into the meeting, someone came over and whispered into my ear, "There's a call for you, Jerry."

I stepped out into the hall and picked up the house phone to be connected.

"Jerry, Don here. Listen, we just got a call from the Greater Cleveland Nursing Home Association and they've retained us, too, to help them through this mess. Think you can drive up there right now and attend a meeting with them?"

I was feeling exhilarated. I was feeling almost like an executive, a real somebody.

"Sure I can," I bounced back.

"Good. Go to the Pick Carter Hotel, downtown Cleveland—it's on Euclid Avenue. It's about an hour and a half drive from where you are. Meet them there. You have a copy of the release in your briefcase. If it hasn't been published by the time you get there, show them your copy, let them read it. It will build their confidence in us. Make your excuses and head out now, and then come back here after the Cleveland meeting, I'll catch you up. Call me at home if it's late when you get in."

"Got it. Pick Carter Hotel. Euclid Avenue," I said.

I hung the phone up, went back into the meeting, and whispered my goodbyes to the director and assured her that Don was on top of the whole thing and would be in contact. She thanked me and walked me to the door.

All my drive to Cleveland, I rehearsed my introductions of the company I worked for, and of me. This was my first toe in the water, talking to a brand-new client, just put under contract. Don was putting a lot of trust in me.

I found my way around downtown Cleveland, asked a cop for Euclid Avenue, and found my way to the hotel. I pulled into an open space on the street for Pick Carter Hotel parking, jumped out, and rushed up the steps into the hotel. The reception was overwhelming. They had already seen a newspaper that had printed the release Don had written, from J. Mark Antil on the front page.

They treated me with the respect and honor of every word Don had written for me in the release. I thought I would spare them the fact that I had not written those brilliant words attacking the state fire marshal, which were now in the headlines. The meeting was short and upbeat.

"Have Don keep us informed. We want to solve this as soon as possible. This coming week, if we can," they said. They took turns shaking my hand and thanking me again and again for the brilliant attack of the state fire marshal.

I rushed from the room feeling pumped, hurried down the hall, and stepped into the hotel elevator. Standing inside, leaning in the back corner of the elevator, was Mike Douglas, the well-known national television personality. I knew his face. He and his television-show guests stayed at the Pick Carter during taping of his daily talk show, which was broadcast out of Cleveland. I was starstruck and shook his hand, introducing myself.

"Just how tall are you?" he asked, looking up.

"Six-ten," I answered.

"My goodness," he said as he got off the elevator. "Such a tall, impressive junior executive," he offered. "Good luck, young man. Nice to meet you."

He waved and walked away.

I'm a junior executive? That's twice today. Television star Mike Douglas himself said I was a junior executive—I continued mumbling this and other blind illusions to myself as I stepped through the shiny brass and glass hotel lobby doors onto the front steps. Just as it would have happened in the movies, a taxi swerved over a lane, pulling up with a screech next to me in my daze. I jumped in the back seat.

"Airport," I announced, as would Clark Gable or Spencer Tracey or Jimmy Stewart. I kept playing the big day over and over in my head, stacking up the virtues of my temporary feelings of self-importance. It was better than winning a basketball game.

My meeting in Columbus at the state capital, being paged for a phone call, then my meeting, as the one and only J. Mark Antil, at the Greater Cleveland Nursing Home Association, and my name on the front pages of the *Columbus Dispatch* and the *Cleveland Plain Dealer*; and I actually met Mike Douglas, and he was such a nice guy, I thought.

The plane landed at the Cincinnati airport in Kentucky, and I hurried off and to the parking area, where I spent twenty minutes looking for my Pontiac. I wanted to get with Don right away and give him a full report on the day.

It was then I paused. I couldn't find my Pontiac anywhere. Should I call the police and report it stolen? I looked down at my dusty cordovan wingtips and mentally retraced my steps all through the day in the life of this Junior Executive—a day that had started at four in the morning; maybe I could remember where I parked it.

"Son of a bitch," I offered to an empty car as I walked by. It dawned on me; I had driven to Cleveland from Columbus and left my car sitting in front of the Pick Carter on Euclid Avenue. It dawned on me as well that I wasn't driving my old Pontiac, but my brand-new Oldsmobile Cutlass I didn't recognize and just stepped around it on Euclid Avenue in Cleveland to catch a cab in front of the hotel.

"I'm such a numb-nuts," rattled through my head. I left the airport parking lot, went inside, got on the next plane back to Cleveland. Don and Russ thought my absentmindedness was hysterical. Russ had to get up and go pee before he wet his pants in his fits of laughter. Don told me he'd pay for the two airplane tickets, this time, but to be more careful next time. The next few months flew by.

Chapter 13

I pulled my Oldsmobile through the alley to the back to park. Don flagged me with a grin from the sidewalk as I drove by, holding his hotdog in one hand, a paper sack for me in the other.

"Big stuff," he shouted. "Let's go upstairs. I'll fill you in. Big stuff."

He reached into the paper sack, lifted out a cheeseburger, and handed it to me as we climbed the back stairs and stepped into his office.

"We're going after a prestige account, the Union Central Life Insurance Company," he said.

"Are you kidding me? I used to work there—for Mike Jones," I said.

"We're dealing with John Lloyd Sr., head guy. I think Mike is in sales promotion."

"Yeah, he is," I said.

"But here's the deal, coincidently," said Don. "Mr. Lloyd's son is a friend of Russ's, and he just invested in or is doing legal work for an old hotel in Columbus—not sure which. The Neil House. It's the oldest hostelry in Ohio, according to him."

"What's a hostelry?" I asked.

"Just a hotel; it's a fancy name for hotel. This one's famous, though, for the underground tunnel between it and the state capitol across the street. Lots of stories of goings-on at the Neil House, you might say, senators sneaking women in and out through the underground tunnel. S'been around a long time. I think rebuilt a time or two. Here's the deal, though. We now have it as an account, but we're not on the clock—just a flat monthly retainer. They'll pay our expenses, but we're not on the clock. They're spending a couple of million renovating it, this is all I know. I think they're taking it public, but I don't know that, either."

"I like Columbus," I said.

"Russ and I talked about it and agreed we would give the account to you. It's your account now, Jerry."

"Are you serious?"

"We figured you can't do any harm while you learn the business on it."

"Thanks, Don," I said. "My own account?"

I knew the Nursing Home Association wasn't my account; I was only acting as a figurehead, giving Don the time to handle the important behind-the-scenes work.

"For real, it's yours," he said.

Russ's office door opened and four men followed billowing clouds of cigar smoke out into the hall. Along with Russ was Doug, his and Don's partner, and another two men. One was young John Lloyd Jr., a vested attorney, an important-looking man with a bold, articulate, officious voice, and the other was a short, portly man who looked to me like Alfred Hitchcock. Russ introduced me first to Mr. Lloyd and then to the other man.

"Jerry, I want you to meet Governor Michael DiSalle," he said casually. "Governor, meet the newest member of our team, Jerry Antil."

I shook the Ohio ex-governor's hand. "How do you do, Governor DiSalle?"

Thoughts of my call to Governor Wallace raced through my head.

"Good to meet you, son."

"Jerry, the governor needs a ride to the airport; think you can arrange it?" asked Russ, biting into his cigar and eyeing the return addresses of two envelopes in his hand, hoping for some client checks in the mail.

"Of course, just give me a second to go pick up some papers from my car. I'll come back up for you Governor."

Five minutes later I came back up to the offices, stepped around Russ and Governor DiSalle and took Don by the arm into his office and pulled the door.

"What's up?" Don asked.

"My cars gone."

"What do you mean, gone?" asked Don.

"It's been stolen."

"Are you kidding me, Jerry?"

"What do I do? I can't drive the governor. I don't have a car."

Don pulled his desk drawer open and picked up a set of car keys.

"There's a '52 Ford out there, black. Take that. Here're the keys."

"A '52 Ford, Don? This is a governor."

"Take the Ford. I'll call the Norwood police about your car missing."

"Okay."

"And keep the driver side window open a bit. The muffler leaks and smokes up pretty badly."

I stepped out of Don's office and asked if the governor won't mind riding in a '52 Ford.

"I've ridden in older cars and a few farm trucks—it'll be my pleasure," said the governor. "Let's go."

"Jerry, go by your place after you drop off the governor," Don said. "Pack a bag and head on up to Columbus. See the GM at the Neil House Hotel; his name is Mark. Stay all the time you need."

"What about my...you know?" I asked.

"I'll take care of it. We'll make a switch later if they find it," said Don, referring to my stolen Oldsmobile.

"They'll put you up at the hotel, Jerry. Get a feel of the place, the hotel business, come up with a plan. Remember our goal—favorable publicity, building awareness for the hotel name."

The governor was a nice man. Congenial and unassuming. He had been with presidents and first ladies, senators, and congressmen. He headed the state for many years and was a popular and respected governor for a long time.

"Governor, do you have any advice for a guy just starting out?" I asked.

"What sort of advice, son?" asked the governor.

"Getting press, getting through all the politics—any ideas?" I asked.

"In politics, always shoot low," he said, smiling at me, waiting for a reaction.

"Always aim low?" I asked. "I give up, what exactly does that mean?"

"If you want to get something done, never attack the primary target—let's say, the governor. If you want to get something done and you haul off and take a shot at the governor, all the governor has to do is say, 'This is something we must look into, so I'll create a subcommittee to make a study and give a report.' In other words, a governor can dodge the bullet of a direct shot."

"So what's the strategy?" I asked.

"Aim and shoot low. Here's an example. Did you work on the article attacking the state fire marshal about the nursing home fire?"

"I sort of helped, but it was mainly Don."

"It was brilliant. You didn't attack the invulnerable governor, who could have dodged the bullet. You shot low, and now the governor can be a hero and reprimand the state fire marshal and tell him to straighten up and fly right. That's how it works. You boys did fine on that one."

"Well, I'll be," I said. "Anything else?"

"Let things be other people's ideas. Seed them, then stand back and let others take the credit, get the glory. You'll get more done that way, in your favor. A newspaper reporter has a job of writing the news. Let them write it. Press releases are not very exciting—they leave nothing to the imagination. Press conferences, with exclusives, are. Stir the batch now and then but let the reporters be the heroes."

"Show biz," I mumbled.

"Entertainment might be a better word, son. People want to be moved, one way or another, and know ultimately that someone is in control and keeping things on track and them informed. Reporters want to be read. A reporter's dream is to make the front page."

I shook the governor's hand and said goodbye, headed back

north to Cincinnati, to my rooming house, and then headed off to Columbus and the Neil House. I tried to remember how simple he'd made it all sound.

Mark was about five-eleven, wore expensive clothes and a colorful tie. He had a smile on his face.

"Hi Jerry, I'm Mark Mowry, general manager. Welcome to the Neil House. How was your trip in?"

Now I had worked in the basement of the Hotel Syracuse when I was twelve, carrying garbage, mopping floors, cleaning sinks in the employee washrooms, and burning waste after sorting through the dirty magazines and naked girl playing cards people would leave in their rooms, but I was never allowed up above the basement. Partly because sanitary engineers, as they called me, weren't a sight they wanted the la-di-da guests to see, and partly because I was underage for a working permit, and my dad didn't want his friend, Mr. Bloom, to get into trouble for putting me on for the summer as a favor to him. This Neil House, old as it was, was magnificent. Pushing through the solid brass and glass revolving doors, you could look up to twelve floors of rooms and railings of intricate wrought iron, long, low-hanging crystal chandeliers, and people moving about on fine oriental rugs scattered throughout the lobby area on marble floors. Across the lobby were four polished brass doors to elevators, some closed and moving as the arrow above them indicated, some open with an elevator man standing at attention with his uniform and bow tie, waiting for guests to step in.

"Welcome, and watch your step," he would say. "Floor, please."

"Twelve," Mark said. "Johnnie, this is Mr. Antil from Cincinnati. He's our guest for an extended stay."

"Welcome, sir," said Johnnie as we came to a stop and he opened the door. "Watch your step, please."

Walking into his office in a corner of the twelfth floor, Mark passed by his secretary. "Ava, get Jerry checked into a suite as our guest and have a key sent up, will you, please? We'll be in my office."

Ava was a dish, to say it politely. She was maybe twenty-two or twenty-three and looked like she had stepped off the front cover of *Vogue* magazine. She smiled at me just before I walked into the back of Mark's office door, bumping my cheek, looking around at her. This sort of thing must have happened a lot, as Mark made no observation or comment about the incident. He offered me a seat, stood in front of his window with a balding head and smiley eyes, and began to tell the story. He started by saying that, at twenty-five, he was the youngest general manager of a major property in the US.

"Just across from Ohio State House, with its ease of access, many of the rich and powerful in Columbus throughout a couple centuries have shared times and spirits here. Our guest book includes Abraham Lincoln, William McKinley, Oscar Wilde, William Howard Taft, Samuel Clemens, Warren G. Harding, Theodore Roosevelt, Ellen Terry, Jenny Lind, Carl Schurz, and Orville Wright. This is the third Neil House. The original was replaced in 1862. This one was built in 1922," Mark said as he sat down.

"Samuel Clemens actually stayed here?" I beamed. "Mark Twain?"

"In your very suite." Mark laughed, knowing the hotel Samuel Clemens had stayed in didn't exist anymore.

I let my imagination believe it—at the time, anyway.

Ava came walking in and handed me a room key.

"Jerry, why don't you go rest up from your drive, then freshen up and we'll meet for dinner at seven, how would that be?" asked Mark.

"Great," I said.

"Good. We'll be dining with John Lloyd this evening. No business. In the morning I will take you both on a tour of the whole facility. Then you can get started."

It sounded so civilized. Elegant, somehow; I'll be dining, I mused to myself.

John Lloyd was the son of Mr. Lloyd, the chairman of the board of Union Central Life Insurance. He had the presence of a president and drank like Ulysses S. Grant. His face was as chiseled as a fine marble bust of Franklin or Adams. He had a commanding voice that was so convincing and powerful and articulate that if he said, "Oops!" after stabbing you, you'd believe he was trying to save your life while pulling the knife from your heart. The man was mesmerizing ... I believe they invented the word "charisma" for people like Mr. John Lloyd Jr. I sat down at the table and was about to learn he was also the best storyteller I had ever heard in my entire life before or since, and I always considered my dad as the best.

Seeing this was a devout drinking crowd, I ordered a drink.

"Cutty and water," I said, as though I'd been around Cape Horn a time or two. I was mimicking Mike Jones from Union Central Life days. That's what he would order. I interrupted the silence and tinkling of cubes.

"Mr. Lloyd, have you ever been in politics? Ever run for office? I bet you'd be a good choice."

That's when my hayride began that particular evening.

Unbeknown to me and only me at that table, it turned out, John Lloyd Jr. had run for office the year before and lost handily. Hell, he was trounced, I was to later learn. I'm not certain that he even voted for himself. Mr. Lloyd looked across the table at me and smiled. He then looked over to Mark and smiled. One by one at the table, he'd look and he'd smile at the waiting eyes around the table, setting me up—this young kid, still wet behind the ears, this punk kid who had known him for a period of, what, maybe seventy-three seconds total, plus the time it took to get his drink? A kid who had probably never read a newspaper in his life— patronizing him, actually having the audacity of saying that he'd be good in some public office. Everyone at the table but me knew what was about to happen. John Lloyd Jr. was about to tell me a story just as seriously as if he were president. My ride began ...

"Son, please call me John."

"Thank you, John," I said

"And thank you for your kind words and generous compliment. You're too kind. I haven't run for public office, but I have had the experience, as a youth around your age, young man, of trying to help one Mr. Phillip Docherty on his run for Congress," John's lie began.

I was soon to learn there was no such person as Phillip Docherty.

"No doubt you've heard of him?" asked John.

"Oh sure," I lied.

I leaned in attentively.

Knowing he had me hooked, John continued, "I took it upon myself to be Phillip Docherty's campaign manager when he first ran for Congress. With the very same perception and brilliance I can see in your eyes, I would drive from town to town all over Ohio, even into rural areas, and patiently go from door to door to ask people for their support. I would never leave their presence until they assured me they would support Mr. Docherty, or give me a very good reason why they weren't supporting him."

"You were doing the numbers," I interrupted. "Did he win?"

John ignored me. He looked at his glass, lifted and took a sip from his Chivas rocks, and continued.

"It was about my fifth week, up near the outskirts of Lima, in the bottom farmland. I parked my car and walked down to the big river—you know, the one that goes through there from Cleveland and Akron. My purpose was to talk with the drawbridge operator, a man named Mr. Portman. I felt perhaps Mr. Portman, in the nature of his business, could influence other voters ..."

"Smart," I interrupted, not realizing there was no river that ran from both Cleveland and Akron.

"My intentions were to cross the drawbridge after speaking with him and to go visit the village people on the other side of the river. Mr. Portman was sitting there on a chair rocking, leaning back, balancing the chair on two legs with his back to the rail. I politely introduced myself to Mr. Portman and took pride in telling him in great detail about my candidate running for Congress, Phillip Docherty. I told him of my candidate's many features and benefits and that it would be my personal pleasure to know I could be assured of his vote for my man Phillip Docherty before I crossed the river and went along my way."

"Smart, really smart," I said.

John sipped his Chivas.

"Mr. Portman paused the rocking back and forth on the chair and made a bold, rather startling announcement. He said to me ..."

John paused, took another sip, turned an eye to me, and said:

"Jerry, I just know, as a writer, you would appreciate its flavor, the local color, if you will, so let me, for you, see if I can do justice and capture the essence of Mr. Portman's dialect."

"Thank you," I said. I was honored, as a writer.

John continued:

"So that's when Mr. Portman looked up at me and said, 'I'm sorry, son, I can't's hold it in any longer. I've been biting my tongue—but I knowed the Docherty boy since he was knee-high to a grasshopper, I did. Why, he used to be the gateman at this *chere* very drawbridge during a whole summer one time, and they's no way—I wouldn't never vote for the man, not if he was the only candidate running for the only office. Nope. No siree bub. Not today, Henry, declared the ferryman, just as he spit a chaw of his tobacco over the rail.

"'My goodness,' I responded, 'of course,'" John continued. "'Sir,' I said, 'may I ask you what caused such an overwhelming lack of confidence in my candidate?'

"'It were the bull,' said Mr. Portman.

"'A bull?' I asked the man.

"'It were Ike Cranston's show bull," said Mr. Portman. "Won blue every year at the state fair, he did. Cranston called him Jebodiah. Don't knowed where'd he got that from, maybe the Bible, but old Jebodiah one day up and got constipated. You knows how it happens on occasion. Well Cranston was beside himself, what with it being the "season" and they was herds of heifers coming to their own that needed caring, so to tell. Well it was then when Cranston gets the brainstorm that all was needed for constipation was soapy water in Jebodiah's plumbing and that may clear the pipes, as be said, sort of speakin'. He got him a bucket of warm soapy water, and looked for a funnel he would need to put the suds in the bull, when he took a gander at his grand pappy's Confederate bugle hanging on a tenpenny on the barn wall. He took the bugle and carried it and the bucket around to the rear of the stall old Jebodiah was standing in, a sadder sight you never did see in that bull's eyes. Well, *plook*—in goes the bugle in the bull's personal, sticking it in enough to hold her steady, and then ole man Cranston poured the whole bucket of warm soapy suds in through the bugle and stood to one side. Jebodiah chortled a little, snorted a bit, and then he shook. He pawed first with the left hoof, then the right. Suddenly, and with no warning t'all, his head rose out straight and he let out a big gruntin' bull holler, his eyes turning in circles, and that was when he let out the biggest fart … making that old bugle blare …

"'BLAAAAAAAAAAAT

"'… right through the bugle sure enough, and that scared hell out of the bull, and he bolted and crashed plumb through the barn wall, running wild down in the pasture. Why he ran and twisted and turned and bucked and kicked and every time he twisted and turned he would fart and ever time he farted the bugle would …

"'BLAAAAAAAAAAAT

"'… Jebodiah would kick and stomp and fart, and the bugle would blow …

"'BLAAAAAAAAAAAT

"'… making him bolt and run off again. Old Jebodiah headed down the hill squirming and twisting and a-farting …

"'BLAAAAAAAAAAAT,   BLAAAAAAAAAAAT, BLAAAAAAAAAAAT

"'… and he headed towards this drawbridge right chere, see? That's when your candidate boy Docherty—he was a running the drawbridge all summer, wouldn't you know—Docherty went and pulled on the lever and the drawbridge lifted up and Jebodiah he fell headfirst in the river— and drowned. Took a week to tow that ole prize bull out. Nope. I'll never vote for the boy. Not on your tin type.'

"'Mr. Portman, you mean to tell me that because young Phillip Docherty accidently raised up the drawbridge causing your friend's bull to drown, you won't vote for him?

"'Ain't the reason t'all,' said Mr. Portman.

"Then why, sir?"

"'Well sonny, I figure it this way. Any dumb son of a bitch that can't tell the difference between a tugboat whistle from a bull blowing a bugle out his asshole got no reason being in Congress.'"

Chapter 14

I was in Mark's office by nine the next morning, chatting with Ava until Mark and John showed up. There was a silver tray with coffee service on it for us. I poured a cup and walked around, looking out the twelfth-floor windows at downtown Columbus and the capitol.

"How's your suite?" asked Ava.

"I love it. I feel like a president or something," I said.

Ava smiled.

"You heard what happened to me last night?" I asked.

"No telling with this crowd," she said. "Tell me."

"I said something stupid and Mr. Lloyd told me a story about a bull I halfway believed," I said.

"Oh, Jebodiah the bull, eh?"

"Yes! Jebodiah! You've heard him tell it?" I asked.

That's his famous story. You should feel honored." She laughed. "He doesn't tell *Jebodiah* to just anyone."

Mark walked in. "Ready for your tour, Jerry?"

"Are we waiting for Mr. Lloyd?" I asked.

"I just left him at breakfast," said Mark. "He's headed off to a meeting and then back to Cincinnati."

"Oh," I said.

"He said to tell you hello and that he looks forward to your working on our publicity."

"Did he say that?"

"He did."

"I really put my foot in my mouth last night," I said.

"He said you're a good sport. He had fun last evening and was pleased you got a chuckle out of it. That's just the way John is— a character. Let's get down to work."

Ava winked a *told ya* at me and Mark held the door open and began the full tour. We started on the twelfth floor. With his master key he opened the empty suites to show me, and to give me some anecdotes of their history. We went down one more floor. He explained that on the mezzanine there would be a large swimming pool, suspended over what was now the lobby.

"Glass bottom?" I chided. I figured if suspended, why not make it glass-bottomed?

"Well, maybe a carpeted one, not sure of the glass-bottom thing," Mark quipped.

The truth was it was too early to know what the final hotel designs were. Open to the imagination, was the buzz. Waiting for money and an architect, was the reality. Only thing certain was that the renovation was going forward.

"Out with the old and in with the new?" I asked.

"Everything goes," Mike answered.

This was when my mind began to whir. I was looking forward to a project I hadn't even dreamed up yet and to what I thought I could bring to the party when I did. We walked the halls and looked behind doors. I thought back and summoned up everything my dad, Big Mike, had taught me, what Mr. V had taught me, Mike Jones—and, of course, Don Gaffney and my newest acquaintance Ex-Governor DiSalle.

I was ready.

Ava and I had lunch in the lounge. I gave her a list of things I would need, including scratch pads and ballpoint pens and such. I told her I was going up to my suite to make some calls and would come by the office later to get them.

As I stepped off the elevator on my floor, she held her hand out and shook mine.

"Good luck, Jerry," she said. "Anything else I can get you?"

"Can you have ice cubes sent up for drinking water?" I asked.

"I can. See you later, I hope?" she asked.

I don't know what it was, but her handshake and that dazzling smile gave me a confidence I could remember getting after listening to Superman on the radio when I was a kid. I knew I could do anything.

I paged through my phonebook, then remembered the power of telephone operators and picked the phone up from the receiver and waited.

"Hotel operator, how may I assist you?"

"Operator, my name is Jerry Antil. I'm working on a project with Mr. Mowry. Can you get the *Columbus Dispatch* for me, please?"

"Yes, Mr. Antil, one moment."

"*Columbus Dispatch*, hello."

"Hello," I began, "Is this the newspaper?"

"This is the *Dispatch*, sir."

"I wonder if you can help me," I said. "I'm in big trouble—
"

"I'm sorry," she started.

"Oh, it's not like I'm pregnant or anything like that ..."

The phone operator broke into a nose-snorting laugh and muffled giggle.

"Sir, how can I help you?" she asked.

"I'm looking for a crackerjack reporter," I blurted. "You know the type, like with a trench coat with his collar up, maybe drinks too much, always quitting or getting fired but never does because he's too good, like maybe Clark Gable, or was it Cary Grant in that—I can't think of the movie—with Rosalind Russell?"

"That would be Ned Stout," she said without a moment's hesitation.

"Really? Ned Stout is his real name?" I asked.

"Yep, Ned Stout, he's who you want, I think," she answered.

"What's your name, operator?" I asked.

"Sir, we're not permitted—"

"How can I thank you if I don't know your name?" I asked.

"Carol," she answered. "Would you like me to ring Mr. Stout?"

"Thank you, Carol, I'll call him later. You've been a big help," I said.

"You want me to ring him now?" asked Carol.

"No, but thanks, Carol. I'll call him later when I'm better organized."

"Good luck," said Carol.

I hung up and picked up the receiver again.

"Hotel operator, how may I assist you?"

"Operator, this is Jerry Antil. How can I send flowers to someone?"

"I can connect you to the florist shop," she said. "You may charge them to your room."

A moment later the florist answered. "Neil House Flowers, hello."

"My name is Jerry Antil, I'm a guest at the hotel. I want a dozen roses sent over to the *Columbus Dispatch*. Deliver them to 'Carol the Telephone Operator,' and have the card read, 'Thank you for your help.' Sign it 'Jerry Antil, the Neil House,' and charge them to my room."

"Yes, sir."

"Thank you. Bye."

Click.

There was a knock on my door. I opened it and a bell captain carried in a tray and set it on the desk. It had a filled silver ice bucket and some glasses and a pitcher of water. I fumbled through my pockets and could only come up with three tens. I signed the check and gave him a ten.

"Thank you, sir," he nearly shouted with a thankful grin and left.

I grabbed a handful of cubes and plunked them into a glass tumbler, sat back down on my bed, and picked up the phone again.

"Hotel operator, how may I assist you?"

"Operator, this is Jerry Antil, I'm …"

"We know you now, Mr. Antil. How may I …"

"*Columbus Dispatch*, please."

"One moment, Mr. Antil."

"*Columbus Dispatch*, hello."

"Ned Stout, please," I asked.

Eight rings later: "Yeah?"

"Is this Ned Stout?"

"Yeah."

"My name is Jerry Antil, I'm at the Neil House, and I have an exclusive story for you. I'm giving it to nobody but you."

"Who you with?" he asked.

I picked up my glass full of cubes and rattled it near the receiver.

"Come let me buy you a drink and I'll give you the scoop. It's an exclusive. Deal?"

"Okay. Give me an hour. What's your name again?"

"Jerry Antil, you'll know me when you walk in—I'm six-foot-ten."

"For real?" he asked.

"Yes."

Click.

I changed my shirt and tie, rushed out and caught an elevator to the lobby floor. I went into the lounge and said hello to the maître d' and gave him ten dollars.

"I have an important meeting in an hour, so do you know what my name is?"

"Yes, of course, it's Mr. Antil," he said.

"Good. Please make sure that anyone who waits on our table knows who I am. It's vital I make a good first impression on the man I'm meeting. Are we good?"

"We're good," said the maître d'.

I moved toward the lounge entrance, turned, and pointed at a corner booth. "Hold that booth for me, can you?"

"Of course. No worries, Mr. Antil," said the maître d'.

I hurried across the lobby, looking up at the large brass clock on the wall. I still had twenty-five minutes before Ned Stout would arrive. I got on the elevator.

"Hello, Johnny," I said to the operator.

"Hello, sir, having a good day? What floor?"

"Call me Jerry. Can you take me to twelve, please?"

I walked into the head office. Ava was in Mark's office,

sitting on the chair in front of his desk and taking dictation. Mark caught my eye and waved me in. Ava looked back and smiled.

I pulled my checkbook out.

"Mark, can I get a check cashed? I need tip money."

"How much do you need?" he asked.

"I need a hundred. Twenty fives should do it for now. Yeah, that should do it," I said.

"You're a wise young man. You've picked up on service in the hotel world of the gratuity. Gratuities are the better part of some of these people's incomes," he said.

"I just need stuff to happen when I need it to happen, I guess. Picked the habit up on court playing for a few winning teams. I figured hotel people went for tips like basketball players went for points and assists," I said.

"Ava has a cash box in her desk."

"I do," said Ava.

"Go see if you have twenty fives for Jerry," said Mark.

Ava stepped out, returned and handed me the five-dollar bills. I wrote a check to "Cash" and handed it to her. She went back to her desk to answer the phone. I told Mark I was about to meet the *Columbus Dispatch*, didn't know what would come of it, just fishing for a break, an idea, I told him.

"Anything you need, call me," said Mark.

As I walked from his office, Ava motioned. She covered the mouthpiece and whispered, "Call me if you want dinner later. That is if you're doing nothing." She smiled.

"Okay," I said, first bumping into the coffee table by the sofa in the waiting area, then stepping around it. I headed out and to the elevator, rode down to the lobby, and stood about thirty feet back from the front hotel doors, looking for the man I thought would be Ned Stout. The clock ticked away, people came and went. I looked over toward the lounge. I could see the maître d' looking at his wristwatch and then up at me. Then it happened. Two men. Across Broad Street, on the corner, one was flipping out a cigarette, looking like Detective Sam Spade in a scruffy trench coat, running fingers through his hair as he stepped off the curb and headed this way. The other was holding a four-by-five camera with a flash. I edged toward the lounge and stood just inside as though I were looking the place over. The man in the trench coat, maybe late twenties, perhaps early thirties, a quiet, inquisitive demeanor, caught my eye and walked past the maître d'. I extended my hand.

"Ned Stout?" I asked.

"I am. What's your name again?" he asked.

"Jerry Antil. Let's go sit over there in the corner booth and I'll fill you in."

"You are a tall one. Six-ten, you say?" he asked.

"I'll be at the bar," said the man with the camera.

I motioned the maître d' to take care of him, the check was on me.

Ned followed me over to the booth. I offered to take his coat. He sat down in the booth with it on, opening the front buttons.

The maître d' was right behind us.

"May I offer you gentlemen a cocktail?" he asked.

"Cutty and water for me. Ned?" I asked.

"You got Crown Royal?" he asked.

"We do," said the maître d'.

"Rocks," said Ned.

His hands were folded on the table in front of him.

"You going to take notes?" I asked, wondering if he had a pad or something to write on in case he needed to.

"Yeah," he said.

He didn't move a muscle.

The drinks came and he grasped his with his left hand. I moved mine closer to the center of the table, as my arms were longer. I fumbled through my brain for an ice-breaking statement.

"This is a pretty famous hotel, but I would guess you already knew that. Lincoln stayed here and Mark Twain, but the original hotel burned down."

"Why am I here?" asked Ned Stout.

"I asked you to come over is to tell you that they are going to completely remodel the hotel, spend a couple million dollars, bring it into the sixties."

Ned didn't move. Took a sip from his drink, waiting.

"Of course, when they remodel, everything will have to go. Out with the old and in with the new, as they say."

"'Spect so," said Ned.

"So," (I let my imagination go wild,) "I was thinking we would have a free-for-all grab bag of furniture, you know, let people come pick up our old furniture, maybe do something good with it."

Ned gave me a "that's interesting" look, but still no movement toward his pad. His lack of interest in a furniture giveaway might have been a good thing, I thought, as I had no idea if I could ever get approval for a grab-bag of hotel furniture.

I sipped my Cutty.

"They're building a swimming pool on the second floor; did I tell you that?"

"Where?" asked Ned Stout.

I pointed out to the lobby. "Up where the mezzanine is now, just hanging there, maybe with a glass bottom."

Still nothing.

"Maybe a carpeted bottom," I added.

Ned let go of his drink.

"Carpet the bottom of a pool?" Ned asked, finally digging into his pocket for a small spiral pad and his ballpoint pen.

I got his attention. I almost had a heart attack.

"Yeah, wall to wall, probably, not sure what color," I said, lifting my Cutty for a slurp.

"So what about the furniture and things? Everything?" asked Ned.

"Everything," I said.

"Will it be like a free-for-all grab-bag?" he asked.

"Something like that—a grab-bag," I said.

Ned motioned for the man with the camera to come over.

"Get something, maybe a chick lifting a chair or lamp or something."

Ned polished down his drink, shook my hand, stood up, buttoned his trench coat, lighted a cigarette, shook my hand again, and left the hotel. Although we'd speak on the phone on occasion, that would be the last time I would ever see the man who started everything for me— Ned Stout.

The hotel's assistant manager was walking through the lobby. I flagged him to hold up a second. I saw a girl and her fella sitting at the counter. They had sporting equipment with them, in a canvas bag, including a football helmet on the seat between them.

"Can I get you to pose for a picture for the newspaper, maybe?" I asked her.

"Sure," she squealed.

"Put that helmet on. We're promoting a furniture thing here—we'll give you both tickets to be first in line, for the pic."

The girl donned the helmet.

"See that man over there, standing by those two side chairs?" I asked.

"Yes," she said.

"Walk over to him, pick up one of those chairs, and smile for the camera."

She smiled, walked over, picked up the chair, and grinned for the camera. The photographer popped the flashbulb once, turned, and walked out of the hotel.

"We live in Toledo and won't be back," said her husband. "We were here for a tournament."

"How about dinner on us, then?" I asked.

"Sure," he said.

I caught an elevator to my floor, took my coat and slacks off, hung them up as the tailor had instructed, took my shirt off, crumpling it and throwing it on the sofa, and sat on the bed, ready to collapse. I was emotionally spent. I picked up the phone.

"Hello, Mr. Antil," said the operator.

"Hi. call me Jerry. Can you ring Ava in Mr. Mowry's office?" I asked.

"Hello?" asked Ava.

"You mentioned dinner?" I asked.

"Yes. How did it go?" she asked.

"I don't have the foggiest. The man barely talked to me. We'll see. Do you want to have dinner with me?"

"What time?"

"How about seven?"

"Seven is good," said Ava.

"Can you call and wake me at six so I can get ready?" I asked.

"Sleep tight," she said.

Click.

My phone rang at six.

"Wake up, sleepy head," said Ava.

"I'm up," I mumbled.

"I'm at home, but I'll see you in the lounge at seven," said Ava.

Click.

I picked up the phone, again.

"Hotel operator—hi, Mr. Antil. How may I assist you?"

"Can I get shirts laundered in the hotel?"

"Yes, I'll send someone up."

Click.

While waiting, I buffed my shoes with underwear and laid out a fresh shirt, my suit, and tie. The bellhop took my shirts and a five-dollar bill and promised to have them back, on hangers, heavy starched by morning. I gave him another five and we made an arrangement. Every day he would come up and pick up my shirts from the chair in the corner and then return them and hang them in the closet for me. I always felt fresher in a cleaned and starched shirt, sometimes changing it several times a day in a world where air conditioning was not commonplace.

When I walked into the Neil House lounge, the bar to the left was crowded, people stacked deep, the beginning stages of the Friday sunset mating ritual in downtown Columbus. Off to the right, in the corner, sitting back against the wall, delicately fingering the stem of a Manhattan glass, was a vision of loveliness, in a cocktail dress and eyes that could light up Broadway. She smiled up through fresh, rose-red lips. I melted into the booth.

"How was your day, big guy?" Ava asked.

The waiter walked up with a tray and set a Cutty and water in front of me.

"I took the liberty," she said.

I lifted the glass, she lifted hers, and we toasted to the day, to Ned Stout and to the *Columbus Dispatch*, and to a wing and a prayer.

"Do you have a girlfriend?" she asked.

"Yes, sort of," I said.

"You must miss her," she said, taking a sip, leaving lipstick on the rim of her glass, watching my eyes.

"I miss kissing," I said.

Ava smiled. It was an "Awww, that's so sweet" smile, like a sister would smile.

"I don't know if I impressed Ned Stout today or just played a fool, stuttering and stammering around. I wish I knew," I said. "Do you have a boyfriend?"

"Not at the moment," she said. "How long has it been since you were with your sweetheart, Jerry?"

I looked up, raised my hand, and counted on my fingers.

"Two, three—dang—almost three and a half years now," I said. "Well, I'll be."

"You mean days, don't you?"

"Huh?"

You said years," said Ava.

I lifted my hand and counted again. "Nope, it's years. Time sure flies," I said.

"Let me get this straight, Jerry. You have a girlfriend, but you haven't seen her in over three years? Oh, I get it; she's in the WAVES or the WACS or something, right?"

"She's in the convent. She left me when I was a sophomore at Xavier."

Ava's eyes melted like she was on a big movie screen and a little boy was telling her how he wanted a puppy like Lassie for Christmas and how he would love it and hold it and take it for walks and play with it and be its best friend.

"You like to kiss?" I asked her.

The maraschino cherry balanced between her teeth popped from her mouth onto the table. "Come again?" she asked.

"You like to kiss?" I asked again.

"Every girl likes to be kissed, Jerry, but I don't want to disappoint you."

"How could you disappoint me?" I asked.

"If you're looking for more," she whispered.

"I don't know anything about more," I admitted. "I just kiss."

"Don't you see other girls in Cincinnati?" she asked.

"Ava, my best girl went into the convent. I kissed her goodbye on July fourth in 1959 and waited for her through working with a guy named Mr. V, a guy named Mike Jones, and now a guy named Don Gaffney, and I've been too busy learning how to become a writer and a marketing guy and going to night school, and you're about the most beautiful girl I have seen that wasn't on a magazine cover in a drugstore, so you want to go up to my suite and kiss or what?"

Ava finished the last of her drink. "I'm leaving ..." she said.

"I'm sorry," I offered.

"... for our office on the twelfth floor. You wait here, and then go to your suite. I'll take the stairs down to it in about fifteen minutes."

"Holy Cobako," I said, almost choking on my scotch. I waited a full ten seconds after I saw her get on the elevator, dropped two fives on the table and slipped out of the lounge.

Now my kissing wasn't the movie kissing, where they spin around through the door, kick it closed, and then both get slammed up against the wall in a lip-lock, her leg coming up around his butt while he's pulling her skirt up to get at her panties as she's tugging at his shirt, popping a few buttons off.

Mine was more like the scene on the yacht in *Some Like It Hot*, with Tony Curtis and Marilyn Monroe, and all they did was kiss and his glasses still steamed up.

When Ava stepped into my suite, the door closed behind her gently. I walked to her, put my arm deep around the small of her back, near her waist, leaned down, planted my lips on hers for leverage, and straightened up, lifting her to me for an opening kiss to set the mood. It was long and soft and slow, with dreamy, half-opened eyes, she a few inches off the floor and me in heaven. Carrying her, I turned and walked us over to the sofa, where we sat down and smooched far into a dreamy Friday night.

"I have to go," Ava moaned. "Mark wants me to come in in the morning. I need to get some sleep."

"I'll walk you up the stairs to your office," I offered.

"No, I'm fine. Just give me your shirt," she said.

"My shirt?" I asked.

"There's lipstick all over it. No sense in giving the bellman and laundry staff something to talk about. I'll take it to my laundry."

I took it off and handed it to her. I kissed her good night, one last time, taking her breath away.

"We never had dinner," I said.

"I know, wasn't it wonderful?" she said. "Good night, big guy. You sure can kiss," she whispered.

"Like riding a bicycle," I said. "How far away do you live?"

"Fifteen minutes. I'm fine."

"Night."

I listened for the stairwell door to close. When it did, I sighed, smelled the rouge, the lipstick, and the shampoo of her hair, stepped back over to my bed, jumped up and off my feet in celebration, and bounced down onto the middle of the bed.

KAFLUNK went the staves, crashing to the floor under the bed's mattress.

"Hotel operator, how may I assist you, Jerry?"

"Operator, I think I broke my bed. Can you send someone up, please?"

Chapter 15

Ring, ring, ring. Ring, ring, ring.
The phone was obnoxious. Saturday morning, no telling what time it was. I reached for it, fumbled around with my eyes closed.

"What time is it?" I said into the receiver.

"Time you came up for coffee and breakfast—my office, fifteen minutes." It was Mark. "I have news. We'll eat in my office."

Click.

I rolled over, opened my eyes, and lifted my head.

"Oh shit," I said.

My pillow was covered with smudges of lipstick. Lipstick had rubbed off my face onto the pillowcase all night. I sat up, put my feet on the floor, and thought. I remembered late last night two maintenance men coming up to fix my bed, the mattress down flat on the floor. I wondered if they had spread the word throughout the hotel staff how my bed had crashed down. There was no telling what they thought went on last night; why not give the maids some lipstick on the pillowcase so they really have something to talk about? I jumped up, stepped into the shower, shaved, put my suit on, and headed up to see Mark for breakfast.

As I pushed the office's door open, I could see Mark's silhouette—the morning sun was in the window behind him—sitting in his office chair, his hands raised high above his head with what looked like a big newspaper in them.

"You did it, you talented son of a bitch, you did it," he shouted.

"Is that good or bad?" my morning brain let me mumble.

"It's something we haven't done in this hotel since Mark Twain slept here, young man—we made full headlines, and you did it. Congratulations, Jerry, you did it." Mark threw a copy of the paper at me with a broad smile.

The front-page headline read, "STAMPEDE LOOMING AT THE NEIL HOUSE." It was Ned Stout's doing for sure. A few paragraphs into the article there was a mention of the possibility of a carpeted swimming pool.

"Where's Ava?" I asked.

"She called in, wanted to sleep in today. I told her to stay home, but she said she would be in by noon. Let's order breakfast," said Mark. "We have to figure this grab-bag thing out."

I still wasn't confident whether or not I had overstepped my authority. "Are we going to do it?" I asked.

"Jerry, this is million-dollar publicity. We're riding it all the way."

I knew a "fast break" when I saw one. The ball was in my court now. My mind started organizing the details of a plan.

About the time Ava walked in, the phone started ringing off the hook. She was beaming a smile at me with the newspaper article in hand.

"Ava, I'm going to need a room with a desk in it," I said, "a telephone with four or five outside lines, and Yellow Pages for New York City, Chicago, and Los Angeles. Can you train the hotel operators that every call or inquiry regarding this event must come to me, or they should at least take a message for me to respond to personally?"

"I'll arrange everything," she said.

"She's the best," said Mark.

Mark turned to his staff in the room and said, "Let Jerry call the shots on this one."

Little did he know, Ava and I were a great team. We worked together smooth as silk. Neither Ava nor I had out-of-control or competitive egos; we just had the drive it took and the confidence to want to make a difference and make things happen. We were in it for the sport. In the next few weeks every media outlet—network television, radio, major city and national newspaper—was called and provided an expense-free suite in the hotel for the day of the "Grab Bag."

And they came in droves, the press and the people.

On the day of the event, press from all over the country filled every complimentary corner suite in the hotel. More than a thousand five hundred people were counted inside—mostly ladies—and more lined up around the entire block to get into the hotel when the fun began. They would each get a coupon with their name on it and be able to come in and tag a piece of furniture, which would then be inventoried in their name and given to them when the hotel was remodeled. Flair Radio, a full weekend national radio program, covered it live; CBS, NBC, and ABC networks did as well. The *Christian Science Monitor* and *Chicago Tribune* featured it on their front page covers—along with more than three hundred English-speaking newspapers, who wrote about it, and all the Columbus, Cincinnati, and Cleveland television stations. People were sending letters from all over the world telling about their honeymoons in the hotel; others mailed in hotel room keys they had stolen.

This musty old "grand lady" of a hotel, the Neil House, was raised from an almost forgotten something—a hostelry—this one special Saturday morning and greeted its next sunset, by that day's end, a rising star again. The Neil House was "Queen of the Pile" once again. Public awareness for her and her remodeling was number one. Reconstruction and the raising of remodeling capital virtually assured.

When the full day of *grab bag* dust settled, most of the hotel worker bees agreed to go home and rest up and we would meet for brunch the next day and talk about our victory and what follow-through was needed.

Ava and I went to my suite, turned the radio on to listen to the news about the hotel on the hour and half hour, and kissed. It was about the time we were stretched out on the sofa, kissing and looking into each other's eyes in the glow of the radio dial, when the news came on with:

"BULLETIN, BULLETIN, BULLETIN. An earthquake has shaken Alaska. Major damage and destruction throughout the state; information unclear at this time, but we will keep you posted. WE REPEAT, there has been a major earthquake in Alaska. Stay tuned to this station for more information as it comes in."

I looked into Ava's eyes.

"You thinking what I'm thinking?" she asked.

"The Neil House is no longer the news for radio or television?" I asked.

"Looks like," she said, chin down with a sad face, looking up into my eyes.

I felt that Superman thing I felt when Ava first shook my hand. I reached over my head, trying to kiss her while my hand fumbled and grabbed the phone receiver. I brought it to my ear.

"Hotel operator, how can I help you, Jerry?" asked the operator.

"Can you get me the AP office on the line?" I asked.

"Did you survive today?" she asked.

"I did."

"What's an AP office, Jerry?"

"The Associated Press. It'll be listed as the Associated Press," I said.

"I'll ring you when I have them. By the way, we had seventeen hundred calls into the hotel switchboard today," she said.

The phone rang. I already had the receiver to my ear and my finger was holding the phone switch button down. I let it go.

"This is Jerry Antil at the Neil House," I said.

"Jerry, AP desk here, whatcha got?"

"Columbus's Neil House hotel is coming to the aid of the Red Cross in Alaska, for the Alaskan earthquake tragedy. We're donating as many sheets, blankets, and pillows as they ask us for, to help out. The Neil House is doing this to say thanks to America and everyone who ever stayed here for remembering her today, and hopes other hotels will follow suit."

"How do you spell Antil?"

"A-N-T-I-L."

"I'll call back for confirmation."

Click.

The phone rang again.

"This is Jerry Antil with the Neil House."

"Can you confirm a story for us?"

"About the blankets and sheets and pillows for the Red Cross in Alaska? Sure can," I said.

It wasn't fifteen minutes later when the radio blasted:

"BULLETIN, BULLETIN, BULLETIN. Dateline, Columbus, Ohio. The Neil House hotel is sending blankets, sheets, and pillows to the Red Cross for use in Alaska, to help the Alaskan earthquake victims. We repeat, the Neil House hotel in Columbus asks all hotels to follow their lead and send blankets and sheets to the Red Cross for the Alaskan earthquake."

I was so exhausted and emotionally spent, I fell asleep soon after the news broadcast vindicating our day's efforts. Ava gave me a peck on the cheek, got up, and went home. It was a day never to be forgotten. In terms of drawing a strong media crowd of VIPs to a party—it would never get any better than that.

On Sunday Don Gaffney called me and was ecstatic about the results of the phenomenal Neil House publicity "stunt."

"You did everything right, Jerry," said Don. "Virtually every paper in the US picked it up. Russ and I are proud of you. We can't afford more money, but we've made you vice president. Think of it, twenty-one, and you're the vice president of the largest public relations agency in the Midwest. I'll talk with the guys about more money and call you Monday. Jerry, great job."

"Thanks, Don. I appreciate it."

"Congratulations."

"It feels good."

"Jerry, I hate to be the bearer of bad news in this 'feel good' moment, but I have some bad news."

"Like what?" I asked.

"Your Oldsmobile wasn't stolen."

"What do you mean?"

"It was repossessed."

"Huh?"

"They repossessed it for nonpayment."

"How could I make payments when they never sent me a coupon book?"

"Is that true? You never got your coupon book?"

"Never, I swear."

"Let me put you on 'hold' and I'll call them. Hold on."

"Okay."

Three minutes later.

"Jerry, they said they sent it. Is your address, 2398 Dana Avenue, Jerry?"

"No, that's the address for Sodality House at Xavier."

"That's where they sent the coupon book— you gave them the wrong address."

"Shit. I gave them the wrong address. Can I pay it now and get it back?"

"They say no— they've already wholesaled it. Sorry."

"Son of a bitch," I said.

"Jerry you've got to get more organized. Slow down and get organized."

"Son of a bitch," I said.

"Well you've got the Ford. Enjoy. And congratulations, Jerry...job well done there at the hotel.

On the following Monday Don called and hinted to me that their third partner thought I was a flash-in-the-pan, an upstart and what kind of a professional gets a car repossessed. He was toying with the old "it's him or me" ever since they had made me vice president without asking him first. The anti-"me"-guy pressure was wearing on Don and Russ.

It wasn't too awfully long, after a few more PR projects— for Gold Medal, the popcorn machine and ice slushing cone machine manufacturer, demonstrating their money-making potential for Little League baseball games; for Horizon Hills tri-level apartments; for getting a Revlon executive, his wife, and daughter featured in a "Sunday Living" spread in the newspaper; and for writing and producing radio commercials for the elegant George and the Dragon restaurant—when the third partner pressed the issue of dumping me or else, again to the breaking point.

I could have duked it out but I wasn't all that happy with not being able to convince the agency to step into the sixties and include sixteen-millimeter film footage for television news as part of their News Release program as easily as I convinced them to get a teletype machine. Besides, the asshole partner had a lock on a big client that paid the rent and a couple of our paychecks, so he'd win a toss between him and me. I only had potential. Don let me go without a fight. He said his hands were tied; the partner with the paying accounts would have to win. I decided to go into the industrial motion picture business, writing and producing movies for industry. Don remained one of my best friends my entire life.

As severance Don and Russ gave me the '52 Ford. I grabbed a suit and drove up to see Ava. Mark was delighted to see me and comped my room and meals for as long as I wanted. Ava was more or less dating the architect working on the hotel's new design, but for old times' sake, we more or less managed to get some serious kissing in.

It was a Monday afternoon when a man came into the lobby of the hotel looking for me. I was just lucky to be there, as I was about to head back to Cincinnati to try to find work. He was a short stocky man with rolled-up shirtsleeves, suspenders, a tie, and horn-rimmed glasses. He kept palming his thinning hair back on his head. His pinky finger had a star sapphire ring on it.

"Mr. Antil pleased to meet you," he said, pumping my hand. "I own a car dealership, on the east side. I have patents on a gadget I want to franchise, wondered if you'd come take a look at it, see what you can do with it."

"Do with it?"

"Get it on television, like you did the Neil House. Boy, what a story that was. Columbus hasn't seen anything like that one in years. I watched every minute ever since it first hit the front page of the newspaper and I just had to meet the person who dreamed that whole thing up."

He had called Ava, asking for the people who did the hotel promotion. She told him she would have me call if I came to town. After I told her I was no longer with Adams, Gaffney & Grant, she got the man on the phone and told him I was the one who had handled the entire promotion and was in the city if he wanted to meet me.

"Let me drive you to my operation, show you my idea, and then you just think about it. Sound like a plan?"

We got in his car and drove through the downtown. He had a new car dealership on the right side of a huge full block-long lot and a used car dealership to its left. We drove between them to the back and parked by what looked like three automotive bays with no fronts or backs on them, standing out on their own away from the other main buildings.

"What is that?" I asked.

"It's a three-bay coin operated 'do it yourself' car wash, Jerry. I have several patents on it and I'm going to franchise it nationwide. I want to see if you can get it on television," he said.

I walked into a bay. There was a narrow red plastic hose hanging from the ceiling, leading down to a metal wand with a handle and trigger.

"It's called *WandaMagic* Car Wash," he said. "You like it?"

"Can I see it work?" I asked.

The man whistled to someone near the service bay and soon a car was pulling into a bay. We put a quarter into the slot holding the grip and trigger; the handle and wand became a high-pressured spray.

"The water comes through a soap tub on the side of the building, and it cleans the surface without scratching the vehicle," he said. "Then you turn this here switch and it goes to clear hot water for a good rinsing."

"Amazing," I said.

I used it on the front window of the car, removing bug smears from it.

"Amazing," I said again.

"It'll be one hell of a franchise," he said. "I just know it. I can see them all over the country."

I set the wand down in a pipe stirrup and we started walking between the lots toward his office to talk.

"I'll pay handsomely if you can get *WandaMagic* on television," he said.

"What if I do manage to get it on local television, mister, what good will that do nationally?" I asked.

"Simple. I get copies of the film they use on the television news and send them around the country to people who maybe want a franchise. Hell, people believe the news. It'll help them make up their mind."

I was impressed.

"What's your budget?" I asked.

He paused and turned. His palm slid back up over his thinning hair.

"You tell me," he said, letting his *used-car* negotiating techniques of never making the first offer step in.

I wasn't quite ready to heed Don's advice to get organized. I didn't have thirty or forty bucks to my name but the free lodging and food at the hotel where I was still a star fogged my sensibilities somewhat.

"How about that white Cadillac Coupe de Ville hardtop convertible over there— that one with the red leather?" I asked, pointing. It was a beauty: a cream white, long and sleek Caddy, with flaring tail fins.

"Why, son, that car ain't but a year old—you know what she's worth?" he hemmed.

"The use of it for one full year, then—you insure it—just like a company car," I hawed back.

"You got yourself a deal, young man. The day you get *WandaMagic* on television is the day you drive that Caddy off the lot, for a whole year—on me. Better do it soon, son, or she'll be sold out from under us. I never turn down a car sale and she's a pretty one." He grinned.

We shook hands, got in his car, and drove back to the Neil House. As he pulled in front and idled the engine, I asked, "What if it doesn't get on television but makes it in the newspaper?"

"Won't do me any good; on television or we have no deal. Work for you, son?"

We shook hands again with a clearer understanding.

I went up and kissed Ava goodbye a few times, borrowed

the Columbus phone book and Yellow Pages from the room, checked out, and drove back to my room in Cincinnati to read them.

Chapter 16

I knew I had to come up with an idea for the car wash in Columbus— but I also knew I had to eat. I needed to be earning money soon. The car wash guy insisted on getting his car wash invention on television. I had a good feel for the newspaper and radio. I picked it up working at AG&G. Although I tried to get Russ and Don to include 16mm film footage along with press releases, I was less familiar with the workings of television. I drove over to the WKRC television station and sat in the lobby like a shark, listening and observing, looking for ideas. A guy my age was sitting there with a Bolex sixteen-millimeter movie camera in one hand and a briefcase in the other. He was sitting on the front edge of the sofa like he was ready for a sprint. Young as he was, he had thinning red hair, almost like it was shaved, maybe quarter-inch barber's shears. His eyes were a blank stare, mouth held in a forced, fake smile.

"Are you a news cameraman?" I asked.

"Any kind of film," he said. "This"—holding up his Bolex camera—"and I have a Graflex four-by-five, and thirty-five-millimeter, and even a two-and-a-quarter-by-two-and-a-quarter."

"You freelance or do you work for the station?" I asked.

"I'm a news stringer."

"What's that?"

"They pay me to bring in news footage. I do freelance, too," he said.

"Let me understand how this works. You see news and shoot it and bring it in?" I asked.

"Well, sometimes, maybe—but mostly they call me to go shoot something they want me to shoot, I bring it in, and they pay me," he said. "What do you do?"

"I do some writing, some PR, but seeing your movie camera you've got me thinking about maybe getting into writing training films or sales films or maybe even television commercials for companies," I said. "Can a guy make a living doing training films? Sales films?"

"If you produce them," he said.

"What do you mean, produce them?" I asked.

"A writer gets paid to write. A photographer, like me, gets paid to shoot. A producer gets a thousand dollars a minute to put it all together. Produce them," he asserted.

"A thousand dollars a minute? Are you serious?" I asked. "Does that mean like if I come up with a fifteen-minute film, somebody would pay me fifteen thousand dollars for it?"

"Pretty much."

"Holy shit."

"Look, producing is getting things and people together—a writer and a cinematographer and a lab that will process and edit film for you. You're a writer, pay me to be your cinematographer and use MPO, a lab in Memphis—they'll cut and splice it all to your script and send it back finished. You get a thousand bucks a minute," he said.

"How do I get it to Memphis?" I asked. The cotton bale at the Memphis Airport and Forrest City's Jim Crow glanced through my memory.

"Railway Express. You take the film cans to the train depot and send them Railway Express. Takes a couple of days is all, and they'll get it and go to work."

"What do they cost?" I asked.

"Maybe two hundred and fifty dollars for a television commercial, three-fifty if you make some changes to what they do. On a movie fifteen or twenty minutes long, maybe twelve to fifteen hundred."

"What's your name?" I asked.

"Jim Riding," he said.

"Jerry Antil," I said, shaking his hand.

He picked up a magazine from the coffee table with a front cover sporting a beautiful girl on it with a headline about Halloween astrological signs and smiled.

"What's your sign?" he asked with a big grin, eyeing the beauty on the cover.

"Aries," I said.

Jim pointed to me. "Aries. Mr. Jerry here is an Aries—of the mind."

He tore a corner from the page of the magazine and wrote his number on a picture of a carved pumpkin and handed it to me.

"Let me ask you something," I said.

"Don't lose this number— but you can find me here if you do," he said.

"What if someone has a news story, do they call you?" I asked.

"Just call a television station, ask for their news desk. They'll call their stringers if they think it's news. Hey, I got to go. Call me if you need something shot," he said as someone called him into the newsroom.

I looked at the cover girl in a Halloween costume, the pumpkin with the scratching of his name and telephone number, stood up, and went out to my Ford. I stared at some clouds for maybe ten seconds, got in and drove to Columbus and checked back into the Neil House. My room and board was still being comped by Mark. The bottom half of the guest-room floors were closed off and the reconstruction had begun. The smell of concrete scented the lobby air. Ava brought a Coke to my room to say hello. We got a few kisses in standing up and I asked her if she would help me if I needed her. She took my cheeks in her hands for a long tender, passionate kiss.

"Anything," she said.

"Thanks," I said.

"But call me at home if it's got nothing to do with the hotel," said Ava.

I drove to a company I found in the yellow pages. They sold manufactured mobile homes, homes people would pull with their cars for camping and touring. I sat with the owner of the company and told him I had an idea I felt would become newsworthy. I asked for his participation and for a fee of $250 to cover my time over the past couple of weeks if I got one of his house trailers on television. He agreed, we shook on it and I rehearsed him on details he needed to get done, the timing and to call me when he was ready. I drove back to the hotel.

"Hello, Mark Mowry's office," said Ava.

"Can you talk?" I asked.

"Yes, hi."

"I need your help later. Can you do it?"

"Everybody's gone to a dinner with the attorneys taking us public. They won't be in until morning. My evening's free. What's up?"

When I got the call from the house trailer guy, Ava and I drove to the car dealer's lot, sat in the car and waited. At ten to six Ava stepped out of my car, went to the corner phone booth and waited for my signal.

Right on the button, at six o'clock, a medium size house trailer came rolling down the street, pulled by a Chevy. As it slowed to turn into the *WandaMagic* Car Wash behind the dealership, on closer look you could see its windows were soaped for Halloween—soaped in orange jack-o-lantern faces, black scary cats and tombstones, ghosts and goblins. Ava picked up the pay phone and, one at a time, dialed every television station in Columbus. "There's a house going through a car wash. It's hysterical," she reported to news directors. She gave them the location. "It's true, there's a whole house in the carwash," she said. By the time the house trailer was in the washing bay and the quarters put in the wash, the television film camera stringers had shown up, and then two reporters. No one was interviewed, but a lot of footage was shot by the television stations. It was happy, fun footage celebrating Halloween, ghosts and goblins, and the absurdity of bringing a house through a carwash. It hit every eleven o'clock television news show in town— all the morning shows the next morning. Ava and I had dinner in my room and watched it on television between kisses. The next morning I drove to the car dealership, picked up my Cadillac Coupe de Ville with its red leather upholstery, and got paid $50 for my 1952 Ford by the happy patent holder of the *WandaMagic* Car Wash process who said this franchise will make him millions. I drove to the mobile home dealership, collected my $250 and headed to

Cincinnati for some mostaccioli and meatballs at Chico's.

Chapter 17

Twenty-two, a couple hundred bucks in my pocket and brimming with more confidence than a good feel of the practical, I was about to drive into the biggest creative learning renaissance of my life in a long, sleek, cream-colored 1962 Cadillac Coupe de Ville hardtop convertible with rich, rose-red leather upholstery and an electric antenna that came out of nowhere and went up when I turned the radio on. I christened the moment, taking her up for a stretch to 110 miles per hour on a straight, level portion of the road somewhere between Columbus, the approaching seven hills of Cincinnati, and my intrepid spirit. So what if it was a used Caddy? Just like Elvis, but six years younger, I had me a Cadillac—for a year, anyway. It floated like a swan.

What I wasn't aware of was that a Cadillac was about to take me through my own coming of age as well— in my twenties.

As I drove into the Cincinnati skyline, I wondered if I should go to the "Over 21" dance at the Alms Hotel again later tonight. I had only been to the dance a few times, back when I was nineteen, working at Union Central Life Insurance for Mike Jones. At six-ten no one checked my age. The "Over 21" dance had big-band dance music, sounds like Glenn Miller and Tommy Dorsey. Fifty or more white-linen-clothed tables were speckled with women in their twenties and thirties in earrings and painted faces sitting and waiting to meet a man, to talk to or to dance with, like in the movie *Marty*. Men in sport coats and ties and wet-combed hair circled the room cautiously, weaving about tables like quarter horses looking for strays who might look up, catch their eye, make a suitable first impression, or, truth be known, just say "yes" if asked to dance. Being turned down for a dance could set a young man's spirit back months in his natural mating development.

Back when I was at Union Central, at nineteen, I thought I would try it to see if the "Over 21" could help me forget my love-lost girlfriend, who was now a nun. I remember circling the tables in the room, I met a girl standing by a tall rubber plant, had two nice slow dances, talking a bit, but when I discovered she was twenty-nine to my nineteen, I made up some lame excuse and politely left for home at the Sodality House. The next Thursday, when someone yelled up from the front hall by the pay phone saying there was a girl on the phone asking for a Jerry Antil, my girl is out of the convent was the first thing that whipped through my brain. Maybe she had come out at last. I could skip four steps down at once without losing my balance. I did it and grabbed the phone.

"Hello?" I hoped.

"Hello, Jerry, this is Brenda."

"Who?"

"Brenda. We met and danced Saturday, at the Alms, do you remember me?"

"Oh, yeah, hi, I remember—yeah, hi," I answered.

"Jerry, you'll never guess."

"Guess?"

"I have two tickets to Moonlight Gardens to see Buddy Morrow and his Marlboro Orchestra for Saturday night—isn't that a dream?" she said.

"Wow, that's great," I answered.

Then it came.

"You wouldn't happen to know some tall, dark, and handsome guy who would want to use one of my tickets and go with me, would you? Huh, big fella?" she hinted.

As my brother Dick once said, about my complete lack of understanding in the mating game business, "You're dumb as a stick, you know that?" He said it to me when I was eight, just before Mom made him wash the dishes for saying it. Once again proving my brother right, my completely sincere answer to Brenda's tricky question was:

"Hey, I'll ask around for you. I'll ask some guys, should be somebody, I'll ask around, call me tomorrow."

There was a click on the phone.

I was so backward I thought we must have gotten disconnected.

But that was then, when I was nineteen—*dumb as a stick*—

and now was now. I was a new twenty-two pent up stallion with a Cadillac and the always fresh memory of Ava's sweet lips to rekindle my confidence. I figured I would make my rooming house the first stop, take a quick shower, change my clothes before heading over to Chico's and then to the Alms Over 21 Dance.

I turned into the driveway of my rooming house and parked under the oak tree, just off the side of the drive so others could pull around; it was the perfect spot from which to look down at my Caddy from the bathroom shower. I shared the third floor with one other roomer, who announced his presence by stacking empty wine bottles in the waste bucket next to the refrigerator. The rumor was he was a LIFE Magazine photographer, but I never saw or met him. The carpeted stairs up the very tightly turned third flight were steep and sweltering. At the top, my room door was across from the community refrigerator. There was enough space to open just one of the three doors at a time—the refrigerator door being one of the three. I pulled on its door to check my shelf for a cold soft drink. Except for a white, unsealed envelope resting on it, my shelf was bare. My name was scrawled in quiet cursive on the envelope's front. The note read: "Jerry—You're behind eight weeks, sweetie, can you bring $80 by?" Then: "Have you seen one of your hand towels? I found a sock in the bathroom; I put it on your dresser, leave a note if it's not yours. Agnes."

A dry-cleaning tycoon had purchased four large homes along the street in front of his mansion, supposedly to protect it from encroaching riffraff. As I got wise, I figured it out that he was only buying surrounding homes to his mansion to keep blacks out of his neighborhood— that is when I decided I would look for a place and move out when I could. But before that a friendly, matronly lady with a ready smile and even disposition, Agnes managed them all, collected the rents, and changed the bed linens and towels in each room every week. I found the washcloth where I'd put it forgetfully, on top of the refrigerator in the hall—out of my mind and her vision. With it was the matching sock to the one Agnes had found in the bathroom. A washcloth wasn't something that would go far, and with my height, looking on top of things for things was always a good idea. I put eighty dollars in the envelope and put it and the hand towel on my dresser, the sock in the drawer and a note: *"Agnes, what happened to my television. Do you know what happened to my television?"*

Larry McDermott's new Caddy was parked in front of Chico's. I pulled in the space behind it, got out, compared them both, and walked into the restaurant.

"Don't bump your head," said Carlo with a smile. He gazed out the window at my wheels, and I could tell he couldn't wait to hear the story of how I got it. But tonight was Larry's night. This dinner, with eight around the table was a happy celebration—everything was on the house. Larry made a special introduction of his lady and announced they were going to get married. I was the one who had introduced him to her—Ruth, a single lady near his age who worked at Union Central Life Insurance. She too had red hair, was beautiful and a timid quiet, with a wonderful smile.

When I had first seen her and her demeanor at Union Central, I thought of Larry right off. He was a perfect gentleman, a good friend of Mr. V's, and a confirmed bachelor—perfect for her. I had given him Ruth's number at work six months before and now they were getting married. To celebrate, I ordered sausage with my spaghetti. Larry asked me about three advertising agencies he had given my name to and who were waiting for my call. He wanted to know if they were on my list of film prospects to call on. One, downtown, handled Kenner Toys, one north on Montgomery Road handled Red Barn restaurants, and one was an agency downtown for Frisch's Big Boy restaurants. I stuck the names and numbers into my pocket, enjoyed my dinner and Larry's and Ruth's celebration, and headed off to the "Over 21" dance at the Alms.

I first saw her walking from the side parking lot to the front of the hotel.

She was medium height, blonde, confident, and beautiful, with breasts like the ones I saw on the Marilyn Monroe calendar on the kitchen wall at Leonard's Coffee Shop back in Homer.

I stopped and waited, holding the brass front door of the Alms Hotel for her. She looked up, caught my eye, and squeaked.

"I know you from somewhere, don't I? Where do I know you from?" she sassed, smiling up at me with a tease, brushing by.

She walked into the hotel, stepping ahead of me in high, patent-leather heels, just to the center of the marble lobby, then she paused and turned around as if to get a look at me; but my sense told me it was for me to get a good look at her. Watching her move in that black sweater and black tight skirt gave me a better understanding of the term "sweater girl."

"Have you figured out where we met?" she asked, as though she meant it.

"Not sure," I gushed like a toothless hillbilly, moving in her direction.

"Basketball," she declared. "That's it. Basketball. Where do you play basketball?" she asked, letting me walk to where she stood. "My God, how tall are you?"

"Six-ten, but that's in shoes. I used to play at X, now I play around, some industrial ball. Want to dance?"

I was blending my sentences like lumpy mashed potatoes. I was asking a girl to dance while standing in the middle of the lobby of a hotel. We ambled over, paid our entry, and walked into the darkened ballroom.

"I don't dance, I like the music," she said. "Order me a drink, will ya, honey? Bloody Mary. Stalk of celery—tell them not too hot. Over there," she said, pointing to a table. "Come sit and talk."

As we walked toward the table, I handed a waitress walking toward us a five-dollar bill to make a detour and ordered our drinks. I took a seat next to the blonde, dripping with the confidence this Greek goddess spewed—a knockout girl who had just picked me out of a crowd.

"What do you mean, you don't dance?" I asked.

"I'm not athletic. But I do like tall boys, especially basketball players," she said.

She leaned her shoulder into my chest and smiled.

"Let me see your hand," she asked.

I rested my hand on the table. She looked at it, then turned her head up at me with a smile.

She wasn't an Ava. Ava was more of a sleek runway-model type—a Jaguar or an Austin Healey. This girl was more robust than a 1952 Cadillac grill, a Marilyn Monroe or a Jayne Mansfield type; but unlike both of them, this one was here live and in person, sitting at my table tonight. Close enough to win the draw.

"I dance," she said. "But not tonight. Not in the mood. I just came to find some nice man who would take me to see Ray Charles."

"Who?"

"Ray Charles."

"When?"

"Next Friday. You like Ray Charles, honey?"

It was about this time when guys started to line up at a distance, walking up to the table one at a time, like lottery winners, to ask her to dance. She wouldn't look up at them—shooed each away like flies, with a flick of her hand. They'd give me a sneer and walk away.

"I like Ray Charles," I said. "Where?"

"It's a neighborhood piano-bar-lounge thing on a bad side of Hamilton, sort of a club. He's only here two nights. I just have to go see him. He doesn't play until ten-thirty or so, but I heard he'll play long after last call and as late as people ask. It's just a bar, not many tables, I think."

"What's your name?" I asked.

"Eileen. Want to go with me?"

"It could be dangerous," I said.

"I don't care," said Eileen.

"I like his sound, his voice," I said. "I heard he's blind."

"I love Ray Charles," said Eileen.

Eileen touched my tie, her thumb and forefinger delicately sliding down its length.

"What's your name?" she asked.

"I'll take you."

"You will? What's your name?"

"Jerry."

"There'll be mostly coloreds there. Are you okay with that? I like Jerry. Strong name. What's your sign?"

"Aries," I said.

"Shit," she said.

"I'll take you, I'll drive," I said. "What's wrong with Aries?"

"I'll tell you when I know you better. You mean it, you'll take me?"

"Sure."

"You're an angel," she said.

"Can I say something without pissing you off?" I asked.

"You can try," said Eileen. She smiled.

"I play basketball with guys like Ray Charles. Don't call them colored, call them black. That shows respect."

Eileen pulled on my tie bringing my face to her lips. She pecked my lips twice while she pulled a pen from her purse and wrote her number and address on a cocktail napkin.

"Good," I said, "next Friday ... perfect."

"Here," she added, folding the napkin and handing it to me. "I never answer the phone. Pick me up Friday. I promise—you won't be sorry, Aries man."

Business done, Eileen snapped her purse closed, tipped her drink back, and plopped it down, empty, on the table. She stood up. "I'll see you then, Aries Jerry."

She turned to walk away, stopped, turned back, leaned down, put her arms around my neck from behind, and kissed me on the cheek.

"See you Friday, honey," she whispered into my ear. "Be a good little boy tonight and don't stay out too late." She smiled, turned again, and left the hotel.

I got what I came for, I thought. I had met a lady—well, a dish—so I quit while I was ahead and got up to be a good boy and go home like she had recommended. I gave Eileen enough time to find her car and drive off, then I left the hotel dance myself.

When I got back to my room there was a note taped to my door. *"Jerry, two men came and took your television for nonpayment. I tried to explain how busy you were, but they didn't seem to care. Sorry."* signed Agnes.

Don's words of my needing to get organized ripped through my brain. And, just as my dad had taught me, late through that night and most of the following day I did my homework of making a list of three agencies physically surrounding each of the agency prospects Larry had given me. Within the week I would call on twenty agencies, selling my services of writing and producing films.

The Kenner Toy agency said yes to a three-thousand-dollar budget for a fifty-eight-second commercial for a toy submarine. They advanced me a thousand for props. Their product was an eight-inch-long gray plastic toy submarine that would float in a tub and fill itself with water, causing it to sink and giving the illusion it was diving. A small plug on its stern would be filled with baking soda, which created oxygen under water and made it come to the surface again. It was fun, and I immediately went Hollywood. I imagined the bellowing submarine horn from all the war movies—

AAAAAAUUUUUUUUGAAAAAAAA

AAAAAAUUUUUUUUGAAAAAAAA

—with the officer yelling, "Dive! Dive!" as the opening to my commercial. I knew a good sound man at the FM radio station who could lift it from somewhere. I could envision the submarine coming to the surface in a bathtub with a happy boy getting his ears scrubbed, but right at this moment I needed an ocean. I went to a woodworking and cabinet shop down in the industrial district and contracted them to build a four-foot-tall, six-foot-long tank made of three-quarter-inch marine plywood with a half-inch clear plastic window on a one-by-three-foot area on one side of the tank.

"Let me get this straight," said the man. "You want a wood box so you can fill it with water? Maybe you might oughta rethink— "

"PT boats and D-Day landing craft used in World War II were made of plywood," I said.

"They were?" he asked.

"Marine plywood."

"I didn't know that."

"They made them in New Orleans."

"They did? I didn't know that."

"It's a no-brainer. My cameraman will shoot the action through the window from an angle looking up at the diving submarine. I'll decorate the insides with art—including mines and miniature torpedoes and maybe even fish. The wood man scratched his head.

"I can build it all right. Question is, will it work? Can't promise that," he cautioned.

"We'll never know until we try," I said.

I paid him cash in advance, and he promised results in a week or two.

Following that payment, I had seven hundred dollars left, less the fifty-dollar bill I dropped pulling the wad out of my jeans pocket; a gust of wind blew it down a drain on Fourth Street. I finally opened a bank account on the same corner, got a check book and in the name of R & A Studios I rented a carpeted two-room, second-floor office just below Clifton Avenue, because it led to Vine Street and down into the heart of downtown Cincinnati, where the action seemed to be. I ordered a telephone; figured we didn't need desks—my new partner, the cameraman I met at the television station and I could use the floor. We needed the space mostly for storing his equipment and making film sales and production calls.

Frisch's Big Boy was a "sit down" restaurant chain featuring a double-patty hamburger—the "Big Boy." They needed a film to show their franchisees the great service provided them, and their agency wanted to see me in three weeks. Another fast food company, Red Barn's ad agency wanted to see me in four weeks about another project. Things were picking up quickly, primarily because, outside of New York or L.A., industrial film production was a fledgling industry; in Cincinnati we had little competition for the "small stuff." Big jobs on commercials went through the New York agencies.

I knew I wanted to write and produce, so I had to find

someone else to do the sales. Until I found someone, I would have to farm out the writing. I called the newspaper and ran a classified ad for a commissioned sales rep.

On Friday I left my rooming house at dusk to make my way to Eileen's neighborhood, looking for her house while I could still see the street numbers. Through the front-door window of what appeared to be her parents' house, I could see Eileen stepping down the stairs to the front hall, each bounce in her step unraveling another part of her body in a rhythm and motion all her own. Her dark red V-neck sweater was so form fitting it looked like fuzzy body paint. A scarf around her neck hung loosely—camouflaging a revealing cleavage in case her father walked in as she was leaving, was my guess. We stepped out onto the stoop and turned to walk down the steps to the sidewalk.

"Isn't that a beauty?" she asked, pointing to the Cadillac, thinking I was parked behind it.

"Like it?" I asked, walking her toward it. I pulled the door open for her to get in.

"Holy shit," she whispered with a grin. She sat down on the edge of the seat, lifted her legs around and in, and stared up at me with a whole new big smile. I walked around, got in, and started it up.

"Did you borrow this?" she asked, rubbing her palm on the leather seat between us.

"It's mine," I said.

Eileen slid over next to me and placed her hand on the top of my thigh, laying her head on my shoulder as a warmer, more understanding hello. We slowly rolled through her neighborhood, as only a long Cadillac could, and headed on our way up to Hamilton. Eileen turned the car radio on and tuned in a station just as the disc jockey was pausing the music for a live commercial.

"All you happy listeners, don't miss the shocking—the horrific—he's a giant on screen and off—he's Eegah—alive and on stage tonight only. Eegah—on stage at the Twin Drive-In theatre on Reading Road. Tallest person at the Twin tonight wins a king-size bed. So grab your girl, grab your guy—take a chance—

head on down to the Twin Drive-In and meet Eegah, biggest man in the world and star of the movie Eegah, so horrifying, you'll lock your car doors. This could be a friend, a neighbor—why, it could even be you—tallest person in the theatre tonight will win a king-size bed."

I looked over at Eileen; she looked up at me. No thought about it, I made a complete U-turn and headed the half mile back up to the Twin Drive-In movie, bought two tickets, and found a place to park, to wait for the show to start and the stage lights to come on. I opened my window enough to hang the speaker on it and sat back to wait. Eileen's perfume filled the car as she turned in her seat and faced me.

"You're bound to win the bed. You're the tallest guy I've ever seen," she said, reaching her hand out and resting it on the side of my neck.

"Could be," I said. "Could be."

"A beautiful Cadillac, now this. Are you always this lucky?" Eileen asked.

The television series *Mr. Lucky* popped into my brain. I lowered my head, lifted my brows.

"They call me Mr. Lucky," I said. Then I smiled.

"Kiss me, damn it," she said. "Just kiss me."

I obliged and her arms sprung, wrapping around my neck like a coil, cashmere breasts pinning my shoulders back, her tongue darting, introducing me to a new sensation—French kissing. I had heard about it and talked about it, but this was a first, and my emotions were mixed on it. Jury was still out. Oh, it was a kiss all right, but my usual kissing style was traditional dreamy-eyed and poetic and soft—a slow dance type with the tastes of lips and the feel of a lip pull or two on soft willing lips. This French kissing was more like push-ups for the tongue—but I was willing to learn.

By the time I was about to get the hang of this French-kissing thing, right about the same time her sweater had ridden like a pleated drape up the front of her satin bra, the stage floodlights came on and the announcer was telling everyone to line up and meet Eegah, the biggest man on earth. Eileen turned, adjusted her hair, and pulled her sweater down, squinting at the flood lamps now lighting up the inside of the car. It was then I was oh-so aware of a slight problem I was having. Seemed as though this French-kissing thing, or maybe it was the warm cashmere, had brought life to a few things—well, at least one thing—and now I wasn't certain I would be able to stand up and walk to the stage.

I'd always thought of this "issue" as a morning thing. It was like a "kickstand" for my bicycle that kept me from rolling over in bed easily. The more I thought about my present situation, the more I was beginning to add two and two together—for the first time in my life. My parents weren't good about giving sex talks. With eight in the family, and living in dairy farm country, they probably thought we'd pay attention enough to pick up the art form somewhere. The more I thought about it, the more I was beginning to understand that writers didn't have to be all that bright—they just had to be observant.

"Things" subsided long enough for me to be able to get out of the car, stand, and get in line behind near fifty guys all lined up to meet the biggest man on earth, Eegah, now on stage in a furry cannibal costume. Slowly, one by one, guys who had piled out of cars and lined up would turn around, look up at my height—step out of line and retreat to their cars. When I finally climbed the steps to the stage, even Eegah, who was seven-one, winced at my height just inches from his. Tall people always look very tall to other tall people—don't ask me why.

He leaned in like a good sport and shook my hand with a friendly grin. The disc jockey took down my name and address and told me the king-size bed would be delivered the following week. The actor who played Eegah, Richard Kiel, would go on to play "Jaws" in the James Bond movies. For the moment I had to get off the stage and back to Eileen, and then on to Hamilton to see Ray Charles. In the car Eileen welcomed me with another long kiss with the tongue push-ups. I was getting the hang of it, now putting my arms around her bare waist, what with her sweater pulling up when she raised her shoulders. At one point—and with our windows foggy by that time—Eileen sat up, slid over to the other side of the front seat, pulled her sweater up over her white satin breasts, over her head, shook her hair around in an attempt to straighten it, and flipped the cashmere sweater onto the car's dashboard.

"I love the smell of this car," she said. I was staring at white bare shoulders and a bra filled to capacity—hardly the look of the bras I'd seen in the past, wrinkled and hanging on a backyard clothesline. Glancing over at me with a smile in her eyes, as if I knew exactly what I was doing, Eileen reached around and put both arms around behind her back, leaned her head down, and off popped her bra—breasts standing straight out without confinement.

"How did you do that?" I asked.

"Do what?" she asked.

"That," I said.

"What?" she asked. Her hands now covering her nipples, as though she were all of a sudden taken shy.

"How do you put both your arms behind your back like that? Do it again, will ya? I want to see that."

"What?" she asked.

"I want to see you do that. The arms thing, you know," I said.

Eileen wrinkled her eyebrows in a perplexing glance, took her bra in her hand and put it around herself with the hooks in front of her. She hooked them, then turned the whole apparatus around her body like a conveyor belt until the clips were behind her; she then pulled the front satin sails up over her breasts and adjusted her shoulder straps. She paused and looked me in the eyes.

"Are you making fun?" she asked.

"I'm dead serious. I've never seen that done before. Can you do it again?" I asked.

Eileen put both arms around behind her back and did it again. Both arms went around to the middle of her back, to my fascination, as she unfastened her bra, again. This time she watched me warily; she wasn't certain "Aries Jerry" in his Cadillac was serious or funning her. Off popped the bra, tossed onto the dashboard with her sweater, and over she came for kissing, which led to touching. I had grown up in the country and had seen breasts before, suckling babies, and didn't think much of them as sexual objects. Hers were mighty proud and perky, fun to touch and watch, no question, but I was enjoying the French kissing better. She called me Mr. Lucky, and at that moment, with her hand nudging my kickstand, I couldn't have agreed with her more. We continued heavy petting for about an hour before she startled, realizing we had to leave to go see Ray Charles in Hamilton. We sat up, rearranged our clothing, she fastened and raised the sails of her bra, pulled her sweater on, and I drove slowly out of the drive-in movie with fond thoughts of a new king-size bed, my first bout of French kisses, the warm feeling of a woman's anatomy, and some answers to this young writer's age-old curiosities: the word "hand" can be a verb, and "blow" can be a metaphor—a figure of speech.

Ray Charles's performance was like an album for the ages, filling the smoke filled evening and my memory bank with a new sound, a new energy, a voice like a fine smoky cello delivered with a genuine smile and expressive eyebrows that seemed to communicate with twenty-twenty vision; everyone sitting around that piano and room could sense we were in the presence of greatness—a coming world-renowned legend one day very soon—Woolworth's be damned.

We sat within feet of his piano and stayed. At the end of the evening, I returned Eileen safely back to her home, kissed a good bit—but I missed Ava's lips and style—and jumped into film production headfirst with little or no time to think of women. Although my sexual curiosity was reaching a peak, I would never see Eileen again— but I could and would conjure memories of her look and feel, as needed if a *situation* ever came up— as be said.

Chapter 18

I called and woke my partner at his parents' home to meet me at the cabinet-woodworking shop near downtown to have a look at the prop I'd ordered and to see what lighting would be necessary for the toy submarine commercial. I thought he might be good at giving me ideas on what I might use to decorate the underwater scene for best reality.

"She's out on the back dock. Let's go have a look," said the cabinet man, leading us around table saws and tall stacks of lumber to a rear loading dock door.

The box was impressive, at first sight. It stood four feet high, just as ordered, looked sturdy with double-glued brass screws adding to the support of hardwood boards firmly doubled up and holding the corner joints in place. It had a most impressive boat-like look and feel about it—like a miniature Noah's Ark. The window built in its one side was a thick clear Plexiglas. My partner got down on his knees and peered in through the side window of the large box.

"Why didn't we just go to a pet store and use a fish aquarium?" he asked, holding his thumbs and forefingers in a square to get a sense of a potential shot angle.

"Got a garden hose around here, so we can try her out?" I asked, ignoring my partner's perfectly simple solution, spit out like he was closing the barn door after the horse had already left the barn.

"Here you go," said the cabinet maker.

The man handed me the hose.

"Tell me when you're ready, I'll turn it on," he said.

I stretched the hose and set the nozzle inside the box on the floor. The water turned the wood dark golden reddish brown, then almost black. We just waited; it would be a long slow process filling a wooden vessel this large with water.

The water was soon at a foot and no leaks. We were impressed. My partner was beginning to think it was a good idea. Two feet, still no leaks. Three feet and there was a bit of seepage coming out from around the edges of the Plexiglas window.

"No problem," offered my partner. "The leak around the window seal won't hinder a clear shot through the window."

By this time he was becoming sold on the concept and he committed to finding the best shots and angles, lying on his back on the dock, hands extended out in front of him, one eye closed, blocking a shot—when, without any warning, the entire box exploded, all four sides bursting apart like a popped waxed-paper cup, water plummeting onto the carpentry plant floor and out over the loading dock onto parked cars. The windowed side of the box slapped down on my partner like a flyswatter. No one was hurt, but everyone got soaked and we left wanting a drink of something other than water to calm our nerves.

The near explosion scared hell out of us but wound us up in giggles and stomach-churning tears of laughter. My partner and I left the box, now flat as a rug on the floor of the dock—went and found a pet store and shot the underwater scene there; had a sound man cut in a sound track we lifted from an old war movie and spliced that to my partner's nephew sitting in a sudsy bathtub playing with the submarine. The client was happy with the result.

Following this I made it a point to share my ideas with my partner for his feedback before I pulled off some impulsive *imaginative* chicanery. I was becoming impressed at the clarity a good photographer like my partner could give an idea. Especially someone trained to shoot the news, quickly—as it happened—and accurately.

In time, my partner and I interviewed half a dozen guys and picked one to rep us—sell our services—giving him a car allowance and a ten-percent commission on sales. We rarely saw him, but he did manage to open some doors for us. We went on to produce more than twenty or so films or commercials, enjoying our work— but seldom making a thousand dollars a minute for longer films. It was my guess the thousand dollars a minute was good bar talk around ladies – not reality. We were honored with a Certificate of Achievement from a Kodak Film Festival for commercials we produced for Cincinnati's Coney Island theme park. Our film lab had entered it in the contest. I wasn't getting rich, but I was learning by the minute.

Word on the street in Cincinnati was a big movie by Blake Edwards, *The Great Race*, starring Tony Curtis, Jack Lemmon, Peter Falk, Keenan Wynn, and Natalie Wood, was partially being shot down in the bluegrass, rolling hills near Louisville. Jake Sweeney, a large Pontiac dealer in Cincinnati, gave my partner and me two brand-new Pontiacs to use to drive down near Louisville, plus five hundred dollars each, if we could find the film company's secret filming place and get pictures of stars admiring the new Pontiac Grand Prix cars or just holding his Jake Sweeney license-plate frame with an endorsing smile. Jack Lemmon and Peter Falk were nowhere to be seen—reportedly shooting pool at a local bar, waiting for their shooting call. Tony Curtis was helicoptered in for the movie's opening balloon-rising scene and the kissing scene and then was lifted out by helicopter just as quickly. The only star we found was Keenan Wynn, who happily leaned on a Pontiac and held the license-plate frame up, mugging for the camera. He was a nice man. The 1964 Pontiac was the fastest car I had ever driven in my life—from zero to a hundred miles per hour in less than a quarter mile. It made my Caddy feel like a slow boat to China. The Pontiac Grand Prix was so fast I was afraid of it.

After that, the industrial film we created for the Frisch's Big Boy restaurant chain, to show their franchisees the quality of the support they were receiving from headquarters, was entitled *Thought for Food,* and was my first foray into working for a franchise company. It was so important I flew to Pam Music studios in Dallas, Texas, to have the movie's music written and scored by Euel Box, a smiling, soft-spoken Dallas gentleman who went on to become a friend. He was later nominated for an Academy Award and won a Golden Globe for his original score in the movie *Benji*. Frisch's Big Boy loved the music, but didn't order it and, once again, my impulsive imagination ate up all our profits on a film.

Despite differences, my partner and I managed to produce excellent work. He liked the shorter, more artsy projects, as a photographer might. Make your money and run. I wanted more meaty work—films that said something, carried a message. By the end of a year, the time was coming when I had to give the Cadillac back to the dealer in Columbus. There were two things I had to do before I did that, however, and I was dedicated to accomplishing both.

The first I had to do before returning my Cadillac was to get a replacement vehicle. Buick Motors had imported a small, low-priced car to compete with the VW Bug; it was called the Opel— a low-cost (less than $1,200) city commuter car. I wrote their first press releases when I was with Adams, Gaffney and Grant. This time I wrote and produced three television commercials for the Schott-Lippert Buick dealership on Montgomery Road in full trade for three of their Opels. My partner got one of them, I got one and one we sold for cash, paid production lab costs and split the change. Mine was red with a sunroof my head would fit through if I was in silly enough moods. I could drive with the sunroof closed if I crouched like a pretzel. The car would stall out if I drove through water. Stall out at a hint of a deep pothole puddle splash. I would have to get out, lift the hood, and towel off the wires before the engine would spark again. Other than that predictable inconvenience, the car zipped about quite economically. I was all set with owning my own car again. Fully paid for.

My second goal before returning the Cadillac was to lose my virginity. In my early twenties, it was high time. I got in the Caddy for a last big adventure before heading north to Columbus to return it. I drove to the Sodality House, parked on the lawn, and left it idling with the driver door open; I ran up the stone steps and up the wooden stairs into the television room, where there was a scattering of guys.

"All those who haven't been laid, raise your hand," I announced.

Not an arm went up.

"All those who have been laid, raise your arm," I announced.

Not an arm went up.

"Okay, well, any of you liars who want to go to Newport, Kentucky, to do the deed, my car's leaving in two minutes—be in it." I turned on my heel and left the room, first peeking into my old room to check it out before I went down the stairs. Two guys were in the back seat and one was riding shotgun by the time I got to my car. I didn't know any of them. I didn't need to know any of them. I got in and, without a word, drove downtown to the Cincinnati side of the suspension bridge, where I parked at a three-hour meter.

"Why are you parking here?" asked one of the guys.

"Don't want to risk getting this car stolen in Newport. We can walk the bridge over to Covington, then a block or two to Newport—find a place to do the deed somewhere and walk back to the car," I announced, much as a drill sergeant would.

We piled out, paid the nickel and walked the suspension bridge across the Ohio River. We found the Newport, Kentucky, portion within blocks of Covington and stepped into an empty diner, sitting on the stools to reconnoiter. A girl in a starched white waitress uniform without a stain on it stood alone behind the counter, just in front of a tall, mirrored wall.

"Coffee?" I asked.

"We don't have coffee," she answered.

"No coffee?" I asked, looking around for the tall coffee urns. "Too early?"

"Where you from?" she asked.

"Xavier—well, they are. From Cincinnati," I said.

"Got driver's licenses?" she asked.

"Sure, why?" I asked.

"Let me see your driver's licenses."

We each flashed our driver's license, to her satisfaction.

"We're not looking to buy drinks," I said.

"Want girls?" she offered.

"Yeah," I said.

"We've got girls." She stood there, waiting for our reaction.

She wanted driver's licenses to prove we were from across the river and not local, not cops.

We all stood at attention, like a drum line with nervous smiles on our faces. Then the girl said, "This way, follow me," and pushed on the large mirror, which was a door behind her.

"See that chandelier hanging back there?"

"I see it," one of the guys said.

"Go back by that chandelier and wait—there's a bar back there. First drink is free. That's where the girls are."

We sat at the bar and ordered beers. The red velveteen wallpapered room was filled with girls of every shape, girls walking about in garter belts, some in bikini bottoms with no tops, girls with silk robes opened in the front and nothing on but lacey panties. One of the guys turned and offered that he didn't want one who looked too much like his sister; another didn't want one who looked like his high school girlfriend. I was about to mention my preferences and guidelines when a hand came around my waist from behind and rested on the kickstand, accompanied by a warm, humid whisper in my ear.

"You got eleven dollars, handsome?"

"Yes," I stuttered.

"How'd you like to come upstairs for some fun, honey?"

Sight unseen I found myself blindly following a perky butt peeking out from under black satin panties with satin garter straps and sheer stockings. I was following her upstairs like a zombie as she held my hand, appropriately, like she was a teacher leading a blind schoolboy.

Afterward, back downstairs in the bar, two of the guys announced that they were staying until they ran out of money, which included everything in one of their Christmas-gift money envelopes and the other's traveling-home-after-the-holiday money, and for the remaining two of us not to worry about them getting back to the Sodality House. One had put cab fare in his sock and would hang onto that. The other one and I walked out through the diner, sheepishly thanked the waitress, who was now doing a crossword puzzle, and we walked back across the suspension bridge.

"Jesus, that was quick," he said. "How about you?"

"Did your room have a little sink in the corner, and did she make you stand there while she washed your thingy by hand with warm Ivory soapy water?" I asked.

"Oh yeah," sighed the guy as we walked.

"I don't think I'll ever smell Ivory soap again and not get a hard-on," I said.

"That part was almost better than the sex," he observed.

"Remember the Martin and Lewis movie?' I asked.

"Which one?"

"When they were in the army," I said.

"Yes," he said.

"Dean would yell at Jerry to 'drop and give him twenty'— push-ups. Remember?"

"I remember," he said.

"Well, for me, this screw was more like 'drop and give me two,'" I said.

"One, for me," he said.

By then we had reached the Cadillac.

"Did you wash your hands?" I asked.

"No," he answered.

"Don't touch the leather."

I drove to the Sodality House, dropped him off and went to my rooming house and took a shower. I headed to Columbus, dropped the car off, and grabbed a Greyhound bus back to Cincinnati. Ava was no longer at the Neil House hotel, so no goodbye kisses.

The film partnership was waning. It seemed both my partner and I were going off in different directions of interest. Money was sparse. Living at home my partner wasn't as motivated as I was to have to pay rent and buy food. He was leaning more toward commercials, more arty film work. I was leaning toward training and sales films so I could write. We began to flounder. I liked the whole research process of learning about companies by producing films for them. Closing our business down and dissolving our partnership came much sooner and more easily than we had both anticipated. One day four of our checks bounced, including our office rent check. Neither of us ever took anything more from the account than twenty-five dollars a week each— him for spending money, me for food, gas, and room rent money, so we had no idea what was going on with the bounced checks. Although we paid bills with most of it we had several thousand dollars in the account, or so we thought. Since the phone had been cut off because of a returned check, we went to the bank and discovered our salesperson had written a series of small forged checks to his name, as if they were paychecks or draw checks, emptying the bank account and then some.

We talked with the police. They said they could put a warrant out for him for stealing checks from the checkbook, but said the guy probably left the state by now. Our office landlord overheard and forgave the last month's rent. My partner and I counted the money we had left in our pockets, went to the Perkins Pancake House in downtown Cincinnati, ordered a breakfast, some blueberry pancakes and a few cups of coffee, talked about the good times, shook hands, and went our separate ways.

Chapter 19

I was so spoiled by basketball scholarships and hotels that let me live, eat and drink free and a Cadillac car at no expense I was totally untrained on responsible management of my finances. The good news was I hardly ever carried cash, so I wasn't feeling the pinch of being out of it. I knew Agnes wouldn't throw me out of the rooming house—I was her favorite tall friend—besides I knew if I wanted to be a prick, the owner of the rooming house probably would let me stay there free just so he could protect his street from blacks moving in— the bastard. I knew Carlo would keep me fed—his mother would slap him if he didn't; most everyone I called friends were family in a way. They practically watched me grow up. So what if I was low on funds? I was long on experience as a result of one of the most productive and learning times of my life—which, on its own merit, made me float.

I would always metaphorically float, as though I was on the Mississippi, if I felt a life experience could one day be a chapter in a book. The forged check thief would spend it and hit a brick wall with nothing to show for it. Every dollar he had stolen meant something my partner and I had learned and would have all our lives. I wanted to start over again, anyway, yet this time using what I knew to do more, learn more—and like an octopus, to do it all at once. I hopped down the rooming house steps a few at a time, out off the stoop, and jumped in the Opel to drive over and see Mr. V. It had been a while since we caught up. He dropped what he was doing, bought us a couple of Coca-Colas, and we roamed the halls and talked like old times.

"Jerry, have you ever heard from the girl in the convent?" he started.

"Only in my nightmares, occasionally. She's in a wedding veil becoming the bride of the Lord. Did you know nuns wore wedding rings, Mr. V? My dream is I arm wrestle God for her and always lose. He's taller," I said sarcastically.

"A wonderful heartbreaker love story it was, Jerry—almost a Romeo and Juliet. One day you will write it," he said. "It won't be sad when you do. It will be beautiful."

The thought occurred to me of trying to explain the slight turn of events in my status—my adventure in the brothel in Newport, where I had driven three innocents from the Sodality House to join me in hell, just so we could be "done with it" once and for all, done with that one, single life experience that hung like a cloud over every guy in his late teens or twenties—but I tempered myself. A gentleman never discusses these sorts of things. A Catholic gentleman only confesses them behind a closed door.

"Have you ever met David Frisch, Mr. V?" I asked.

"Yes, I have."

"He owns Frisch's Big Boy restaurants."

"I know him well," he said.

"We did a movie for him, *Thought for Food*, for his franchise convention," I said.

"Wonderful title—very clever," said Mr. V.

"I know. The title wasn't mine, it was my partner's idea," I said.

"Well, you produced the movie, probably wrote much of it, so it was yours as well," said Mr. V.

"You know what Mr. Frisch told me?"

"No, what?" asked Mr. V.

"I had asked him how he dreamed up the 'Big Boy' idea—you know, the double hamburger he invented. I wanted to learn the big secret of his discovery, his inspiration for the Big Boy. Know what he said?"

"Tell me, I'm certain it's a story in itself," said Mr. V.

"He told me this guy Bob Wian and him kind of got together and talked and dreamed it up. He said they sat around trying to come up with a way to get people to buy two hamburgers when they only wanted one. Isn't that fantastic, Mr. V? They divided the country and went to town with the Big Boy. Bob's Big Boy in the west, Frisch's Big Boy in the east."

"How simple. What a great story. I must use that sometime," said Mr. V.

"Mr. V, we lost all our money—my partner and me—but it's okay, we were ready to split up anyway. I want to do bigger things. Maybe several things at once, I'm thinking. Any ideas, Mr. V? Any ideas how I can earn some fast cash just to get me by?" I asked.

"I don't need any writing, if that's what you're thinking," said Mr. V.

We sat on the outside steps of Albers Hall, looking over the oily, cracked parkway at the football stadium.

"How's the XU building fund drive coming?" I asked.

"It's very promising," said Mr. V. "Things are going well. Jerry, you might consider going out and talking to the folks at the Gibson Greeting Card Company. There could be a release there for a writer's talent you may not have considered—greeting cards. You also might try creating an advertising campaign on your own, an idea for a product and then seeing if the agency for the product would buy it from you or pay you for it. Do it on speculation. Film work, too, Jerry—you enjoy that; don't give that up too soon. Perhaps you can find some bigger film projects, important ones— like maybe for a city or state, or perhaps a series of films for one company that would absorb your talents. Let me think about it some. By the way, there's a new art museum downtown featuring kinetics—motion—you might check it out."

"What's kinetics?" I asked.

"Art that moves, mobiles, film, motion," said Mr. V.

"I'll check it out," I said.

"Let's grab a hotdog and a cream soda next week; I'll have some more ideas for you," said Mr. V.

"You said advertising, Mr. V, what did you have in mind?" I asked.

"Get with someone who knows the workings of the advertising agency business," he said. "Learn what an agency might be looking for in ways of creative. Then create something, do something creative for one of their clients, on spec—take the risk to see if they would buy it."

"That's a good one. Thanks. I knew you'd have a ton of

ideas, like always. If you think of anything else—painting rooms, even—I'll do it. I'm going to go ask Agnes at the rooming house if they need any rooms painted in return for my rent. I painted rooms in Milwaukee in high school for extra money," I said.

"A man of many talents," Mr. V said. "I didn't know you painted."

"Yeah, my dad moved us to Milwaukee in my senior year in high school; he got a job there, so we all moved. While we were there he got me jobs at an animal hospital and painting rooms. I don't even need a ladder," I said.

"I have a painting job that should take two weekends. Fifty dollars, if you're interested in painting the wrought-iron fence in my back yard black," he said. "It needs a good going-over with a wire brush first, though and some rust preservative primer."

"Done," I said. "I'll do it this weekend."

"Another fifty if you want to paint the inside of my garage. It's all stucco and concrete," said Mr. V.

"A room paint job is only worth $15, Mr. V," I said. "I'll do the garage but for $15. Sixty-five bucks will get me to winter." I laughed.

"Jerry, check out the Gibson Greeting Card Company in the meantime, and consider the advertising idea," said Mr. V. "Something will jump out at you. You've always had a knack for making things happen."

I said hello to Mrs. Burke, left the building, and drove to Ashland Avenue, where I walked through Mr. V's yard, sizing up the wrought-iron fence. I pulled the garage door open and checked that out. I figured a weekend on each would get the job done. On the way back to the rooming house, I thought I would loop around the McMillan neighborhood and the Catholic Youth Organization club to see if there was any roundball pickup games going on. There were none.

I drove by a large restored Elizabethan three-story house with a tasteful, freshly painted sign in the yard. "Cye Landy Advertising." I had not heard of an agency by that name. It wasn't on my list of agencies. The house looked like a stately old mansion. In the driveway portico was a classic Mercedes Gull-wing, a silver roadster with doors that opened out like wings. I had only seen one in a movie. I became intrigued with the car and the word advertising on the sign. I pulled in front, parked at the curb, and walked the drive and up the steps to the open front door. I stepped inside. It was decorated nicely; I could smell fresh paint. There were a few empty desks on the first floor. It may have been lunch time, I thought, or they could just be moving in.

I stood by the opened front door and heard voices coming from upstairs; they were moving around a second-floor open hallway. The quieter of the two voices seemed to be a woman and in command. The softer voice was getting closer, as though it was coming down the grand staircase; my view of all but the landing was blocked by an interior wall ahead of me about twelve feet. No one knew I was in the waiting area. I paused, stood there holding the door open, seeing the reflection of the Mercedes Gull-wing in the door window. I waited, listened, and watched.

A delicate bared heel pouted out from a navy blue pump with a perfect white leather bow as it first stepped down onto the glossy, varnished stair landing. I started my visual journey up a lovely calf, to hips that could make me forget my name, then up to a wide, white, flat front collar with a bow-like lapel framing a cleavage that gave whole new meanings to the great divide and double-breasted. She looked like she had stepped off the cover of *Harper's Bazaar*. She was truly a vision. The black straw brim of her hat was tipped down, covering her eyes like a Mata Hari of an age gone by. I could only imagine a face. As she paused on the landing, the brim lifted slightly, baring the perfect heart-shaped pout of ruby-red lips. Her lips opened just enough to mouth a whispered, curious "Who are you?" in my direction.

I knew it was a long shot and out of my league. Nothing ventured, nothing gained. My true motives for standing there were cloudy, so I made it up as I went along.

"I saw your sign," I stuttered.

"It's not my sign," she whispered.

"Oh," I whimpered.

"What's on your mind?" she whispered.

The last thing on my mind at that moment was advertising. Ava's eyes, her lipstick on a cocktail glass, Eileen's cashmere soft warm breasts, and a bar of Ivory soap sparked through my memory like flashbulbs.

This lady was in a league above, a league of her own.

"Advertising," I said.

"Then you need Cye," the whisper mouthed.

"No Cye," I blurted, almost interrupting her. "I'm thinking Chico's, Italian. Do you like spaghetti?"

Please no Cye, I thought to myself.

"You want to talk advertising?" she asked.

"Advertising, yes, absolutely. But no Cye. How about seven, does seven tonight work for you? I'm pretty much open at seven," I stammered.

"I do like Italian." She smiled.

"Good. It's on Montgomery Road, near Dana Avenue in Norwood." I turned, adjusting my tie in confidence, and started walking toward the door, hoping to get away with it. I turned back and paused, just to have one more gander.

"Carlo, he's the owner. He has bibs for dinner guests, so you won't get sauce on your … ah, your … pretty dress," I said.

This time she gave me that look. I knew she had that feeling I was flirting with her.

"I won't need a bib. I'm a neat and tidy lady, especially when I talk advertising," her lips whispered a bit more loudly, certain to reach my ear. I caught a hint of beginnings of a pursed-lipped snicker just as she tipped the well-trained hat brim even lower to cover it.

As usual, I became the blubbering hillbilly idiot.

"Well I need a bib, I've been known to drool, ya see," I said, looking over my shoulder.

I turned, walked out of the building, tripped down the first two steps, bumped my knee on the car fender, jumped in my Opel, and sped off.

She was the most electrifying thing I'd seen north of the

Ohio River, since Ava at the Neil House. I was going to give it a good old college try. Question was, would she show up at Chico's, where I could sign the check, and if so, was the Mercedes hers and would she be alone or with the Cye guy?

I headed on up to Gibson Greeting Card to ask for opportunities. I did have a contact with them as my ex-partner and I had shot some footage of one of their card lines for a sales meeting and catalogue. While in the waiting room, I met a large Hawaiian man in his early thirties—a high school English teacher looking to pick up freelance writing jobs with Gibson.

"What's your area?" I asked.

"Literature maven," he said. "I think personal greetings and advertising can benefit from tying into good literature. People are becoming more sophisticated."

"What's your personal goal?" I asked. It was something my dad would ask me.

"To become nouveau riche and get a convertible with leopard-skin seat covers," he replied. Then he bellowed a jocular laugh.

"Seven o'clock, a little Italian restaurant on Montgomery Road—Chico's. Can you be there tonight? I've got an idea. I'll buy."

"My wife ...," he started.

"Bring her," I finished.

"Aloha," he said.

I wrote down his name and phone number just in case he didn't show. I liked his presence, his style.

The receptionist told me to go upstairs and ask for Bud Townsend. He remembered me from the project I had worked on for their sales manager. He offered me a job, analyzing seasonal card sales. He had a project of identifying companies in the Thomas Register that manufactured or sold "attachment" ideas and samples such as miniature dried flowers, ribbons, tokens, bells, and trinkets for the artists to consider as attachments to greeting cards. He also asked me to come up with a way to measure the impact on card sales every time a house poet of theirs, the renowned poetess

Helen Steiner Rice, appeared live to read her poetry on *The Lawrence Welk Show*. I soon learned that the number-one selling Christmas card each year, whether it was a single card or box set, was always the card that showed a Christmas star breaking through a dark blue sky over a tall church steeple and the words "Silent Night."

At Gibson Greeting Card, I would get to meet and become close with a gold standard in creative—Jack E. Schneider, humorist and illustrator extraordinaire, who specialized in their new tall, slim line humorous cards. He was a wry, solemn-faced wit, an ex-marine who thought, knew, and spewed funny, often without cracking a smile. Jack and I would go on to write humorous radio commercials together.

I went home, went through all my pants pockets for any money I could find, put on a suit and headed for Chico's at six fifty-five.

"Don't bump your head," said Carlo.

"Hi Carlo," I said.

"Where've you been, stranger?"

"Going nuts," I said.

"Where's the Caddy?" he asked.

"Driving that Opal. I'll tell you later."

"You've got company."

"Is she here already?"

"Jerry, you should never keep a lady waiting."

I looked around. In the far corner the lady in black was sitting in the circular booth. Her hat was not with her. Seeing my silhouette blocking a setting sun coming through the front-door window, her head tipped down and a finger pulled her horned-rimmed sunglasses down just enough to beam two big beautiful green eyes in my direction.

"Uh-oh," I told Carlo. "I think I'm in lust."

"The opera begins," said Carlo.

"Will you look at those eyes?" I asked.

"Have you seen her car?" he asked in a whisper.

"The big M with the wings?" I asked.

"There can't be two of them in all of Cincinnati," Carlo whispered.

"I don't know about the car but there's only one of her in town, that's for sure, and she's at my table tonight," I said.

"I have no idea what you're up to, but God bless you, my friend," said Carlo.

"I don't know, either, just trying to land on my feet is all. Mr. V gave me an idea."

"He's a smart man. Tell him hello for me when you see him."

"Carlo, I've never gone on the make before."

"On the make. Is that what I think it means?"

"I may need tickets to the symphony for this one." I chided, "This is a class act."

"It is what I thought it means," said Carlo.

"Wish me luck."

"Old violinists only get the cheap seats, but I can get you backstage."

"For real, backstage?" I asked, totally impressed.

"First things first, one thing at a time, my friend: your lady awaits. First your heart attack, then the symphony tickets," he quipped. "Now if you need any help …"

"There's two more coming—a Hawaiian guy and his wife."

"It only gets better," said Carlo.

"Will you send them over?"

"I will."

"And Carlo, my friend, when the check comes and I sign it, try to pretend you know I can afford it and I'm not flat broke on my ass again, which I am."

"Jerry, have I ever, one time, ever even hinted …?"

"Never."

"You break my heart," he added.

"Wish me luck. All I know is she must know advertising."

"The possibilities are endless," moaned Carlo.

"I can't afford her, I'm sure—I don't even know what she does or can do," I said.

"Good point—wine will be by the bottle tonight," said Carlo.

"Thank you, my friend," I said.

"How much did he clip you for, that crook bastard?" he said.

"Who told you?" I said.

"I cashed a check for him that would have bounced. Your name was forged on it but I knew it wasn't your signature so I checked your signature on tabs," he said. "It was for six dollars, a lunch. I never deposited it. I got his license number and gave it and the check to the police," he said.

"Maybe a few thousand—not sure. I never knew how to balance a checkbook. I'd write checks and forget to enter them in the checkbook. I'm a mess, but hey, such is life. Next time no checkbooks lying around, right?" I asked.

"Go eat, enjoy, love, be fruitful and multiply," said Carlo with a smile, winking at the prize waiting for me in the booth. "And if there are any heart attacks, don't mention my restaurant by name."

I walked back toward the corner, pulling my suit coat off and rolling my shirt sleeves up one cuff flap along the way, just as if I were coming home.

"I was beginning to wonder if you were going to show," she offered.

I ignored her. I was parsing my thoughts, sparring between flirting and business, trying to come up with what to say to one of the loveliest ladies I'd ever sat with. I stalled as I folded and hung the coat over the back of a chair in front of the booth, sat down, and slid in.

"Don't want marinara on my suit coat," I said.

"I hate when that happens," she said. And then, impatiently, "Okay, it's quaint and the food is no doubt wonderful, but why am I here and who are you? I don't even know your name."

I extended my hand. "I'm Jerry. Jerry Antil," I stuttered.

"Doreen," she said, shaking my hand, looking me straight

in the eye. "I'm Doreen Baker."

"Doreen? Doreen. Well imagine that, Doreen. It suits you, it certainly does."

"Are you looking for an agency?" she asked.

"Doreen, it was just a moment ago I had no idea what was in my future. I didn't have a clue what direction I was going. Then a wise man suggested I do something in advertising, but before I do, he said, first find and meet someone who knows the working ends of the advertising agency business. Doreen, you obviously know the advertising business, and you were an angel heaven-sent within the hour of that wise man making the suggestion. Why, even your car has wings," I said.

Carlo walked up to the table.

"Would you like to see a wine list?" he asked, like the maître d' at Delmonico's.

"I'm not sure I'm staying," suggested the mystery lady.

"Carlo, meet Doreen. Doreen, please meet my dear friend, Carlo. Carlo, the lady would like you to open the driest red wine you have in the house and let it breathe," I said. I had seen it in a movie.

Doreen took her sunglasses off, folded them, and set them on the table, thinking.

"It's not my agency. I'm considering becoming an account executive there," she said.

"So you know the business. What does an account executive do?" I asked. "I could never figure the difference between an account executive and an account manager."

She did a double-take look at me. "Is this a test?" she asked.

"I really don't know, and it's important I do," I said.

My young age and agency inexperience shined through me like a sandlot baseball flying through a living room window. My height had camouflaged my age.

"Does your mother know you're out tonight, little boy?" she mused.

"Yes, and I have to be in bed by eleven, and I'm not

supposed to talk to strangers, so isn't it wonderful we've been introduced? Don't for a minute confuse my height, nice suit, and good looks with being smart. I'm a writer and writers don't get out much. We're not all that bright."

She smiled.

The wine came, and the tall Hawaiian, his wife in a t-shirt and no bra, was by now standing right behind Carlo as he uncorked it. Some women had begun to go braless as a statement of feminism in the sixties. In the later sixties, some burned their bras as a statement of protest. This well-endowed young lady was more native, one might say.

"Carlo, better bring another bottle. Folks, meet Doreen. Doreen, meet English—teacher and literature maven—and his wife, flower child. Have a seat. English, what is your name, anyway? Mine is Jerry."

"Philip, but I like English, let's stick with that. My wife is Elle."

Elle bounced into the booth next to Doreen, who scooted over closer toward me. English sat in one of the chairs. Carlo had two bottles open and poured a taster slug of the first for me to test. I placed fingers on the round base of the wine glass and pushed it slowly but firmly over in front of Doreen.

"Doreen would know best, Carlo," I said. "She'll do us the honors."

She was caught by surprise with that one, picked the glass delicately, lifted it to her lips. I took my prowess to a newer level. It was like a chess game now. She was beautiful, mysterious, and worldly. I was not letting go. I needed her brains, but I wanted her.

Doreen lifted the glass and tasted the wine, washed it in her mouth, swallowed, and said, "That's a nice wine; very nice, indeed."

Carlo beamed and began to pour.

"This is good, children, everyone enjoy," he said.

"Carlo, my friend—my new friends Doreen here, and have you met English and his wife, Elle? Carlo, we are about to have the most important, most productive powwow in all of Cincinnati tonight. Our future rests upon the evening. We don't want to see a menu. Will you kindly get with the chef and bring specialties of the house until we cry uncle?" I asked.

"Welcome to our house, Jerry's friends. Our house is your house. Enjoy the wine, your palates are about to be treated. Abbondanza," said Carlo.

"To Chico's," I said, lifting my glass in toast.

"To Chico's," everyone said in unison, sipping from theirs.

Carlo bowed as he would after a violin solo and backed toward the kitchen. In a minute or two the sound system came on and we could hear the needle scratching across and settling in on a record of Italian opera that would play throughout our dinner.

"Thanks for coming," I began. "Do any of you believe in vibes? Karma?" I asked

Everyone agreed that they did.

"Well, we are more than just ships passing in the night. A friend of mine gave me an idea to try in advertising, and within the day he suggested it I met English here, who wants to take literature into advertising, and then I met Doreen, who obviously knows the inner workings of the advertising business. Let's feast while I tell you of my friend's idea. Then you can give me your thoughts. Dinner is on me."

I lifted my glass, as did everyone at the table, in anticipation.

"To us," I said. "To English, Doreen, and Jerry—and whatever story we may write or adventures we may choose to travel together."

Everyone sipped. English beamed. Doreen moved a bit closer to me in the booth. The food started coming as if it would never stop.

"I want to use our talents as a team and come up with a 'spec' advertising campaign for someone, each of us contributing our time and talents, splitting whatever money we get three ways. We can all do it on the side—keep doing what you do for a living. Doreen here can sell our idea to an agency. What's your goal, again, English?" I asked.

"To become nouveau riche—leopard seat covers on a new convertible," he said. He contained his laughing bellow and smiled.

Doreen laughed, looked over at me, and winked approval.

"And Doreen, we'll deliver the goods and you'll be account executive and take it to the agency and knock their socks off as only you can," I said.

"I thought you didn't know what an account executive was," she said, poking my ribs like maybe I had been teasing her earlier.

"I don't … not for sure, anyway … but I figured if you were one, you were the best there was at it. Anyone looking at you would know that," I said.

"Awwww," she said, leaning over and giving me a peck on the cheek. "That's so sweet."

"This is a family restaurant," sparked Carlo with a smirk, bringing two platters of food. "No kissing at the table."

"The wine is wonderful, Carlo, it's the best Italian red I've had in some time," Doreen said. "What is it?"

"Okay, you can kiss at the table, but keep one foot on the floor when you do," Carlo said, bringing two bowls and setting them down. "It's an Italian blend."

We feasted and laughed far into the evening. Somehow we all knew this was right, just as we knew it wasn't permanent. It felt good, we clicked—each a personality, each his or her own star at the table … just maybe we had the chemistry to make something happen, maybe not. We were eager and willing to give it a chance to find out.

As the coffee came—Carlo had placed three coffee beans floating in each cup for good luck—Doreen asked, "What's next? Do we have any idea of where to start?"

"I need to ask around with some of my contacts. I'll need a week," I said. "Can we do this again next Sunday night—seven? I'll have some ideas, a plan by then, maybe."

Everyone agreed to meet again next Sunday. Carlo walked us to the door, asking Doreen if she would like candles for our next dinner and what color. His mother came out, met and said hello to everyone. The whole establishment had enjoyed our celebration, felt our energy, celebrated with us. We stepped onto Montgomery Road to watch Doreen open her winged doors, climb in, and close them down like a spaceship. English and I waved, walked to our cars, and drove away as Carlo stood on the sidewalk smiling at the evening's full moon.

Chapter 20

My plan was to drive up to Fort Wayne, talk with my dad, maybe go fishing and pick his brains. Throughout his career he had hired and used advertising agencies. He knew and had worked with the most famous people—Duncan Hines, Walt Disney. He could give me some solid direction.

Dad was sitting on the back steps as I drove in. He was untangling a fishing line and adding sinkers to it with pliers, wearing a colorful Hawaiian shirt, not his usual suit and tie.

"Jerry me boy," he yelled as I drove in and parked on the side lawn. "You're just in time for supper. Your mother's in college until five, we'll have stuffed green peppers. I made a batch today, ground beef and rice, just like New Orleans."

He stood and shook my hand with a big grin, welcoming me home.

"How long can you stay?" he asked.

"I need to pick your brain—go back tomorrow," I said. "Can we go fishing and talk?"

"I know the perfect spot," he said. "I've never tried it, but we'll rent a boat. It's an abandoned stone quarry the state has stocked with croppy or bass, not sure which. I'll get poles ready; we'll go in the morning."

Mom's Ford drove in and parked on the lawn next to my car. She got out, carrying schoolbooks like she was a teenager.

"Oh, how wonderful," she said, holding up her free arm and waiting for a big hug and kiss on the cheek. "My boy is home."

Dad went out of his way to show off Mom's college transcript and announced she would be graduating with a cap and gown ceremony in June with the St. Joseph's students.

"I'm busting my buttons for your mother, son," he beamed. "In her sixties, eight children, twenty-one grandchildren and she's graduating with honors with kids.

"That's amazing, Mom. What are you gonna do with your degree?" I asked.

"I'll be teaching at the grade school. I'm praying I'll get a job with the Catholic Diocese of Fort Wayne, as a child guidance counselor, and work toward my master's and maybe my doctorate."

Dad beamed with pride.

"Let's eat," he shouted. "Mommy, put your books and papers on the sofa and come to the table."

He held the screen door open for Mom and then me. He leaned out and balanced his fishing pole on the outside wall and came into the kitchen.

Spooning two stuffed green peppers onto my plate, and some sliced, boiled summer squash, I said, "Mom and Dad, I'm doing good. Got a few things planned that I'll make work out. Can't tell you about them, until I get into them, not sure what may happen."

"That's why stories start, '*Once upon a time*,'" quipped Mom. "An adventure can't be an adventure and told to others until the adventurer has lived it themselves, the whole story."

Dad was busting to tell me some news.

"Your mommy sent the last check back to Syracuse, and everyone has been paid in full. It took some time, but not a single person went unpaid."

I knew Dad lost everything—but I didn't know he owed people a lot of money.

Dad and Mom had happy faces with their accomplishment.

Long before I was born Mom and Dad had moved to central New York State just after the 1929 stock market crash, when the Great Depression started. He became a partner in a bakery with a man he was best friends with. Electricity became available, and the two young men figured out how to finance a huge Peterson oven—which took three weeks to preheat—and started serving bread, cakes, and pies to all the Roosevelt Administration's CCC camps, Pine Camp military base, and the grocers in central New York—nearly 90,000 loaves a day. The bakery had more than one plant and ultimately became one of the largest independent wholesale bakeries in the United States.

When his best friend and bakery partner died in 1949, Dad's interest in the bakery waned, but he created some national baking brands like Duncan Hines. Then he got tuberculosis, the number-one killer in the early fifties. He spent a debilitating, demoralizing year in a sanitarium. With a piece of his lung surgically removed, he was cured. He sold his interest in the bakery and invested that and everything he and Mom had put away, plus a lot of new debt, into building a restaurant that failed the summer before my senior year in school with the kids I'd grown up with since the second grade.

Dad had no choice at sixty but to go off looking for a job, anywhere in the country. We had grown up on an eighty-four-acre estate, which had once been a county park with a seventy-foot waterfall and large picnicking pavilion. My dad bought it from the county in 1938. He converted the pavilion into a five-bedroom, two-bath home after the War. Investing his retirement money poorly, he lost that home and Mom moved three of us into a room over our failed restaurant, for a month before moving to Milwaukee, where Dad got a job with a bakery. During my senior year, five of us lived in a single-room studio apartment in the high rise low-rent Marshall Arms apartment hotel in downtown Milwaukee. I was so insecure from the moves in my senior year, I didn't go to the city high school Basketball All-Star dinner I had earned an invitation to at sixteen.

We moved to two different second-floor walkups in Fort Wayne, Indiana, first on Oliver Street, next on Bowser Street, and then a whole house on Dewald Street, where Mom could teach grade school at St. Pat's the following summer before I started at Xavier. That's when Dad bought Mom this home on Belle Avenue, a modest, five small rooms on a corner lot near downtown Fort Wayne, a long cry from growing up on an eighty-four-acre estate, but with just as much love and happiness.

It wasn't until my third bite of my first stuffed green pepper that I was to learn that they weren't poor all this time—just acting responsibly. Dad made good money, as he had all his life, both in Milwaukee and here in Fort Wayne, following the bust. By their own choice, each week, Dad would hand Mom his paycheck and every week Mom would keep careful records, write dozens of checks, stuffing them in dozens of envelopes, and mail them back "home" to pay off all the creditors so no one would lose a nickel from investing their confidence in my dad, Big Mike.

"Everyone has been paid in full, with interest," Dad beamed. "Now we can live a little and I can go fishing, Jerry me boy."

I felt ashamed about having a car and a television repossessed. I wished I could learn to be more responsible like my dad…but then I had an afterthought— maybe it was my mother.

I later learned together they had sent more than eighty thousand dollars, ($700,000 in 2020 money) over the course of five years, to pay the debts back home, with interest—sometimes checks as small as five dollars a week. When my dad died in the seventies, two decades after having left central New York, his body was shipped back to rest at the St. Mary's Cemetery in Cortland, New York. Standing room only at Big Mike's funeral mass at St. Mary's church. Several thousand people to say goodbye to a nice man, Big Mike.

I rowed the boat to the middle of the quarry.

"No sense dropping anchor," said Dad. "I don't think there's a bottom."

"Dad, I'm into a few things now. Me and some others are going to come up with a advertising campaign for a company or a product and make it so good the agency will buy it from us, or pay us a royalty or something. Has that ever been done?"

"Happens a lot, more than you would think, someone having a better idea. Even happened to you, don't you remember, Jerry me boy? You cast off that side, I'll cast this side."

"What d'ya mean? It happened to me?"

"When did you get your horse, Jack?"

"I was twelve, I think, maybe thirteen."

"Do you remember the time I had you with me, we were at the radio station in Syracuse—WSYR—in the studio listening to the man play music in the background on the old player piano while an announcer read commercials for the new Donald Duck bread we were coming out with for Walt Disney?"

"I remember, Dad. I remember telling you the man should be playing Disney music—like, 'Hi ho, hi ho, it's off to work we go,' and not the dumb music he was playing for that announcer man— and you had them start over and do it. I remember."

"Seems to me you had a horse not long after that, it seems to me," Dad said, wriggling his eyebrows and smiling.

"I got my horse for that idea?" I asked in amazement, reeling in and putting a fresh worm on the line.

"It helped," said Dad. "One of the agency men told me about a horse he knew was available at a reasonable price— turned out to be your Jack. What's your idea now, son?" he asked. "How can I help?"

"I need an idea about a company or product you think we should try to come up with a campaign for. Got any ideas?"

"Remember Arthur Godfrey, son?"

"Yes, of course. I remember him."

"Arthur Godfrey was the best there was at advertising a product."

"I remember we'd listen to him on the radio in the car. I remember Mom crying when she heard him announce the funeral for President Roosevelt when we were still in Cortland," I said.

"That's the man. He was considered one of the most influential radio and television voices in the 1940s and early 1950s, made several brand names a household word, he did. Remember Lipton, son?"

"Sure, he'd make the tea and I think even Lipton's cup-of-soup and taste it and say, 'Ahhhhhhhh,' that he loved it. I could almost smell it through the radio."

"Seems to me Lipton's Tea could use a little competition," hinted Dad.

"Like who?" I asked, reeling in a bass.

"Do some homework, son. Check out who's handling Tetley Tea as an account. You might just give them a try," said Dad.

"Tetley Tea, Dad?"

"Who better than Tetley? Go for a number two. Lipton got the jump on them in the forties. They need a home run," said Dad.

I breathed a sigh of relief. Not only did I understand the strategy on why Tetley Tea was the good choice, I felt I could sell the idea to English and Doreen.

"You know those tall funny cards, Dad? You know the tall greeting cards?"

"I do, indeed," said Dad.

"I'm meeting the guy later this week who writes them. Jack Schneider."

Dad took my fishing pole so I could be free to row.

"Okay, let me think," he said. "Something I can borrow from the old vaudeville days of the 1920s. See what he thinks of this ... 'It's your birthday, show everyone how young you are, lean over backward and pick up a handkerchief in your teeth.' Open the card to: 'Now pick up your teeth.'"

"I'll tell him for sure, Dad, for sure."

I packed my Opel, said my goodbyes and headed back to Cincinnati to let new adventures begin.

Leaving the Fort Wayne city limits, I reflected on my short visit, on what incredible parents I had, how they didn't think twice and sacrificed all those years with no help from anyone, to pay those debts to the people who trusted them. All the time, for my two years at Xavier, before they even put food on their own table, they saw to it I got five dollars every week I was in college. I thought about my job with Union Central Life and how Dad sent me money for custom shirts; and the time he drove me to Cincinnati and bought me the suits and shoes so I could sell my writing services.

I didn't wipe my tears. I wanted to feel them in the air. I wanted never to forget my roots.

As the skyline of Cincinnati reappeared, my mind began churning once again, alive, ready to do battle. I'd call Don Gaffney and ask him if he knows who handles Tetley, and on Thursday I'd go have a hotdog and crème soda with Mr. V.

Six weeks later, I would mail Dad a check from Hallmark Cards for $65. They bought his gag.

Chapter 21

Today was Wednesday, and dinner at Chico's with Doreen and English was still set for Sunday, and I had to get with Mr. V tomorrow and paint his fence Saturday. I wasn't convinced that I wanted to start working at Gibson Monday for extra cash to help produce our spec campaign. Other than a small stash, I was broke but I felt it was time to start working on my timetable, not other people's timetables, if I was to mushroom like I wanted. I could understand how a clerk could make a career of contacting vendors or suppliers, gathering samples. Not my style. I was trained by my dad. I didn't want a job at Gibson slowing me down.

I headed over to see Mr. V for that hotdog and crème soda.

"I may take a job with Gibson, but I'm trying to talk myself out of it," I said. "It could let me learn some things while I stack up some cash."

"Stacking up cash is always a good idea. I thought it could," said Mr. V.

"Did you know they have a full floor filled with artists sitting under skylights who do hand separations of the colors of each card for printing?" I asked.

"I know the photographic separation process; I wasn't aware of Gibson's process. That is such precision; they do have a reputation for producing high-quality work. What a skill that must be. Like watchmaking patience, eye, and steady hand," said Mr. V.

"Tetley Tea," I said.

"Tetley Tea?" asked Mr. V.

"It's the product we're going to create a spec campaign for. My dad thinks Lipton needs some big competition and thinks Tetley would be motivated to listen," I said.

"Interesting," said Mr. V. "Do you have a plan?"

"I have to call Don Gaffney, find out who their agency is first and then try to set an appointment in a month. I think that's all the time we'll need."

Mr. V went to his bookshelf, pulled a directory of advertisers, and sat back down at his desk, paging through it. He slipped on some reading glasses. His eyes lit up as he came upon a listing on a page.

"Hello?" asked Mr. V, as would Sherlock Holmes.

"What?" I asked.

"Ogilvy & Mather," said Mr. V.

"You're kidding me," I said.

"Their agency is Ogilvy & Mather, New York City."

"Ogilvy & Mather?" I asked.

"Yes," said Mr. V.

"Ogilvy & Mather handle Tetley Tea?"

"According to this they do," said Mr. V.

"We don't have a prayer," I said.

"Excuse me?" asked Mr. V.

"I read his book, Mr. V—David Ogilvy's—*Confessions of an Advertising Man*. He's world famous, he's an advertising genius. We don't stand a chance," I whimpered.

Mr. V put his finger on the listing, the book open and lying flat on his desk, and looked up at me wryly over the tops of the rims.

"Excuse me? Is this the Jerry I know? Is this the 'long stem is in the lobby' Jerry Antil? The Ohio Nursing Home Association J. Mark Antil? The Neil House Hotel Jerry Antil?" He grinned.

"But David Ogilvy, Mr. V," I said.

Mr. V looked down and read the listing to himself.

"Jerry, say the agency knows you want to try to sell them an idea and they will see you in a month, would you still be willing to go ahead with your plans for doing something for their client, Tetley Tea?" asked Mr. V.

He had a look of confidence in his face. His confidence in me reminded me that most of the things I'd accomplished had been because I took a chance.

"Yes," I said.

"Good answer," said Mr. V.

Mr. V lifted his phone from his credenza to his desk, and dialed the operator. This was so untypical of him; usually he would ask Mrs. Burke to place calls for him.

"Operator, I want …"

He proceeded to read the number from the listing in the directory, then he waited for a connection.

"Yes, good morning, this is Edward VonderHaar, Xavier University, calling for Mr. Heekin. Is he available?"

I had no idea what he was up to or who he was calling. I sat, watched, and listened to a one-sided conversation.

"Hello, Jim? Ed VonderHaar here, how are you?" he asked. "Congratulations on your promotion. You will do well, I'm certain of it. … Thank you. … Your dad is an important part of the university, a very important part. … Yes. … Jim, I have a question for you. Some talented young folks I am aware of have a desire to bring an idea to Ogilvy & Mather for consideration by you for one of your existing clients. Any chance they could get an audience? … They're thinking in thirty days. … Yes, take it down, if you will. The young man is Jerry Antil. A-N-T-I-L, Jerry. He will call you in thirty days or so and ask for an appointment … Thank you so much, Jim—and much success with your new post … Goodbye."

I sat and waited.

"Jerry, that happened to be Jim Heekin. He was recently made president and CEO of Ogilvy & Mather. He is waiting for your call in about thirty days and will see you personally," said Mr. V.

"I don't know what to say," I said.

"This is the chance you were looking for—give it your all and good luck."

"I know Heekin—where from? Heekin Can? Heekin Advertising?" I asked.

"Right on both counts, and you're set for thirty days," said Mr. V. "Mr. Jim Heekin has been in New York some time now with Ogilvy. His family is the Heekins, the canning people. I took a chance and called him," said Mr. V. "Jerry, if you haven't already, please go check out the Kinetic Art Exhibit in the gallery downtown before it leaves, you might get some ideas from it. They have many film works on exhibit."

I drove downtown, parked at a meter, and went into the art gallery near Fountain Square.

The gallery was a narrow, deep storefront freshly painted with white walls, track and spot lighting, and a shiny, lacquered, hardwood floor. The gallery was filled with *objets d'art*—each of which moved about, swayed back and forth, or made sounds. The country, in the sixties, was into movement and togetherness. Miró suspended mobiles, kinetics—strands of tubing swaying and chiming together, sights, sounds, happenings. A "happening" in the day could be something as simple as thirty people in a park, an old junker car and a sledgehammer. One at a time a passerby would take a slam or two with the sledgehammer until the car was a flat sheet of metal on the ground. Another group might try to see how many people they could squeeze into a phone booth. The record, in the early sixties, was fifteen whole bodies and twenty-five whole and partial bodies. I walked over and stood by a continuous reel of sixteen-millimeter film clacking and flashing and projecting images in black and white on the wall.

A tall man, midthirties, examining the Miró mobile hanging in the corner, caught my eye. He had a head of disheveled sparkling golden hair, a rumpled trench coat with its collar up, motorcycle goggles pulled down and hanging around his neck, corduroy pants, and work boots. He was holding gloves in one hand. He walked over to me.

"Is that your work?" he asked.

"No, I'm just visiting. Someone told me about it. Nice gallery," I said.

"Are you interested in film?" he asked. He began scratching his head like Will Rogers. He stood tall and had the honest, disheveled look of Peter O'Toole in *Lawrence of Arabia*. I kept my eyes on the moving film image projected on the wall.

"I've produced a few—had a good business going, some pretty good films—had to get out, though," I said.

"Do tell," he said.

"Take this film here, being projected on the wall: it looks like someone just reached in a black film-loading bag and scratched through the frame cells with a pin and then processed the unexposed film, giving it an animated look. Maybe they did it in a darkroom before they processed the film," I said.

"Processed?"

"Developed."

"Is there a lot of difference between sixteen-millimeter and thirty-five?" he asked.

"Mostly cost of equipment. They both can be rented. Cost of lab work is probably more with thirty-five. But technically they both still shoot at twenty-four frames a second," I said.

"Twenty-four frames a second? Both? Does that mean for every second of movie twenty-four pictures have traveled on the screen?"

"Pretty much."

"Fascinating," he said, dropping a glove to the floor and leaning down to pick it up. "Is sound hard to shoot?"

"I don't know how to shoot sound; that's Hollywood. I record separately—sound-over or they call it voice-over—and splice it in," I said.

"Is that difficult? Splicing in the sound?"

"No, it's just a magnetic track; you put the sound at twenty-eight frames is all. I stick to sixteen-millimeter, though. For the things I produced no need for thirty-five."

"You mentioned twenty-four frames, now you speak of twenty-eight frames. Can you unravel the mystery for me?" he asked.

"Film goes through the camera and projector lens at twenty-four frames a second," I said.

"Yes, I got that much," he said.

"The sound for the frame of the picture in the projector lens is being read on an optical or magnetic strip on the side of the frame four frames behind it, or precisely on the twenty-eighth frame. It has to be on the twenty-eighth frame because that's where they put the sound reader on projectors."

"The tiny little microphone?" he asked.

"The tiny little microphone—the sound reader," I said.

"Wow!" shouted this Lawrence of Arabia character, turning about on one foot, losing his balance just learning how simple it appeared to be. "Have you met any stars in this movie business of yours?" he asked.

"At Symphony Hall I met some movie stars. Mel Tormé— he was doing *Brigadoon*, David Janssen was in *Mr. Roberts* there, Keenan Wynn was in *The Great Race* movie, and some others, but none of them were in my movies. My films were for businesses— you know, like commercials and sales films."

"I can just imagine. It's a whole new world!" he said.

"It's a pretty simple business, but I'm a bad businessman. I like it so I can write," I said. "I just want to be a writer."

"Interesting," said the man, "most interesting; why'd you get out of this wonderful film business? It didn't pay?"

"It's supposed to pay a thousand a minute, suppose to pay really well— I just wasn't good at the business part; decided to do something else," I said.

"A thousand dollars a minute?" he asked. He turned toward the wall and the movie being projected on it and started calculating with his fingers the seconds and minutes in his head.

"Well, with training or sales films, up to that, more for commercials—but a lot of that includes writing and production and lab costs; depends. Thousand a minute is just a guide. It's supposed to be profitable, though," I said.

"What if you had a partner who was good at business?" the man asked.

"I don't have the money it takes; I'm trying something else," I said.

He put out his hand and introduced himself. "A. Chase Shaffer," he said. "Just call me Chase."

"I'm Jerry Antil. Nice to meet you."

"What capital would a film company need, Jerry Antil?"

"For film production?" I asked.

"Yes, to get it started—to get it 'rolling'—ha, ha, ha, ha!"

"I'd need a van to haul things around—oh, and an apartment, one where I can fit a desk; a desk, money to live on, some selling costs, postage, mailings and long-distance charges. I wouldn't do it unless I could get business in all the surrounding states. I'd have to scout around and line up freelance film crews. Oh, and I'd need a lawyer to write it up, an agreement, that is."

"I'm a lawyer," said Chase.

I turned and looked at him. He had an honest face.

"How about a thousand a month," he said, "for six months, just to try it—just to see if we like it together? For your van—we'll call it the 'Antil Mobile'—your living and selling expenses? I'll put it up, the van plus a thousand every month, for six months. You do your thing, get the business, write and produce films, and I'll do the contracts, collect the money, and pay the bills. If we have sales, I get my money back first, after bills are paid, of course, and then we split the profits. In six months we decide to go on or call it quits," he said.

"I could go for that. Six months?" I asked.

"Six months," said Chase.

"I could go for that," I said.

Chase went on to tell me that he was a practicing attorney and owned several office buildings in downtown Cincinnati and apartment buildings in Mount Adams. His family had graced him with a small fortune upon his graduation from law school, which included more than ten thousand shares of Polaroid stock and some IBM—the hottest stocks on the market since the 1950s and a high rise office building or two downtown. I told him about my experiences with Adams, Gaffney & Grant, some of the companies I'd produced films for, and about the possibility of projects with Gibson on Monday.

"How about it?" Chase asked, offering his hand with a sparkle in his eye.

"Deal!" I said, shaking it.

"Come with me, Jerry Antil," he said walking in long graceful strides toward the gallery door.

"Where to?" I asked.

"I want to show you something," he said.

We left the gallery. He was distracted, buckling the belt

around his trench coat as he walked me to a motorcycle resting by the curb.

"Nice bike; is it Italian?" I asked.

"Get on," he said, "I want to show you something." He pulled on his goggles and adjusted the straps.

This was when the opening scene of *Lawrence of Arabia* flashed through my mind, where *Sir Lawrence* raced a motorcycle that looked like this one, dressed just like he was dressed, and crashed it while the movie was dissolving to people walking out of his funeral.

"My car is just over there," I said. "Why don't I follow you."

"I'll bring you right back, this will be quicker. Hop on, Jerry Antil," he said. "Don't dally!"

He mounted his motorcycle, stepped up on the starter pedal, and with a heave started it in one try. As he took it off its kickstand, he revved it and balanced it upright. I lifted a leg over the motorcycle, set my foot on the ground on the other side, and sat down behind him.

"My God, how tall are you, man?" he shouted through the noise.

"Six-ten," I shouted back, grabbing the sides of his trench coat belt to hang on.

"Lift your feet, put them on the foot pegs," he said. "Ready?"

"Ready," I shouted back.

"Avanti!" he screamed as we putted off.

He circled the Fountain Square fountains, wobbling slightly while pulling his left glove on, waited for a bus to pull away from an intersection, and off we went down Vine, down past Fifth Street, Fourth Street, catching every light down toward the parkway. At one red light, we came to a stop in the middle lane just before we were about to turn left; while we were stopped, I could feel a leg cramp. I straightened my legs and stood, adjusting my trousers, and he took off with me standing there tall, bent over, and bowlegged, appearing to be pulling my pants down in the middle of downtown traffic, a car behind me now honking. Noticing the lighter ride, Chase flagged his head back twice, signaling his awareness of my dilemma, and circled two completely illegal U-turns and came back for me like we had it rehearsed, laughing. He took me up to Mount Adams, a trendy upscale neighborhood nestled on top of one of Cincinnati's seven beautiful hills. He owned a dozen or so town homes there, slanting up the streets, homes he had divided and converted into luxury apartments. We parked in front of the one he wanted to show me. It was nice, way too expensive for me. I told him I had already found a place over on Price Hill, but on the west side, a studio with a nice view, half the price of Mount Adams, in a new high-rise.

Chase and I shook on our deal. He said he would have papers to sign the following day and I should go buy a van to use for film making. He would buy it from me if we ended the business. Just as we walked back to his motorcycle, a fellow came out of one of his apartments, walking toward a new Corvette. Chase introduced me to him—Peter Sealey, my age. Peter was a brand manager at Procter & Gamble. He had intense, interested eyes, thinning hair, a look of all business, as if he cared about every detail. Chase suggested Peter and I would have some things in common, with my being a writer and film producer and Peter being a brain at Procter & Gamble, one of the most sophisticated consumer marketing companies in the world. He told Peter about our new venture and that he was about to take me back downtown to get my car.

"Film man," said Peter.

"I try," I said.

"What sort of things have you worked on?" Peter asked.

"Kenner Toy, Frisch's, Coney Island," I said.

"Impressive," said Peter. "Let's have a drink sometime, talk." He shook my hand and stepped toward his Corvette.

"Peter Sealey, Jerry Antil here needs a ride downtown; are you going that way, by chance?" asked Chase, paging through a group of envelopes the postman had handed him walking by.

Peter offered to drive me. I shook Chase's hand and

crawled into the Corvette. Peter worked on the Crisco brand and the Duncan Hines cake-mix brand. I told him my dad had started the Duncan Hines baking brand, in Cortland, New York. He perked as he pulled over at Fountain Square.

"Where're you headed now?" I asked, getting out of the car.

"I was thinking of a piano lounge I know, simple jazz. Maybe the Busy Bee, nothing concrete," he said.

"It's Friday, the Bee will be hopping with pick-ups," I said.

"Want to meet there? We can talk the film business and Duncan Hines, check out the ladies," said Peter.

Busy Bee was a popular after-work cocktail lounge on Ludlow Avenue. A delightful blend of nubile college girls bouncing around and the dressier twentyish or thirtyish office-working girls on the prowl. All lovely for the discerning girlwatcher; by our own admission, Peter and I were the best at it, admiring the beautiful pulchritude moving about the busy bar area, every detail.

"I've never been good at picking up girls at bars," I said. "I think I'm too tall. I can't hear them half the time, they can't hear me. Look at those guys in the thick of those fine ladies over there, Pete; they're getting all the action at eye level. I'm working on an advertising lady with a Mercedes—not sure I have a chance. I think she's in her late twenties; I'm way too young for her."

"If she's pushing thirty and she's in advertising, Jere—best you choose your words carefully." Peter grinned. "Never use words like 'blitz,' 'short,' 'mini,' advertising terms that carry subliminal messages." Peter sipped his Irish whiskey with a devilish grin. "Thrust, that's it—'thrust' would be a good word. Deep and thrust."

"I'm beyond that, Peter," I said. "We've been talking so much business I wouldn't know how to start something. I think I'm committed to coming up with an ad campaign with her, on spec. I haven't even tried to kiss her good night."

Contact lenses had just come on the market in the eyeglass world, and only a few could afford them in the early days. Peter looked up with a slight squint through his new contacts, assessed the situation, and took another sip of his Irish whiskey.

"Some lovely ladies, no question about it," he said. "Look at them over there—an ample supply, Jerry, plenty to go around." With that, his brain took a sudden turn: "I just read a top-secret five-year study and forecast," he said.

"Top secret? About what?"

"Searle, the drug people, got FDA approval and are about to launch a birth control pill for women ... the first ever in history."

"What does that mean, birth control?" I asked.

"Sex with no babies," said Peter.

"You're kidding, right?" I asked. "There'll be a pill that'll keep a girl from getting pregnant after having sex."

"Exactly."

"Every time, they, you know—?" I asked.

"Every time."

"You pulling my leg, Pete?"

"I saw the secret report," said Peter.

"About a pill?"

"A pill."

"How would it work?" I asked.

"Jerry, all I know is that the world's about to learn that women like sex just as much as men," Peter attested.

"No way," I said.

"Big guy, these are the sixties and the world is about to be catapulted, literally launched into the wildest sexual revolution ever seen in the history of man. I don't intend to miss a minute of it."

"I know they like kissing," I said.

My mind boggled as I thought back to my one and only experience at the brothel in Newport; she seemed bored to tears. Then reality set in, in about the same length of time as my Newport hooker experience came to mind.

"Procter & Gamble—Peter don't you guys make Ivory soap?" I asked.

"We do; why?" he asked.

"Oh, no reason," I said.

"The whole company started with a wooden horse drawn wagon and Ivory soap. It floats," said Peter.

"That sounds great, Pete, the pill thing, but how about tonight? I've got to paint a fence for a guy at seven in the morning. I don't have all night to hunt and beg," I said.

Peter took a sip, looking in full control.

"As I see it," started Peter, "we have alternatives to remedy the situation. Count them—there are two. Third-party endorsement for one," he said, lifting an ice cube from a water glass and putting it in his mouth.

"Huh?" I articulated.

"Third-party endorsement, big guy; it's a proven fact people believe third-party endorsement, will often rely on it. It's a powerful marketing tool," he said, crunching the ice cube.

"You're absolutely right," I said, "I remember that from my PR days and the newspaper and television news releases. People believe what they read in the newspaper or see in the news, as long as it's a third party saying it," I said. "But what's that got to do with a bunch of chicks at the bar tonight and our going home with lipstick on our collars?" I looked at my watch.

Peter held his drink up, in a covert attempt at covering his lips from being read. He leaned in.

"Big guy, I go to that far end of the bar and carefully tell the fine women on that end about you, Jerry Antil, and what a prize you are; you, big guy, go to the other end over there and tell all those fine ladies what a catch I am—the one and only Peter Sealey. They'll believe me about you, they'll believe you about me—it's all third-party. Sometime in the evening, they'll have no alternative, the ladies become the hunters and shift ends of the bar to be close to their target, and you and I leave the place with arm candy—by last call, if it works."

Peter took a slug, clinked my glass, and set his glass down in satisfaction.

"We're not going to do that, of course." I laughed. "You

said you had two ideas. What's the other one?"

"We ask every guy in the place who doesn't have a Corvette or their own private plane to leave and we'd be here alone with the ladies," he said. "I'd even let you choose first."

"Peter, how much do you make?" I asked.

"Jerry, I couldn't possibly spend it all; it's a burden, I know. I mean how many cars or planes does one guy need?" he laughed.

Peter and I left the Busy Bee Lounge and walked to our cars.

"Jere, what are you doing tomorrow afternoon?" he asked.

"I'm painting a fence for a friend, until noon, a little after," I said. "I have to prime it. I maybe there until one or two."

"Can you be at the airport by three?"

"Which one?"

"Cincinnati."

"I can, yes. What's up?"

"I'm taking my plane up. Ride with me to West Virginia," he said. "I'm checking out The Greenbrier—a luxury resort for a possible P&G planning conference. Someone told me I could land on their private runway. Three o'clock, big guy—we can talk Duncan Hines. You might bring a blazer or jacket; they may have a dress code. We'll eat there, be back here by nine or ten."

I woke up early for a Saturday. I pulled on jeans and a T-shirt and drove over to Ashland Avenue to Mr. V's house. I came up with a game plan for the wrought-iron fence. I'd wire-brush one section at a time and then rust coated and painted it one section at a time. By one o'clock I was cleaning the brushes and putting the paint cans on the stoop in the garage leading into the house. Taped to the door was an envelope that had a fifty-dollar bill in it. I folded it in my pocket.

Peter was pulling the chocks from behind the wheels and checking wings and tail parts.

"I chartered a plane this size to fly an old girlfriend to Columbus one time, Peter, but it was canvas. Yours is beautiful, a Beechcraft Bonanza."

"You charted a plane to give a girlfriend a ride? I'm impressed," said Peter.

"She went into the convent, anyway," I said.

"Ouch!" barked Peter, wincing. "What do you do with your women to drive them into the convent?" Peter asked. He laughed.

"I'm beginning to wonder myself," I said.

The engine started, and the propeller sliced efficiently, patiently waiting for the ride down the runway. We taxied behind an American Airlines jet at a gate and around a Delta jet coming in the opposite direction. At one point our plane rested to a pause. Peter picked up a microphone from the dash, thumbed the button.

"This is Bonanza three-three-two-five-Charlie requesting takeoff. I repeat, Bonanza three-three-two-five-Charlie requesting takeoff."

"Go ahead, Bonanza, we see you. You're cleared for takeoff—runway two, south."

"Roger that."

Peter's thumb positioned itself squarely on the throttle and began slowly, methodically pushing it in. The plane responded like the finest Swiss watch. With an emphatic leap we grabbed up into the sky and began climbing with no hesitation. Concentrating on the view of the horizon on his side and out front, still climbing, Peter reached down between the seats and grabbed a lever without turning his head.

"Big guy, there's no better feeling than tucking the tires into the belly of your own Beechcraft Bonanza after a precision takeoff."

Life was a wonderful celebration. Peter punctuated every second of it, championing every single breath. He was on a constant search for excellence and took in each drop of his life experience, like a fine port wine.

"So your father created Duncan Hines. Did he come up with the first cake mix? How did that go?" he asked, watching the horizon.

"I was pretty young, Peter. I think twelve. Dad was an owner of a big bakery that had plants around central New York. A man named Roy Park and the man named Duncan Hines came to him to see what he could do with the Duncan Hines brand. Apparently they had tried various foods with no luck. Dad and his bakery created Duncan Hines bread—it was a whole wheat, shorter, thin sliced premium loaf, Dad called it. That was the first Duncan Hines baking product. They sold the Duncan Hines name for baking—to Procter & Gamble, I guess—for a lot of money, and you guys came up with the cake-mix idea."

"Fascinating, a fascinating story," Peter said. "So you've actually met *the* Duncan Hines?"

"My dad knew him, I only saw pictures," I said.

"Jerry, we have been using every ounce of research to own this market—cake mixes. It has been an incredible journey. We came up with nine flavors of cake mixes. We soon learned that chocolate was the favorite flavor, and the name of the game is shelf space in the store, so we grew that to nine different chocolate flavors, eighteen flavors in all."

Peter pointed down at a mountain range below us.

"We learned that the baker actually equated baking a cake to the joy having a baby. Presenting the cake to a husband or wife or birthday kid was a symbolic gesture—an offering—just as having a baby would be."

"You guessed that?"

"Three thousand interviews told us that."

I was fascinated.

"We actually took it another step. We removed the egg from the cake mix, letting the baker add the egg, 'fresh ingredients.' After that, we broke the chocolate out into a separate bag and let the baker add that as well. That gave a sense it was even fresher—more 'from scratch.'"

"You must spend a bundle on research," I said.

"In this day and age, a homemaker spends three and a half hours a day in the kitchen. The family kitchen has become our laboratory. We study everything. It's what we do. The consumer tells us what they want, when and how they want it, and we merely oblige."

"You sound like my dad," I said. "He was always sensitive to his customer. I heard he would never join the Cortland Country Club or drive a Cadillac because of his customers. He would say his grocers didn't drive Cadillacs and many of them were Italian, black or Jewish. 'I won't drive a Cadillac and make my customers uncomfortable,' he would tell me, 'and I'd sure never join a country club that doesn't accept Italians, blacks or Jews as members.'"

"Smart man," said Peter.

Peter picked up the microphone, thumbed the button, and requested landing permission at Greenbrier. We lofted down like we were in a movie onto a long, rich, green lawn that looked like a velvet carpet leading up to a Taj Mahal—large stucco buildings with endlessly pillared patios and tall windows and striped canvas awnings: the resort.

We got out of the plane, put our jackets on, and walked the grounds in a setting sun. We crossed the patio of the main building and were welcomed into a dining area by a gentleman in a tuxedo, who led us to a table.

"I'll get the sommelier," he said.

"As much as I'd love a fine wine, I'll have to pass," Peter said. "Sir, can you see that my plane gets fueled? We're flying back after dinner and I never drink when I am about to fly. Jere, have a glass of wine, a drink if you'd like one."

"Ginger ale is fine with me," I said.

"Very good. I'll send your waiter, gentlemen and call the runway office."

"Peter, I'm impressed at the depth of your marketing skills. You take it to an entirely new level for me. I know guys who know sales, others know PR, advertising guys—but you're the whole package."

"Big guy, thank God most of the marketing world is still blundering along with pushcarts, selling their wares. Marketing has one and only one single objective: to create and maintain a high level of unaided top-of-mind awareness for your product name and concept. Nothing more and nothing less; all else will fall into place. A lot of people haven't figured that out yet. Every tool of marketing has that single purpose."

"Say it in English," I said.

"Jerry, have you heard of Crisco, of McDonald's, of Hunt's catsup? How about Howard Johnson?"

"I've heard of every one of those," I said. "What's the catch?"

"The catch is your knowing the brand names is a start but not the big game, big guy. I told you the names—or 'aided' you with brands, and you could recall them. That is called 'aided' awareness. Now try this. Name a tissue," he said.

"Kleenex," I said.

"Soup."

"Campbell's."

"Washing machine?"

"Maytag."

"Without assistance, your mind came up with the first brands it could think of. This is called 'unaided top-of-mind' awareness of brands. The goal of marketing. If you went out shopping for those generic items I mentioned, you would have the brands you named already on the top of your mind, in front of any other brands. Being first in line with a consumer is what it's all about. I want the world to think of Duncan Hines when they think of cake, or even dessert for that matter, and of Crisco when they think of cooking. Until your prospective customer has seen your message ten times, they won't begin to understand it much remember it. We see thousands of messages every day— billboards, signs, radio, television—but we retain little." Peter lifted his glass of water and motioned the waiter over.

I didn't know that much about fine dining, other than my expensive dinner or two at the Gourmet Room with my girlfriend, back when I had to ice cupcakes all night for a week to be able to pay for them. There were dinners at the Neil House and my regular fare of mostaccioli and meatballs at Chico's, but my better dining experiences were limited, practically nil. I did remember, however, my mother teaching me that a quality, fine table or fine restaurant would always have butter knives. You could always tell you were at the best, she would say, if they had butter knives. A butter knife was that one single standard that would distinguish a table setting as superior, as the best there was.

I thought of the fun the evening before at the Busy Bee Lounge listening to Peter talk about third-party endorsement at the bar, the laughs we had. I thought of the fascinating care and detail he took in just bringing happiness to a homemaker baking in a kitchen, the satisfaction of a flawless liftoff at the airport.

In the world of marketing, Peter Sealey was a butter knife. I'd never met a person, before or since, like Peter, one you could learn the essence and depth of marketing just having a beer with him ... and whatever I learned from him was always interesting and never boring. To Peter, marketing was a way of life, it was literature, poetry. Peter was my MBA. He could talk marketing at the highest levels as simply and easily as I could write compositions in between classes.

Chapter 22

English and his wife were standing in front of Chico's as I drove up and parked behind Doreen's Mercedes. He stood there in a bright red Hawaiian shirt, holding the door for me. Elle was tucking her T-shirt into her jeans.

"*Après vous*," English said with a deep bow.

"Don't bump your head," chided Chico. "Your lady is waiting, and by the looks of her you will need all your senses."

Doreen was in the corner booth dressed in cleavage and white pearls with ivory-rimmed sunglasses, already sipping a glass of red wine.

"Carlo?" I announced, as if I was entering a bullring. "We'll have what the lady is having. We trust her implicitly."

And the festival began. I started it by telling everyone the good news about my dad's suggested client, Tetley Tea.

"Interesting," said Doreen. "Come up with any ideas yet?"

"I saw it in a coffee cup, with a guy," I said. "Make a cup of tea more masculine, a guy thing somehow."

"Masculine?" asked Doreen. "Who buys tea at the grocery?"

"Damned if I know," I said.

"How about a couple having tea like two people usually have coffee and making it more refined, more accepted, a part of the landscape?" Doreen asked.

"Okay, okay, guys," said English. "Picture this. Picture a warm flickering campfire in a wooded glen by a small lake. Maybe a stacked stone wall behind. There's a thirty-two revolver resting on the stone wall. It's dark, the sky is clear and star studded and there are two men sitting around watching the fire spark. Both of the men have blue porcelain tin coffee cups in their hands, with tea strings and tags hanging over their rims. In the distance, you can hear a wolf howling at the full moon."

English reached, gulped some wine, set the glass down, stared up to the corner of the ceiling like he was about to do a Shakespearean soliloquy, and said:

"First man says: 'Tell me about the rabbits, George.'

"Second man says: 'Lenny, drink your tea.'

"'But I want to hear about the rabbits, George.'

"'Just drink your tea.'

"'What kind of tea is this, George? I like it George.'

"'It's Tetley, Lenny—always look for it in the blue and white box.'

"'I like Tetley Tea, George. Now, tell me about the rabbits, George.'"

Doreen and I sat motionless with our mouths open, mesmerized, stunned, gazing at English, who was in a tickled grin, waiting for some applause. We weren't quite certain if we liked it or not. Flower child was wiping up water she had spilled on the table, checking down to see if her T-shirt had gotten wet.

"Where do I know that from?" I asked, picking up my wine.

"It's John Steinbeck," said Doreen. "It's from *Of Mice and Men*. Lenny and George. George always promised Lenny that one day they would have a place and raise rabbits."

I tweaked my chin, thinking.

"If this is family TV, what's with the gun on the rock pile?" asked Doreen.

"Stone fence," said English. "The gun is resting on the stone fence."

"Wait a minute," I said.

"What?" asked English.

"So didn't George shoot Lenny in the back of the head near a campfire in the woods or by a lake or something?" I gaffed.

English pouted.

"I'm sorry, English; actually, it's quite creative," I said. "I know I couldn't have thought of anything better quite so fast."

"I have a masculine idea that would be great in print," said Doreen. "Imagine a manly full page of war medals spread out on display ... but one of them is a tea bag with the string wrapped over it and the tag hanging down below it, like one of the medals. Caption: 'Only one is awarded for good taste.'"

Carlo piled the table with food.

Our friendships were developing. I only thought it was fair to share what I felt was a downside to our endeavor—now that I'd met Peter Sealey and learned the depth in which a company like Procter & Gamble considered before launching a consumer project.

"Here's the deal, guys," I started. "I just met one of the brightest marketing people I've ever met, beside my dad and Mr. VonderHaar over at X, that is. This guy tells me Procter & Gamble will know what a homemaker is thinking before one even walks into the kitchen, almost which cabinet doors they'll open first, second, and third, and General Foods already knows this homemaker probably loves to serve guests Maxwell House coffee since it 'tastes as good as it smells,' knowing people who don't drink coffee because it tastes bitter love the smell of the roasting coffee beans at the Kroger store, and the television commercial promises Maxwell House tastes as good as it smells and every time they walk through the grocery and smell the roasting beans, they think of Maxwell House," I said, and took a deep breath.

"He's right," said Doreen.

"Guys," I said, "a deal is a deal. I can get to Ogilvy, I already know that. Actually, they're waiting for my call. But here's the new deal. English, if you want to put something together, I'll help you and I will go there and present it. Doreen, that goes for your print ideas, too. Nothing ventured, nothing gained. But I now know that trying to come up with something creative without studying our prospective buyer—they call it a target profile—it's pretty much a gamble. I mean they may like the creative and it may fit, but it's pretty much a long shot. In the meantime, I'm going to try to get some film business and some contract writing."

"I say let's go for it," Doreen said. "I'll put together a series of print ads."

"I'll write commercials, thirties and sixties. Lenny and George, okay with you?" English asked.

"I'll present them," I said. "Make certain the thirties are twenty-eight seconds and the sixties are fifty-eight seconds;

stations need that lead-in, lead-out time—two seconds."

During coffee Doreen invited me to meet her at an FM radio station recording studio later in the week to record some Christmas radio commercials for a client.

"I'll have festive hot buttered rum for you." She winked and leaned into me. "I'll get you in the Christmas spirit."

"Call me when you're ready, English, we'll meet and eat here," I said. "If you need me for anything, call my answering service."

Doreen held my arm closely.

"What if I need you?" she smiled.

"You call me too, when you're ready," I said. We'll meet and eat here then, too. In fact, I'm here practically every night of the week. Any of you, come as often as you like."

"Are you going to meet me for hot buttered rum at the Christmas recording?" asked Doreen.

"I'll be there."

"I want to look festive and Christmassy," said Doreen.

"You mean like a date?" I asked.

"Well, there will be hot buttered rum, music and I do have a new dress— tis the season," she whispered.

While Doreen and English worked out details of their campaign ideas, Peter and I became good friends and met for drinks often, at various places. Sometimes we would take the plane for a ride. I would bring him up to date on my progress in building the film business; he would give me tips on proposal writing, marketing, and writing marketing plans, if a client wasn't sure what they wanted in a sales film.

"First line is your objective. Say it in one sentence, big guy. Make it brief, make it punch; Babe Ruth only used one bat. Then comes the cost; put it right up there in front. Then you tell your strategy—one, two, three—then your execution for each strategy, and, finally, implementation."

"It's like chess," I said. "It's like telling your tactics and strategy but starting the game with a checkmate."

"Exquisite," said Peter. "I couldn't have phrased it better.

Remember to keep it to one page, two at the most. Cost, objective, strategy, execution, and implementation."

I etched it into my brain. As time went on I got a thirty-second spot commercial for Collins, a man running for Congress. I wrote and produced a gorgeous commercial for Cadillac, where I put spotlights in a dealership's garage and a white Cadillac in the middle. The floor was wetted down. I had small mirrors placed under the hood of the car, attached to the water heater, the battery, and the radiator. I had a young man in white coveralls on his knees, a garden hose in one hand, a spotless white washcloth in the other, washing the car, every crevice of the grille. By shooting through the mirrors under the hood, it looked as though you were looking out from the engine through the grille at a man taking the care of a fine watchmaker in cleaning a sparkling chrome grille of the most luxurious automobile on earth. I wrote it without a word. It was produced without a word spoken; a lone cello played *Pachelbel* behind the sound effects of a dripping garden hose.

I got a contract to write and produce a movie for the Marcellus Casket Company, in Syracuse, New York. John F. Kennedy was laid to rest in a Marcellus casket. The work was one of my best. I named it *The Warmth of Wood*.

"Wood, the warmth of wood, the one gift of nature man has lived with, worked with, and died with from the beginning of time. This is wood, mahogany, beginning another part of its journey at the Marcellus Casket Company at Syracuse, New York." The company used the film for many years before reshooting shorter film clips for their casket sales team.

Doreen and English gave me their work, their mockups, scripts, even some recorded spots and wished me luck in New York City. I scoured all my pants pockets and counted out my money, every cent I had on the bed. I had enough to pay for an airline ticket to and from New York, a cab and a cheap hotel for one night only and a cab back to LaGuardia to fly home. I made the appointment. I found the Hotel Chesterfield where I could get a room if I paid in advance for $19. I remember asking the cab driver if he thought they'd have a room and his telling me to 'leave your bag, go check, I'll wait'. I could see my bag and the ad campaign inside it being stolen and winding up in Brooklyn somewhere. I paid the fare and got out with my bag. He screeched off. The Hotel Chesterfield was a dump. A huge dump. All night long I could hear arguments in the hall. I presented our Tetley Tea ideas to Jim Heekin, president of Ogilvy & Mather. He was most cordial and professional, making me feel welcome. He took no calls, closed his door and looked at the work patiently, asked many questions about our central theme and message. We had coffee in his office. I remember wondering why he hadn't offered me Tetley Tea. He finally said our work showed a great deal of creativity, and he liked the approach, but he was having a time trying to put a thread of continuity through it. I wasn't certain what the hell continuity meant – I couldn't even balance a checkbook. The best I could come up with was an "Oh well, we gave it a shot." He passed on our campaign, but said it was a good effort. David Ogilvy was not in the offices or he would have introduced me. He went so far as to say if I was ever in the city again, I was to stop by, and he would introduce me to David Ogilvy.

I flew back to Cincinnati with barely enough to pay for the airport parking. I drove to XU and reported the results to Mr. V. That night I repeated it to Doreen and English at Chico's. We didn't make a dime, but it was a great adventure. Doreen and English shared with me a sense of pride knowing we had created something that had been reviewed by the world-famous Ogilvy agency. English and Doreen each put copies of the work into their portfolios. For me, it was a chapter in a book one day. We had another great dinner; Carlo popped champagne.

During a gentle white Christmas snow fall one evening, Doreen and I sat in a warm leather sofa in a darkened FM radio station recording studio. We had dressed for the occasion, almost as if it were a date. Me in a dark charcoal suit and dress tie— Doreen wrapped in shoulder mink over a low-cut blouse with a pearl necklace. She sat in an Audrey Hepburn-like above the knee puffy black full cocktail skirt over a white petticoat and sheer French silk stockings held up by sensuous black satin garter straps.

We sat together with our hot buttered rums on a leather sofa in the studio listening to the pleasant sounds of a British talent voice Doreen's agency hired to record radio spots, commercials for a high end *exclusive* local retail gift shop. The room was filled with sounds of the faint marching of "Drummer Boy" music in the background. We sipped hot buttered rum, nudging each other on the sofa and stepping around each other in tight studio spaces here and there— eventually calling it a wrap on the recording.

"Can we go to your place?" Doreen asked.

"My place ain't much," I said.

"We don't need much," whispered Doreen.

She smiled.

"And my thermos isn't empty," she added.

The three flights of stairs up to my room next to the refrigerator in the hall were curved, narrow and steep. I followed behind Doreen, catching an occasional glimpse of a parachuting white petticoat and satin garter strap. We wound up celebrating our rum and body bump inspired early Christmas evening rolling on my bed kissing passionately. We took making out to a whole other level—for me, anyway. Kickstand was elevated to new heights and experience. The evening was sweaty and funky and made a lasting impression on us both, to be sure. She was gone when I awoke. When asked, 'what happened to you and Doreen?' I used to say – "As I was to learn over time, two careers running at high rates of speed during the virtual marketing birth and awakening of a fledgling but bourgeoning nation, still in a post-War puberty—people like Doreen and me rarely got a second dance together. I never saw her again, never ran into her." That is what I used to say…but of course that was bullshit. The truth to what really happened was in the throes of passion that Christmas evening in the sack, with a gentle grip she was adjusting kickstand into her private heaven and sitting on it with a sanctioning, "Do you love me, Jerry? I'm very much in love with you."

My brother Dick, the *'You're dumb as a stick'* (when it comes to women) brother was never there when I needed him.

Gently fondling her incredibly firm breasts, it was about

my eighth or ninth thrust with my pelvis when I whispered, "Love?"

Doreen's answer, straddling me as she sensually ground her hips. "I'm so in love with you. You love me, don't you?" for which I queried a metaphoric could it be love— as she was like old enough to be my mother. I sobered up in an empty bed and Doreen never took another call from me or answered her door or any of three letters of apology I wrote her.

The next spring, one night, while I was sitting at the Blind Lemon with a few guys, including Peter, having a drink, unwinding, and passing the time, the most unbelievable—but true—book chapter fiasco adventure was about to unfold without any warning—to any of us. It was a work night; we were just talking girls and marketing, as normal.

"I got this crazy commercial today, a ten-second spot for a driveway sealer," I said.

There were two rounds of drinks delivered while we discussed what in the living hell a driveway sealer even was and what could be said in ten seconds about it.

Sealey ordered coffee and asked if they could make us sandwiches—anything they had would be fine. Sandwiches all around.

"How about having a limo driving up a long, circular, black-topped driveway and then parking in front of a mansion?" I offered.

"Is there a pool next to the mansion?" one guy asked.

"Huh?" I asked.

"A swimming pool. Is there a pool?" he asked.

"Okay, sure, there's a pool."

"Ten seconds?" he asked.

"Ten seconds—well, it's really eight," I said, "and, okay, a pool."

The guy took a sip of his scotch.

"Sounds like a pool scene, Pete … one, maybe two seconds long," he started.

"Pool scene?" Peter asked.

"Where there's a swimming pool, there could be bikinis."

Just the word, "bikini," was about the sexiest thing a young guy could hear or even think about in the early sixties. The song had recently come out—"She wore an itsy bitsy, teeny weenie, yellow polka-dot bikini"—and just hearing the lyrics, every lascivious naughty syllable of it, would be enough to send young men behind closed and locked doors all over America.

I looked at Sealey in question. He stared up at me, thinking of the possibility.

"Bikini scene?!" I mouthed a whisper.

We gazed at each other, imagining the possibilities, looked up, looked back at each other.

"NAHHHHHHH!" we both grunted, dismissing the thought. They weren't even showing bikinis in beach movies yet, just modest two-piece swimsuits.

We ate our sandwiches and went home. The next day I looked through my Yellow Pages, picked up my phone, and dialed a modeling agency, for a chauffeur for the limousine.

"Ma'am, I need a chauffeur in a full uniform, for a television commercial. He'll be driving a limo. Do you have anyone?"

"We'll find candidates and have their sheets sent to you. What's your address?"

I gave her my high-rise studio apartment address.

"I'll have them to you by Saturday, sir."

"There aren't any such things as bikini models, are there for like a pool scene in a television commercial?" I asked. "Nah, I wouldn't think so—never mind."

The modeling agency called other modeling agencies making inquiries about bikini models, I later learned.

Saturday came.

"Come on, Peter, answer your damn phone … please, please, please answer your phone. Pete. Pete."

The phone was picked up.

"This better be good," growled a raspy cotton voice. "Have any idea what time it is on a Saturday morning?"

"Pete, this is Jerry, you have to come over. Get over here quick, please."

"Hah?" he grumbled through a snore.

"Come now, hurry."

"I'm not going anywhere, go back to bed." He hung up.

The phone was picked up.

"This better not be Antil."

"Peter, you got to come—go get Larry, someone else, maybe Walters, come bail me out, please, I need help."

"What on earth?" he grunted. "You in the workhouse?"

Cincinnati had a workhouse, a civilized, nonchain chain gang where drunks and vagrants and petty criminals were automatically sentenced public service to "work things off."

"Worse! Peter, you know when your friend at the Blind Lemmon suggested a bikini pool-party scene?"

"Tell me you didn't, big guy. Please tell me you didn't," prayed Peter.

"I did. I had no idea there was ever a chance, but when I was calling a modeling agency for a chauffeur, I asked about a bikini model," I whimpered.

"And a girl showed up," Peter said. "Way to go, Jere, is she there in your apartment now? Probably underage, too—way to go. Just be a gentleman, tell her thanks, take her stats, and send her on her way home back to her mother."

"Downstairs, in the lobby," I said.

"Well, put something on and go down and tell her there."

"They're all down in the lobby," I muttered.

There was a pause.

Peter's voice raised a notch.

"All?"

"And around the building, in the parking lot. More than a hundred of them, girls in bikinis for an audition, Pete, they're everywhere and more cars are pulling up with even more girls."

I heard a *clunk, clunk, bang,* then an echoed voice: "Shit! Hold on, hold on, I dropped the phone."

"You there, Peter?" I asked.

"Jerry, there are more than a hundred girls in bikinis standing in the lobby of your building and filling the parking lot waiting for an audition, at eight a.m. on a Saturday morning? Are you serious?"

"Dead serious."

"Do you have a building manager?"

"She's standing here," I said.

Peter asked me to ask if there was a party room and could we use it for an hour or two. She agreed and encouraged us to do something soon.

Peter and his friends came over, bailing me out. They set up a table and took names and thanked every girl. I stood behind a Bolex camera on a tripod. It was empty. Gentlemen might be the wrong word but we were polite, sitting there, witnessing, one at a time, the largest bevy of some of the most beautiful, bikini-clad women ever assembled this far inland in the history of Cincinnati, one at a time. One girl came in a long coat. At the table she opened her coat baring herself in panties and bra. "I didn't have a bikini, will this do?" Sometimes Larry was nice enough to ask a girl to jump like she was playing with a beach ball or do jumping jacks like she was at the gym. Jumping jacks were very good.

In the end, there was no pool scene for the driveway sealer commercial. My mom and two older sisters would have disowned me. My dad would have been disappointed, and I knew better. I did hire four girls from two different agencies, but with Pete's help I cleaned it up. I dressed them in classic red and black Chesterfield coats, some in coats with faux fur collars, wearing mittens acting like wholesome college girls coming home for the holidays. I had them climb out of a limo holding stacks of gift packages wrapped with ribbon. The bikini audition became classic P&G brand manager barroom buzz for some time. By the end of the day, although seven angry girlfriends and housewives living in the building slid notes of disapproval under my door or the building manager's door, eleven husbands or bachelors left roses, boxes of candy, three bottles of champagne, and two thank-you notes in front of my apartment door in gratitude. They'd push my doorbell and leave quickly. One married French woman waited in sweatpants and T-shirt for me to answer my door, stepped in handing me two glasses of wine. I had no sooner lifted one of the glasses for a sip when she pushed the door closed behind her, pulled her sweatpants to the floor and stepped out of them bare butt and smiling. She took the other wine glass from my hand, placed a hand flat against my chest and walked me backwards to my bed, finishing her wine and setting the empty glass on the windowsill. I kept my mouth shut the hour or so she was there sitting on my kickstand while rolling her hips in an endless steady rocking motion. After we finished, she did some stretching exercises as if she had just visited the gym, touched her toes a few times, kissed me goodbye and I never saw her again.

A few months later Peter's Corvette was stolen, raced across the bridge into Kentucky, and ultimately flipped over in a police chase. I was standing talking with Chase about the scarcity of profitable film projects the day Peter drove up in his brand-new Buick Riviera. The lines of his new car were classic. The most advanced design of the time.

"Peter, you just have to stop living this quiet, austere life and start spending some money on yourself," I laughed, smelling the new leather of a new space-age car.

"I'm moving," said Peter.

"Where? When?" asked Chase.

"To New York," he said.

"Proctor and Gamble is transferring you?" Chase asked.

"No," said Peter. "McCann Erickson made me an offer I couldn't refuse."

"So you're leaving us for the big city?" I asked.

"New York, big guy, the Big Apple, Gotham City, front porch to the world," he announced. "I'll be in the book—look me up and come see me, crash at my pad anytime."

In the sixties most everyone lived in homes or apartments. Cool people called them *pads*. The term came from 'landing pad' for the frequent business traveler. Over drinks Peter told me about his move to New York, and about a prestigious agency there,

McCann, that owned an exclusive marketing think tank and hired only the best of the best in marketing. He was also heading up the introduction of a new cereal brand, Captain Crunch. He would fly his plane first to Newark and then come back to drive the car.

In days, he was off to New York.

I produced a number of films in the months ahead but was overwhelmed with the last big film contract for Herb Slotnick. It was a series of eight training films and television commercials for Carrol's Hamburgers, a restaurant group in Syracuse that had learned about me from my work with Marcellus Casket. Chase and I shook hands and called it quits after that. In the middle of one production, exhausted, I grabbed a spliced but still unwritten reel of film about making French fries and drove five hours from Syracuse to Manhattan, and down to Peter's apartment at the fashionable Brevoort East near Washington Square. Peter wasn't home.

On arrival, I threaded and started the projector, using the living room wall as a screen, and fell asleep. My plan had been to watch the raw but spliced footage and make notes and write the voice over words as I watched the film. Peter came in from work, me snoring on the sofa, the reel on the projector spinning, film slapping the table with each turn. He rethreaded the film in the projector and turned the Wollensak reel-to-reel tape recorder on and picked up its microphone. He started the projector. Watching the film in one complete pass, he dictated straight through from beginning to end, every word of the final script that was ultimately used in the twenty-eight-minute film on how to make a French fry, while I snored.

"See this? Recognize it right away, don't you? In fact, it's probably one of the most common and ordinary foods in all America, the potato. But wait! There's a story to be told ... it's a story ..."

The client loved it. Not a word was changed. It took exactly twenty-eight minutes for the butter knife to write the entire twenty-eight-minute film about a subject he'd only learned from watching the film—once.

Chapter 23

Partnerless and independent I turned the van over to Chase just about the time I got a call from the City of Ogdensburg, New York, asking me if I could write and produce a film to attract a doctor. I had my heart set on going to New York City to find a job, but I thought I'd investigate the opportunity along the way as it was in New York State. My best friend, Greg Shaban, the guy whose family I'd met at the Horizon Hill apartments when I was working for Adams, Gaffney & Grant, had moved to Detroit where they adopted a boy, Christopher. I moved my belongings into a spare room at their apartment. I remember sitting in Detroit on Eight Mile Road through the Detroit Race riots. We could hear the tank cannon fire downtown. I left the house to go get a pizza and an army jeep with two soldiers with a 50-caliber gun ordered me off the street and back to the house. When it calmed down, I became Christopher's godfather. I then headed off to Ogdensburg to check the town out. Greg loaned me his Gulf credit card in case I needed gas money or had car troubles. I remember getting a speeding ticket in Erie driving from the Ohio border to the New York border through a small section of Pennsylvania. The state police had me follow them to a Justice of the Peace. I was broke anf talked the justice of the peace into accepting my movie projector as security and let me go on the promise I would come back on my way back through and pay the fine. I offered him my hand, in honor, just as Big Mike would have, and I promised.

After a few days visiting the city fathers and driving around Ogdensburg, I told the mayor and chamber of commerce head that a doctor probably wouldn't stay, if he did come, because the city was too rundown. They challenged me to conduct a beautification program for the city and offered me ten thousand dollars, half for the program and half for writing and producing a movie. I accepted the challenge, a six-month contract, payments on a new blue Volkswagen bug, and a draw of sixty-five dollars a week. I asked for a hundred-dollar advance and used part of it to pay my speeding ticket in Erie. With my help and direction, the

Ogdensburg beautification program was embraced by the entire community. Each morning the local radio station would give me an hour to talk, with people calling in. The city's adults came and volunteered their time, money and materials if they had some. Union members, builders, carpenters, and painters volunteered their time to rebuild long park steps down to the reservoir and steps down to the shores of the St. Lawrence Seaway. Businesses donated the materials. The kids in school or home from college joined what we called "The Night Raiders," and we'd start at dusk and end at dawn, and would completely paint a bridge, or paint waste barrels with stenciled flowers, or paint the fire hydrants.

By the time I was wrapping up the beautification program portion of my contract, more than half of the twelve hundred homeowners had made capital improvements to their homes. The townspeople came together with a pride they earned working side by side—a new bond of old establishment and the young on the same team. Governor Rockefeller commented in a conference on the success of Ogdensburg, the pioneer city beautification project we had just completed. Nearing the end of the contract the city fathers called me into a special meeting to tell me they couldn't pay me the balance of what they owed. I was depending on the profits from the film production as a grubstake for me in New York City. They said if I sued them, it would bankrupt the city. "Can I at least have the VW bug?" I asked. They agreed but told me there was a balance due on it and that I would have to make the rest of the payments. Following the governor's commendation, the Duke Foundation asked me to consider writing a book on city beautification management and said they would publish it if I did. Doris Duke offered to let me stay at her home in Hawaii if I needed the space to write.

While I was in Ogdensburg, Greg and his family had moved again, this time to Bellerose Village, Long Island, a few blocks from their kid's grandparents, where they adopted another, a baby girl. Revlon made Greg a vice president and gave him a corner office on the forty-eighth floor, overlooking Madison Avenue.

I left Ogdensburg and headed for Bellerose Village. The day I got there I parked and took a train into the city and walked to the New York Public Library, pulled the telephone books of major northeastern cities, and copied down advertising agency and company names and addresses. I mailed every one of them my updated resume.

I called Peter Sealey and told him I had arrived. Pete was now in charge of the prestigious marketing think tank McCann had set up while he worked on the Captain Crunch cereal launch and some things for the Sprite brand of Coca-Cola USA. Over many drinks and many dinners, Peter would share his brilliance about just how simple marketing was; he would stress how important it was not to complicate it, to keep it focused. I'd listen to every word. He'd proven his theories time and time again, and now, in his midtwenties, had landed his private plane—"Bonanza 3325 Charlie"—at the Newark airport. Through him, I was getting a feel for the advertising agency business, but more importantly marketing at the level of proficiency he had both pioneered and attained.

I would take a train in from Long Island nearly every day for interviews.

Peter said once, "Jerry, you drove to New York City, the Big Apple, Gotham City, front porch of the world, in a blue Volkswagen Bug that hadn't had an oil change in I don't know how many thousand miles, the same weekend the Interpublic Group of agencies filed for bankruptcy and laid off twenty thousand guys, who are on the streets now looking for your job. Despite this, you're getting interviews. Something will happen."

"I was offered and took the job as advertising manager for a National Distiller's chemical division. We lunched every day on expense. At the end of the first month my boss called me in and told me that the mailer I did for their 'dairy machine' product was a big hit. "But I have to terminate you," he added as if it was a lunchtime afterthought.

"What?"

"Sorry."

"You're firing me?" I asked.

"You've left me no choice," he said.

"What's that supposed to mean? Was my mailer a hit or not?"

"You lied on your application?"

"I never lied. What do you mean I lied?"

"You never graduated from Xavier University."

"I never said I graduated from XU."

"Your resume said you were alumnus of Xavier University."

"So?"

"You never graduated."

"Alumnus means graduated but it also means attended. I attended Xavier University. I'm a Xavier alumnus. It's not a lie."

"My decision is irrevocable."

I called Peter to tell him the news of my demise on my first job in the city. We cancelled our dinner plans. He gently told me to keep in touch. I caught a train to Bellerose Village to start the job-hunting process all over.

Manhattan was in Holiday swing and it was party time for the duration. I wound up taking a $2.50 an hour Christmas job at Gertz, a department store on Jamaica Avenue in Queens. I was selling radios and as it turned out I was good at it. I learned from watching my dad selling grocers. He wouldn't sell, he would lay all of his products on a counter and let the grocer select. On Christmas Eve Paul Gertz came into the radio department with a bottle of Chivas Regal.

"Young man, you've broken sales records here. Would you consider a career in retail, with Gertz?" asked Mr. Gertz.

"Thank you, Mr. Gertz, but it's just a Christmas job. I want to be a writer."

"A writer? Interesting. She's gone now but I would have introduced you to Norman Mailer's stepdaughter, she's part time here selling washers and driers," said Mr. Gertz.

"Mailer? *The Naked and the Dead,* Norman Mailer?" I asked.

"The same," said Mr. Gertz.

Some how I read that as a sign that I was on the right path.

"Share your secret, Jerry. Tell us how you managed to break our sales record," the department manager said.

"Well first was, if anyone stepped on that carpet there, I never ask them if I could help them. I would ask, 'What room are you looking for?' and if they said their boy's room or their girl's room or their own bedroom, I'd grab four or five appropriate radios and set them on that counter. They'd always pick at least one."

"Enjoy the scotch, Jerry, and Merry Christmas," said Mr. Gertz, shaking my hand.

It was still my awe, my wow! – it was the Big Apple. To me it was and still is, always, a celebration to go into—or as I like to put it, to "have arrived in"—New York City by way of Penn Station, a tunnel, or even a bridge, it doesn't matter. Every time I went into the city back then, I went by train, the LIRR; and as usual I would be walking from the train up the stairs, smelling the shampoos, the cigarette smoke, and the leather of briefcases throughout the lobby, and listening for the articulate, effervescent train announcer to make my day:

"Train number seventeen foura—theeee Adooorondack Limited—now available for boarding on traaaaaack nuuuumber thirty-eight—general boarding for Albany, Syracuse, Rochester, Buffalo, and stops between. All aboard, please—track number thirty-eight. All aboard, please."

I'd look beyond my jobless disappointment into shop windows, at the men's ties, the bagels, cutlery store items and umbrellas as I'd hurry through the busy underground terminal. I'd take the escalator up to heaven, on the Madison Square Garden side. I couldn't see the 'Garden' and not be reminded of the greats who had played sports there or fought there. I would think of how proud Ducky Castille must have been getting cheered by the crowd during that NIT game. I wondered where he was now— if he was out looking for a job, like me.

I hailed a checker cab—for the leg room—in Madison

Square Garden's portico and made it to a hotel a few blocks from Times Square with twenty minutes to spare for my interview. My dad taught me that *on time* was late so always be early to make a good impression. It was in a busy fourth-floor hotel suite filled with sounds of the streets, the honking and sirens filtering through the cream-colored wooden blinds covering two half-opened corner windows. Three applicants for the same job were sitting around a fold out card table taking a test and two more applicants were ready to leave, waiting for me to come through the door so they could get by.

A man in horn-rimmed glasses, shirt sleeves, and tie walked up to me with three file folders in his hand. He looked beleaguered from the repetition of spending a week on his task—a small part of the back of his shirt was pulled up from his pants—but he appeared fulfilled with his day's accomplishments, with sweaty armpits and five unsharpened pencils sticking up from his shirt pocket. He looked like he had been on this grist mill for days now and was just going through a routine. He smiled.

"Name?" he asked.

"Jerry Antil," I said.

"Oh right," he said, shaking my hand. "Oh good, you're early. Step over here, Mr. Antil, let me bring you up to speed."

We stepped over by the chairs facing the corner window.

"Mr. Antil, are you familiar with AAMCO?" he asked.

"I am," I said.

Turns out, I wasn't. I thought it was American Motors Corporation—Nash and Jeep. Little did I know it was the AAMCO Automatic Transmissions Company. I went through the entire interview, even returning to Long Island, not realizing.

"We like your resume, that's why you're here. Mr. Antil, everyone we consider must take a Wonderlic Personnel Test. Based on those results, we may or may not call you back for a second interview in King of Prussia, Pennsylvania. Are you okay with that?" he asked.

"I thought I was here for Bell Advertising agency, a writing position," I said.

"AAMCO owns Bell Advertising. Bell Advertising is a house agency. You would work for Bell Advertising, if we select you, but your employer would be AAMCO."

"Does this position require a degree? I'm short on hours for a degree," I said so as not to waste his or my time.

"We only judge candidates by Wonderlic."

"What's Wonderlic?"

"They are a thinking ability tester." If you score high, we don't care about degrees. Are you okay with taking the test?"

"I'm fine with being tested," I said. "Where's King of Prussia?"

"Penn to Thirtieth Street Station in Philly. If we call you for a second interview it would be there you would go, our driver would pick you up, drive you to the interview and return you to the station."

"How many interviews?" I asked.

"There will be three interviews. This the first of the three."

"Okay."

"We pay commute and train expenses for interviews. Keep your receipts."

"Okay," I said.

"Good, sit over there." He pointed to an empty chair at the table. "Here's a pencil. The test is in this envelope. You will notice that the envelope is marked with a number three. When you open the envelope, I will give you fifteen seconds to get ready, and then I will begin timer number three and time you for exactly fifteen minutes. When the bell rings and I say stop, you stop, even if you aren't finished. Got it?"

"Got it," I said.

"Put the pencil down when I say stop," he repeated.

"Got it," I repeated.

I sat down, ripped the envelope open, and began figuring out how many feet of gold ribbon I could buy for twenty dollars if it cost a nickel per two feet … and which decimal was smaller … and which looked the same as the above, only upside down.

The thought ran through my head that the last time I took a

test like this, in high school, the guidance counselor had suggested that truck driving might be a good vocation. Then I remembered the note Mrs. Doxtator wrote on a composition I had written later that year: "This was one of the loveliest autumns I have read about."

Ding went the timer bell.

"Time's up, Mr. Antil," said the man, standing at a pencil sharpener.

I put the pencil down, two questions shy of finishing, and stood up. He walked over, picked up my test, and placed it in the envelope along with a sheet he had already filled out and a copy of my resume.

"Call me Jerry," I said.

"Mr. Antil, someone will call this week on our evaluation and what's next. Thanks for coming in. Have a nice day," he said, shaking my hand.

I opened the door, let another applicant step through. With a passion for local color of the greatest city in the world, I left the hotel for my next stop, Times Square. What could be better than a chess game on a second floor of the largest people destination in America? Its sins, the smells and sounds were a metaphor for Manhattan connecting the lights of Broadway to a fashionable Midtown. There was no place else like the '60s Times Square— the crotch of Manhattan. I walked to Forty-second Street, looking forward to hushed noises and smells of a chess game or two at the *"flea house"*—the New York Chess and Checker Club. Along the way I bought a Nathan's hotdog with mustard and relish. Distracted in thought of my interview I walked past the unimposing dark green, paint-chipped wooden door with glass and a gnarled window shade drawn down behind. Then I remembered my oversight, turned back, and found it.

I finished the hotdog before I touched the railing. I reached the top of the creaky stairs to a smoked-filled hall on the second floor where as many as fifty chess, Scrabble, and backgammon games were going on … some for money. Mostly chess, though. It resembled a pool hall for board games. Some chess games were timed by the clock, others by wet cigar stubs, ashtrays and coffee cups— or a *"What the fuck*!?" after a surprise *checkmate.* Observers gathering around the boards, watching every move; the silence was deafening, with an undercurrent of pieces being hammered down in attack sounding like a hooker's spiked heels on a sidewalk, or sets of dice being shaken in leather cups and spilled out like voodoo bones, or clocks being slapped, moving a game forward, or dinging, ending a game. I saw an empty chair at a chess board and stepped over to it. The unshaven man in the T-shirt sized me up and offered me a chance.

"You play the clock?" he asked.

"I play the clock," I said. When you play by the clock, every time you make a move, you hit the clock, stopping it and starting your opponent's clock.

"I'll give you twenty minutes against my five," he said.

This man would have only five minutes of playing time before his clock ran out. I would have twenty.

"I'll give you twenty to my five," he repeated. "Five bucks a game."

I took my suit coat off and rested it on my lap. This was Times Square; I wasn't about to hang it on my chair back.

We began, my twenty minutes on the clock against his five. I was okay until my third move, when I punched the clock and he said:

"You aren't very good, are you?"

The game was over soon. He mated me in seven moves.

"I quit," I said.

"Oh, don't quit, man," said the T-shirt, "please don't quit. I'll give you thirty to my five. For five bucks I'll even give you forty minutes. Okay, an hour for ten bucks, how about it, buddy? Please don't quit."

"Got to go," I said.

"How about Scrabble? Checkers?" the man pleaded. "I'll play you anything—backgammon. Two bucks a game. I'll go two to one—my four bucks to your two. Come on, don't leave—any game."

"I've had enough," I said. "Thanks."

I stood up and put my suit coat on.

My standing up was rejection. His shoulders slumped, his face and head sank down into a depression. He was alone at the board again in the only world he knew—a smoke-filled world that required two filled seats to survive; he had one empty, and he hadn't eaten. He squeezed a Zippo up a tight pantleg and popped it out of his pants pocket like a whitehead, clicked it open, snap-rolled it on the friction of his pant leg, then with an inch of golden flame lighted a Lucky Strike stuck to his lip. He inhaled with deep lung contraction, staring down into his space, exhaling a cloud of smoke in disgust on the queen that had won him his last three games.

I set five dollars on the board, for my loss, and left. My solace from getting beaten so badly came in knowing that becoming proficient at chess required a great number of games. I didn't know what it was about the place, the "*flea house.*" Had its own smell, like a locker room after a game. I had heard many guys on this particular second-floor birdhouse walkup on Forty-second Street were some of the most brilliant chess players in the world, some who lived from cigarette pack to cigarette pack, hoping not to scare off the fish from Long Island—too soon—not until they had some of their folding money stacked up on their side of the board, for maybe some food later, cigarettes, or wine for drinking in the shadows of flashing neon lighting, their midnight sunset.

I decided, for the moment, I would only play chess games for fun. I couldn't afford the fare at the New York Chess and Checker Club in Times Square. But I knew I'd be back, every time I came within blocks of the place, even if it was only to inhale the atmosphere and watch people. I learned that I could play anybody, as long as I played regularly, and improve. I didn't have to pay to learn. I waited for a checker cab and flagged it, heading to Penn Station for a train back to Bellerose.

Within the week I was asked to come down for an interview.

Chapter 24

I stayed in the city the night before so I could catch a 6:30 a.m. train at Penn Station to Thirtieth Street Station in Philadelphia. A company van was waiting to drive me through downtown Philadelphia, up next to the Schuylkill River with its long boats of college rowing teams out practicing, then up through Valley Forge to King of Prussia. I've always had a passion for the daring and the heroes of the Revolutionary War. Being driven through greater Philadelphia, I almost felt like I was revisiting it, although I had never been there before.

AAMCO headquarters was an office/warehouse-like building. A girl came to the lobby, asked me to follow her. We walked through an office area where fifty or sixty people sat at desks shuffling papers. She pushed a door open and directly behind it was an empty warehouse with light glowing through the exit door at the far back end. We headed through the warehouse. On the left was a glassed-off room filled with men at desks talking on their phones, some standing and talking, most sitting.

There were two glass booths with a man in each sitting and wearing earphones and telephone microphones, talking. To the right were metal stairs up to a loft where there appeared to be a training class. It was filled with people sitting at tables, an instructor standing. As we got closer to the far end of the warehouse, I could make out the wall and windows of another office area built against the back wall of the warehouse building. The girl opened and held the door for me and walked me to the first office. The man inside, wearing glasses, looked like he had slept in his wrinkled shirt and tie. He stood and offered his hand.

"John Bannon, Jerry, nice to meet you," he said. "Come in, have a seat."

When John sat down behind his desk, the air conditioning unit in the window just behind his head rumbled on.

"Is this the advertising department?" I asked.

"Bell Agency," said John. "We're a captive house agency for AAMCO. From your resume I would have thought you were older."

John had a simple honesty in his eyes. He appeared to be incisive, intelligent, and reminded me of Mike Jones and John Lennon.

"Other than getting my degree, I've done about everything else," I said.

"First, about me, the empty desk we're trying to fill, and then we'll dig into your bag of tricks. Good for you?" he asked.

"Good for me," I said.

"I'm John Bannon, marketing director of AAMCO Automatic Transmissions, Inc., president of Bell Advertising Agency, and I drink too much. Heard of Miss Rheingold?" he asked.

"Sure, who hasn't?" I asked.

"That was mine," he said. "Advertising VP Rheingold; more recently, VP advertising, Pepsi."

Pete Sealey was a hero of mine—running huge brands, the likes of Duncan Hines, Crisco, Captain Crunch, even Sprite, world-famous brands ... but for some reason, meeting a guy who had handled all of Pepsi Cola—dang, that was like sitting with Babe Ruth. I lost decorum.

"No shit?" I blurted. "*The* Pepsi Cola? The 'Come Alive, You're in the Pepsi Generation' Pepsi?"

John lit a cigarette and laughed. "No shit."

"What's the wildest thing you've ever done?" I asked.

John leaned in, like he was sitting around a campfire.

"Okay, first off, I learned early to never go anywhere without a photographer in my pocket, especially in New York City—fucking city is brimming with stories, why risk missing one?"

"That's the truth," I said, interrupting him. A good photographer can write better than any of us...better stories."

"Shit," John said. "That's good. A good photographer can write better than a writer. You mind if I use that?"

"Be my guest."

"So, where was I?"

"New York City – brimming with stories," I said.

"Oh yeah. A story in New York City is news worldwide. So there was a thing going on—a celebration thing or ceremony, can't remember—at St. Patrick's Cathedral, something with General Dwight D. Eisenhower—Ike—and a bunch of bigwigs attending. I got a seat at it through a contact at a network; my photographer got a seat further back. When it was over and Ike came walking up the aisle with a big friendly smile, I just reached out, held a Pepsi out for him—and he took it with a grin. Snap ... front-page stuff." John beamed, rethinking it in his head.

"Amazing third-party endorsement," I said.

"Whether he wanted to or not," chided John. "You know your stuff," he added.

He went on, "It worked well in football locker rooms, too. Hand a quarterback or some star a can or bottle. Hell, who doesn't like Pepsi? It's like unpaid endorsements. They know it, know the cameras are watching them, and show off drinking it. They'd get printed somewhere, the pictures, they'd make impressions."

"What is AAMCO?" I conceded. "I thought it was American Motors at first."

"It's a franchise. Stands for Anthony A. Martino Company; he had a bunch of shops for years in Philadelphia. What's important for you to know coming in is that it's first and always a franchise business. Pepsi is a franchise. Chevrolet is a franchise. Blue Cross Blue Shield is a franchise. A franchise has offices or businesses all over the country under the company brand—like an AAMCO center that is owned by the individual person, a franchisee. They have to follow the head office rules, but each franchisee owns and operates their own unit for a given period—ten years, in our case. A non-franchise company's branch office is just a company's branch office, run by employees, not owners."

"So a franchisee pays you and buys the rights to operate one of your businesses and keep the profits, if there are any?"

"Yes, and some of them can lose, just like any other business. Buying a franchise from an established company like AAMCO with proven guidelines and operations and procedures manuals can control their risks."

"What do you get out of it?" I asked.

"A royalty; they each pay us a small percentage of their sales to use our brand and follow our guidelines," said John. "Hell, I think the Better Business Bureau is even a franchise. The country runs on franchises. The business this franchise happens to be in is transmission repair. AAMCO Automatic Transmissions is taking transmission repair from the oil puddled alleys of America and putting it on Main Street USA during a recession where people are keeping their cars longer and will need repairs."

"I did lots of things for franchise companies," I said. "Frisch's Big Boy, Carroll's Hamburgers, McDonald's, Red Barn restaurants, more," I said.

"Let me show you the big picture and what the scene is here, see if we fit," John began. "I like your resume—came off as a creative guy with balls, not afraid to try things, made some successes, probably smart enough to have never thought of the money, sometimes rich, but never poor. I told personnel I wanted to meet you, see what you're made of. I liked the read of your resume; sucker was, how many, eight pages?" he asked.

"They gave me a test," I said.

"It's genius," he said, "the tests, not sure whose idea it was. They test everybody. If you make a hundred thirty-eight on the Wonderlic, they automatically make you assistant to the president … they figure you're smart enough to do anything, or figure anything out. With the right score, one day you could be running Parts, the next day Operations or Franchise Sales," he said, lighting another cigarette.

"What'd I get? Can you tell me?" I asked.

"Can't tell you. Oh, hell, I think you're the guy. One thirty-six, respectable," he said. "In the one twenties or less, you wouldn't be here."

John walked me through the agency, introducing me to several writers, including a young guy in horn-rimmed glasses, Andy Mensing, his lead writer; then to Chet Zisk, the art director.

"Chet has been with me all the way—every Rheingold girl,

the whole Pepsi trip. He's the best designer on the east coast."

Chet and I shook hands as John and I turned and went back into his office, this time closing the door.

"Look, Jerry, most people are screwed up when it comes to advertising. They try to make a big job out of it. They don't get it. It's about moving product, getting it out the door. You find someone who falls in love with their product and they'll lose it every time. They'll focus on the romance of it—it's an orgy—but will drop the ball on the task at hand—moving product. We create one, maybe two commercials; I hire an agency in every city to place the commercial where I tell them to place it and they get the fifteen percent."

"Was the Zsa Zsa Gabor television spot yours?" I asked.

"Bob Morgan, the owner and president, dreamed it up, I produced it. It's all we've been running, coast to coast. It's all we need to run. We pound it. We're editing ones with Johnny Unitas and Wilt Chamberlain for follow-up."

"It takes at least eight to ten message impressions of your brand and concept on your target audience to make impact," I said. "You only need one commercial."

John dropped his jaw.

"Well I'll be goddamned, a writer who knows marketing. The job's yours, if you want it, but we still have to talk," John said, waving through the window at his secretary, motioning for two coffees.

"How can you write and not know marketing?" I asked.

"Jerry, in franchising there are two pieces to the puzzle. Most writers don't get it. They come in here trying to dream up the next Zsa Zsa thing, thinking it'll make them a star. They change marketing directors here faster than a broad changes hats. If you got the sense to figure it out, you can own the world," said John.

Our coffee came.

"Keep it coming, Diane," John said to his secretary.

"Franchising is two things. On one hand"—he raised his left arm— "it's *operations*. It's the operations department's job to develop our products and procedures, to train, manage, oversee, mentor, monitor, police the franchise system, the franchisees, and to see they are towing the line on the rigid standards—a uniform set of policies and procedures set forth in the franchise agreement—and that they're making their weekly sales reports and paying their royalty and spending their requirement in advertising. Our operations director is Harold Nedell; he's tough, he's good. He'll come in once in a while, ask for things—some graphics, some point of sale. Don't think about it; just get it done for him."

John raised his other arm.

"*Marketing* is the other arm. Now you may think that Zsa Zsa is our advertising, but you'd be wrong. Belting Zsa Zsa out there is simple cannon fire, it's shrapnel pounding out impressions, building the AAMCO name. It's no-brainer simple. One commercial, one group of buys in cities we have franchised centers in. Advertising to Bell Advertising is 'franchise sales advertising.' That pays the bills. Translated, that means advertising to the portion of the public looking to get into business for themselves. We advertise all over the place for these prospects—a budget of ten thousand dollars a month. That's a shit-pot load of money for the available media. *Wall Street Journal*, *New York Times*, franchise journals—like that is all we have. No one in the country spends near that much. That's why we're the fastest growing franchise."

"Why do you have to spend so much?" I asked.

"We ain't romantic," said John. "Everybody knows a McDonald's and a Big Boy."

"You've got a point," I said.

"Who the hell has a transmission shop on their list of things they want to do when they grow up?"

"Ha!" I guffawed.

"Focus on that, focus on getting people interested in AAMCO as an option for owning a business, and you'll win the prize," said John.

"What's the numbers?" I asked.

"Well, Mr. First Writer in fucking History Ever to Ask Me a Question Like That, I'll tell you," said John. "Ten grand a month in advertising is generating prospect leads or inquiries at the rate of $145 per lead. Approximately one in a hundred of them—someone who calls or contacts us from that advertising—becomes a qualified prospect."

"That's not a lot of prospects," I said.

"Not a lot at all. We're the fastest growing franchise in America. It's like an aphrodisiac," said John. "A lot of guys would just come in here and rest on the laurels we already established. They would just move things around on their desk and try to look important, hang on for the ride. If you don't get caught up with the bullshit, playing the rat-like agility advertising mind games, you could do well. Some ad guys get seduced by the romance of just playing the role."

"You don't know me," I said. "I was offered ten thousand dollars to write and produce a movie for a city in upstate New York, to help them attract a doctor. I spent a three-day weekend there scouting it out and told them a movie could bring a doctor in to look around, maybe go fishing, but it would take more than a movie to make them want to stay—the place was a dump."

"Did you tell them that?" asked John.

"Effen-A-Tweetee, I did."

"Effen-A-Tweetee? Effen-A-Tweetee? Interesting turn of phrase," John laughed.

"I cleaned it up. I can't be held responsible when I'm not at a typewriter," I said.

"Did you really call the city a dump?" he asked.

"Well, not 'dump,' but I said who would want to stay, the shape the city was in—something like that."

"Did they want to tar and feather you?" asked John.

"They offered me ten thousand dollars to conduct a six-month beautification program for their city," I said.

"Did you take it?" asked John.

"I told them to give me sixty-five dollars a week draw and a car. Their chamber of commerce wound up buying me a new VW Bug and giving me a sixty-five dollars a week draw on the balance."

"It was a big hit," said John.

"They couldn't come up with the money they owed me," I said. "They burned me, but yes, it was a success. They ran out of money, but I stayed and finished anyway."

"I read about that project in your resume. I wondered how the hell you fit a city beautification in the middle of twenty film productions. It made as much sense to me as taking a bowling ball on a fishing trip. Want the job or not?" asked John.

"Isn't there another interview?" I asked.

"Only if I wasn't sure. I'm sure," said John.

"I don't know anything about cars," I said.

"Good," said John.

"But I want the job," I said.

"Jobs yours," said John.

"I'll have to commute from the city for a while."

John opened his desk drawer, pulled out a key, and slid it over to me.

"Put this in your pocket. It's a key to a big house in Bridgeport that AAMCO owns—rooms for executives who need to stay over. It's free, maid service, use it as often as you'd like."

"Are writers executives here?" I asked.

"You're now our marketing manager, my assistant. Start Monday, get back there and grab an empty desk—start writing." he laughed.

I spent the next two months commuting to Philadelphia from New York City, looking out my back window of the warehouse, meeting with Jerry Marcus, franchise director. Jerry had a team of twelve franchise sales specialists working for him. One guy, Ned Reid introduced himself to me as the token Negro in Franchise Sales. Ned and I became great friends. We'd go to jazz clubs and golf driving ranges. Every Monday morning Jerry Marcus and I would have a lead report meeting, analyzing the cost per lead by media and overall cost averages. Jerry was also a pilot and took me to a private airport and encouraged me to take lessons. I went every week, took three hours, and was ready for my solo flight.

"Don't do it," said my instructor.

"Why not?" I asked.

"Jerry, when you're in the air you can't be looking at birds and clouds and other distractions. You can't do anything other than keep an eye on the horizon and your wings level."

"I agree," I said. "Marcus and Sealey are good at it, I'm not. Thanks, you probably saved my life."

Then one day it dawned on me like I was making a great discovery. I sat at my desk, put a sheet of paper into my typewriter, and began typing:

AAMCO Automatic Transmissions, Inc.

85% of the people who saw the name AAMCO at the top of this ad won't even begin the sentence you are reading now. Why? They think they have to be mechanics. They're wrong, they need to be executives.

10% won't be able to raise the $17,500 fee required for getting an AAMCO franchise.

The remaining 5% will call or write AAMCO before this [name of media] gets routed to the next name on the list.

The ad was tested in the *Wall Street Journal* and *New York Times* Sunday classifieds. Franchise lead costs dropped in a week from the traditional $145 an inquiry-lead to $35 an inquiry-lead, holding the same conversion and closing percentages. I moved into John's office, now bumping my head on the window air conditioner, and John moved to a start-up retail clothing store franchise concept, Suzanne's.

Over time I called and interviewed advertising agencies and television general managers in 132 metropolitan areas, asking remedial questions on media-buy efficiencies with a focus on repetitive impressions for best impact. I would compare answers, always asking myself how I could do it better, just as Big Mike, Mr. V, and Pete Sealey had taught me. The more local agencies I spoke with and the more television station general managers I had a chance to interview, the more I realized that the entire television broadcasting system was just beginning to come into its own coming of age, as it were. The more I called, the more I was convinced—Peter Sealey was ahead of any marketing curve, and this was a time of television media's puberty.

AAMCO was mushrooming. On any given day I'd have a group coming in wanting me to sponsor an Indy racing car; another group from a company called Hanna-Barbera wanted me to sponsor a new 'blue collar' cartoon series, *The Flintstones.* A gentleman from New York City asked me to meet him for dinner at the famous Bookbinders restaurant, to talk a job proposal. He wanted me to consider heading up marketing for a group of television stations they were organizing, to be called NET—later, PBS. I would get a job offer a month; one seemed more persistent than the others. The president of Bonanza International Food Franchising, Inc., in Dallas called me repeatedly, asking me to consider joining their company as marketing vice president. I had been to Dallas once, working with Euel Box while scoring a movie I was producing. Its heat was all I remembered. I just couldn't see myself in Jeeps, shooting varmints, jumping over rattlers and tumbleweed. I kept wishing him a nice day and going about my business at AAMCO. I was learning franchising from the best, most disciplined franchise marketing company in the US, according to several authorities in the industry, an industry— franchising— that was the hope for America—to turn the country around through entrepreneurship and bring it out of recession. I still had a lot to learn.

Then I got the call.

"Jerry Antil," I said into the phone.

"Mr. Morgan would like to see you in his office."

"When?"

"Now."

A walk to Mr. Morgan's office was always a long walk for anybody. I didn't know what to expect. It was rare, if ever, that the owner of the company would call a lower-management guy like me into his office. When I arrived, I was told to go right in. His desk was a large oval walnut desk on a pedestal. His chair was a tall black leather wing-back; the wall behind him was lined with half empty bookshelves. He was a soft-spoken man, tall and confident. Mr. Morgan always seemed to make it a point, when talking, to tell of the failures he'd had in his business career. Using himself as an example, he would encourage others to never stop trying. Four of his top assistants and his attorney, Marty Katz, sat around the table.

Catching my eye, Mr. Morgan didn't invite me to sit. He looked me in the eye like he had a message to deliver—not conversation.

"We're having issues in New York State," he said. "Big issues."

"What issues, Mr. Morgan?" I asked.

"Problems with a franchisee in Buffalo getting on the wrong side of the wrong person. The attorney general's office in New York State padlocked the doors of all the AAMCO centers, shutting us down statewide. They do not want to understand the structure of the franchising concept—that the actions of one particular independent owner-operator who steps out of compliance with policy and procedure does not represent an entire system, and will be monitored and taken out of the system if actions persist. We police our own in the course of our reporting process, and will remove them for violating their franchise agreement if necessary."

He watched my eyes and let it sink in. Then he continued.

"Good things have been coming out of your department, Jerry. Go to New York and come up with something that will get our centers opened, while we work on it from this end. You have five days at which time we'll try something else. You may go," he said, staring at me with a smile.

Every face sitting around his desk looked pale. After I left and pulled the door, I was certain they would get paler. I had no idea what had happened in Buffalo, but by the looks of the room, whatever it was had happened because of a hole in franchisee contact, training, or monitoring. I walked the hall to my office thinking. I pushed the door open and walked by my secretary.

"Find out when the next train leaves to Penn Station, get me a travel advance in cash, five hundred dollars, and if the mail van is gone, have a cab here an hour before the train to take me."

The company had a van and driver who visited the post office daily to pick up our mail. If he wasn't busy, some executives would ask him to drive instead of waiting for a cab.

"Send Chet in," I said.

Chet Zisk, our designer and art director, was a good friend by now. He came in, closed the door, and stood there waiting.

"Where the hell is there someone who can show me what to do? I only have a hint of what's going on, don't know if I can even talk about it. Have you heard anything?" I asked.

"I talked with Jerry Marcus," Chet said.

"Does Jerry know anything?" I asked.

"You didn't hear this from me. A franchisee in New York, a real hothead, got pissed when an undercover agent took a brand-new car into his shop just to see what his center would do."

"Buffalo," I said.

"Right," said Chet. "When the attorney general's agent called him from a payphone to ask about the car, the franchisee told him the transmission pan was out and there were metal shavings in it and he needed a new transmission—and that's when the agent told him it was a new car and laughed through the phone. The asshole got riled that his mechanic had wasted time, working on the car in vain—a setup—and apparently he left the transmission pan sitting on the front seat."

"Did the mechanic put the metal filings in the transmission pan to make it look like it needed work?" I asked.

"Every new car will have metal filings in its transmission pan," said Chet.

"Shit," I said.

"I heard he told the agent to go fuck himself and to put the transmission pan back himself," said Chet.

"Christ," I said.

"One hothead franchisee that shouldn't have been a franchisee can hurt it for the hundreds of good guys out there. Now all of New York State is closed for AAMCO. We monitor them but have to do better somehow. The Operation Department does, when they check 'em out before they become franchisees—interview them, something."

My secretary pushed my door open.

"Jerry, here's the money; please count it and sign the receipt. A cab will be here in half an hour. What else will you need?" asked my secretary.

"A briefcase with sharpened pencils, legal pads, and Manhattan's Yellow Pages. I can't think of anything else. Thanks," I said.

Chet shook my hand. "Good luck," he said. He started to walk out, paused, and turned. "It was Marcus."

"What about Marcus?" I asked.

"He had you called into Morgan's office. I do know that."

"Why me?" I asked, thinking about the pricey talent sitting around Morgan's desk, each one at much higher pay grades than me.

"He told Morgan you were the only one ever to take the time to figure out the franchise sales-lead thing and you hit it on the nose; he convinced him you're the best to figure this out, too."

"Jerry Marcus said all that?" I asked.

"He's right. Good luck."

"Thanks, Chet," I said.

"And bring me a salami from Katz's Deli," said Chet.

He walked out and back to his art board.

Chapter 25

Whenever I stepped into an edifice of American culture, like Philadelphia's Thirtieth Street Station felt like to me, I would melt into it, taking it in, every inch, every facet, every piece of molding, facial expression of passersby, every mood. I had half an hour—a lifetime; I wanted to absorb the sensuality of this living, breathing part of history, a complex organ in the soul of Philadelphia, one that had seen generations before me; it was a cathedral of adventure's beginnings and ends. What famous, anxious, desperate explorers, winners, defenders, losers, the lost, presidents had walked between the row upon row of long, antique wooden benches or sat right where I was sitting and admired the enormous hand painted murals on the walls? Had movies been shot here?

I listened to the echoes of the train announcer celebrating another live performance, announcing boarding and departure times of my train. I stood up and began to move, following the backs of faceless, expressionless heads walking through the hall and down the steps like the cows had once come down from the pasture at farmer Parker's back in Delphi Falls, slowly, methodically, to a purpose.

I asked a conductor, "Which direction is it to New York?" as I boarded and took a seat facing south, on the east side of the train, so I could see where we'd been. After the first jerk or two, the iron crunch of the cars, we soon came into daylight, and images came to my mind of the slow, mournful train ride for President Kennedy's flag-draped casket—made by the company I'd shot a movie for, Marcellus Casket Company in Syracuse—the memory rippling through my brain with every clacking of the same track that had taken his coffin to its rest. I remembered shaking John Kennedy's hand in front of the Sheraton Gibson hotel in Cincinnati when he was a young senator while I was at Xavier. I traveled back in mind to 1945, when my mother wept while listening to a single quiet voice, the echoing clip clop of horseshoes, the hallowed drumbeats of President Roosevelt's funeral procession on the radio.

The afternoon sun reflection jumped from a home's window and slapped my face, stirring me; I stood up, walked back to the dining car, threw my briefcase on an empty booth table, and ordered two coffees, regular, to save time. I needed to think. I felt I knew and had lived through moments like this before, the uncertainty of these times for AAMCO in New York. I thought back to the loneliness of moving six times when I was sixteen and surviving. The time I spent in jail and survived. I had fallen a lot but there hadn't been a cliff I hadn't been able to climb if I didn't quit trying. Traits my father and mother instilled in me helped me decide a course of action for the problem at hand, calmly. I owed my penchant for recovery to one simple set of guiding principles, my ability to listen to and to learn from the right experiences, the right people, doing what I thought was right and not worrying what others thought.

I carried my coffees to the table, sat down, and pulled out a pad and pencil, and began scribbling my resources. On separate lines, about ten lines spacing between each, I wrote, "Big Mike," "Mr. V," and "Peter S. Sealey." They were my resources. What each of them taught me was all I would need to know. Big Mike had taught me to always do my research—define my universe, then do the numbers, be bigger than life, think outside the box, and don't be afraid what anyone thought; and, of course, when a big dog runs at me, whistle for it. Mr. V taught me that life was a banquet, an adventure, and if I didn't know the rules, make some, and invite everyone, accept the challenges, always keep in motion, and follow my heart and dreams. Peter Sealey—the butter knife of marketing. Define the common denominators (trends). Go for repeat impressions, first by third-party endorsement. He would say a marketing professional's role is to seek out, identify, and define areas of opportunity for your brand or concept, create a simple, one-page plan including objective, strategy, execution, and implementation—and act on it, be decisive, within four fences: budget, ethics, policy, and law. Be relentless in doing it—pound the crap out of your message until everyone in your universe has seen or heard it eight, ten times. I remembered the car ride with Governor Michael DiSalle and his telling me to aim low.

When we arrived, I walked through Penn Station once again but not like I had every other day. It was now with a determination. I knew I had to create something, discover something. I knew I had to do it soon. The escalator up let my imagination once again see the welcoming Madison Square Garden and salute it with a smile, this time taking me back to the 1920s tale of adventure when my dad watched Max Schmeling fight Primo Carnera, and his getting to meet and shake the defeated Carnera's hand; I was reminded that this new fight, for me, wasn't over—this was only round one. With a sense of urgency I decided I wasn't walking this day; I flagged a taxi, looking across Seventh Avenue at the New Yorker hotel, where I knew my dad stayed for meetings in the early 1940s with other bakers from across the country during the creation of the Sunbeam bread brand.

"New York Public Library, Forty-second," I said.

"Which way you want to go, buddy?" yanked the cabby with the out-of-towner test. The library was eight blocks away. Wrong answer could be costly for an unsuspecting out-of-towner. I decided to put the cabby in his place, call him out for trying to run up the fare.

"Oh, I don't know, pal," I said. "I always enjoy a quick route—maybe take the ferry down through Staten Island, maybe up through Westchester and around, run up the meter getting to the library eight blocks from here," I snapped.

"I was just askin', pal, no need to get snippy, I was just askin'," he pouted.

"No, you weren't, you wanted to gouge me by hiking the fare like I was a tourist."

He didn't answer, turned his head forward, avoiding the rearview mirror. He pulled over in front of the library. The fare was $1.75; I handed him a five.

"You're the first impression a lot of people have in New York City, bud. Act nice, pretend they're your family—keep the change."

He didn't say a word, but I could tell he got my meaning, gestured a sheepish thanks for my tip. I got out, stood on the sidewalk, and stared up at the lions still protecting the massive library. I stood there for as long as fifteen minutes before I walked the steps and entered one of the city's great landmarks, a library that had become an icon in the movie *Miracle on 34ᵗʰ Street*, about the bags of letters to Santa Claus.

The library was now an old friend of mine. It was here I spent days finding the names and addresses of those companies throughout the east coast. It was here I hoped to find secrets to the clues I needed. I looked at my watch and had the best part of the day left, so I climbed the steps, entered the kingdom, and walked the great halls of quiet and echo. I saw studying, reading, the careful turning of pages. I walked and looked at the books on the shelves and the molding around the ceiling and the furniture. I came upon four, what looked like voting machines, without the curtain. A lady was sitting in front of one. I paused and watched. It was a microfiche. With the machine she was able to look at a small, card-shaped piece of film from the archives and see an entire old newspaper projected up on the screen. I watched over her shoulder as she manipulated several pages on the screen until she found the article she wanted. I walked to the librarian.

"Ma'am, that machine over there," I said, pointing, "what can it do?"

"Old newspapers, maps, documents, if they have been stored on microfiche in our archives, you can look them up and read them there; it's a service to researchers or students writing papers. What are you looking for?" she asked.

"What say I wanted to see the front page of the *New York Times*, maybe even the front page of every *New York Times* back a year, would it do that for me?" I asked.

"Microfilm, then, sir. You would want that machine on the wall over there. Every *New York Times* has been archived and there are many on each spool, you just have to roll through the spool to the front page. Would you like me to get you started?"

I placed my pencils on the left side of the machine, my

legal pads on the right. My strategy was simple. I was going to look at every front page of the *New York Times* back a year if I had to and see if there was a local subject or topic that appeared more often than others. If I could see what interested a New Yorker enough to reappear on the front page of the *New York Times*, it could be a telling clue for opportunity. I spent the rest of the day, almost to closing, and the following morning turning the dial on the machine, scanning the pages, writing the different storylines on my legal pad, adding hash marks next to repeated topics. By noon the second day I had discovered the winner: Senator Robert F. Kennedy's pet project, the Bedford Stuyvesant Rehabilitation Project. Senator Kennedy was now dead, tragically assassinated in LA, but his legacy lived on. The Bed-Stuy [(*pronounced* Bed-St(eye)] area of Brooklyn was like a war zone. It was a black ghetto, a forgotten slum. There were rumors and stories of taxicabs with white drivers or passengers being turned over by agitated locals and set on fire. I wrote down the address of the Bedford Stuyvesant Restoration Center, closed my briefcase, and walked over to the lady librarian who had been so helpful.

"What's your name? I asked. "I'm Jerry."

"Helen," she answered.

I extended my hand. "Helen, thank you for helping me out," I said.

"Were you able to find what you needed?" she asked.

"I did indeed, thank you for your patience," I said.

"You're welcome, Jerry. Any time," she whispered.

I walked through the great library once more before leaving, letting everything sink in and settle in my mind. I remembered the beautification program I had created and managed for the City of Ogdensburg and how the locals had so much love and loyalty toward their own hometown. Home is home, ran through my brain. Some are unpaved streets, some are echoes of a forgotten past, but they're still home to someone. I stepped out, skipped down the steps, and flagged a cab. This Bed-Stuy place may sound like a ghetto, but it must be home to somebody.

"Bed-Stuy, please, we're going to ..." I started to say to the driver.

"Get out, sir."

"Excuse me?" I asked.

"Ain't going to Bed-Stuy. Get out, sir," said the cabby.

The next three cabs I flagged were with the same result. No one was going to risk driving a white man into Bed-Stuy, putting us in harm's way. I rented a Hertz car and drove myself. I got there without incident, parked, went into the Restoration Center's building, up to the floor where the offices were. I was met by a mid-forties, tastefully tailored woman with the warm smile and quiet demeanor of a Jacqueline Kennedy. The lady graciously extended her hand welcoming me— a white man, into her world. We shook hands with full eye contact, just as my mom and dad taught me.

"I've read a lot of headlines about your Bedford Stuyvesant Restoration," I said.

"We've made some news," the lady said as if she was a bit embarrassed by it.

"Can you explain what you're trying to do here?" I asked.

"Would you like coffee, Mr. Antil?" the lady asked.

"If you'll join me, I'd love a cup. Thank you."

"I'd be delighted, it's fresh," she said.

As she poured coffee into cups already placed on a silver tray on the coffee table this elegant lady told me the story of Bed-Stuy; of how Mayor John Lindsey, Senator Robert F. Kennedy and Senator Jacob Javits were trying to help the community redevelop.

"Mr. Antil, we're trying to motivate the local blacks, my brothers and sisters to step forwards and bootstrap the community into seeing the advantages of creating jobs through commerce. To create their own businesses that everyone could benefit by doing business with each other—the laundry, the grocer, the appliance repair shop—building a grassroots infrastructure, an economy right here in the neighborhood," she explained.

I looked out the window down to the streets, the alleys, which seemed vacant and empty.

"We're trying to attract businesses to come into the area

and give our people a chance," she added.

"Have any stepped up to the plate?" I asked.

"Outside bankers have offered financing to outside developers— but outsiders."

"But not to blacks," I said. "And not to locals."

"Not one," she admitted. "Not a soul. Banks are reluctant to talk to our residents. My Bedford Stuyvesant brothers and sisters have not been acknowledged much less accepted. Outsiders think we created this environment. Most have only learned to survive in it."

"My dad taught me something about people and cultures," I said.

"Yes? And what did your father teach you?" she asked.

"He taught me to never look through a person, look him directly in the eye, maybe break bread with them and you're certain to become friends."

"Such a lovely thought," she said.

"AAMCO is stepping forward, ma'am," I said. "I have the authority to give anyone you select in your community a fully equipped, fully paid-for AAMCO Automatic Transmission Center—complete with intensive and ongoing free training and support," I said.

"God bless you," she said.

She went into her office and came out with a gift for me. It was a picture of Robert F. Kennedy. I carefully tucked it into my briefcase.

"I'll courier you information for a press conference," she said. "Can your people attend?"

"They will be delighted," I assured her.

I returned my car to Hertz, caught a cab to Penn Station, boarded, and slept until I could hear the wheels squeaking at the North Philadelphia station, waking me in time to splash my face and get ready for the next stop at Thirtieth Street Station.

I walked boldly into the executive offices, asking Mr. Morgan's secretary to announce me. She did so immediately and told me to go right in. Three execs were sitting across from Mr.

Morgan.

"Back so soon?" Mr. Morgan asked.

"Just got here," I said.

"That was fast. What'd you find?" asked Mr. Morgan.

I told him what I was able to find and accomplish in the two days and what I had committed to on behalf of the company. I told them about Senator Jacob Javits's and Robert F. Kennedy's passion for this project and how no one had come forward to help the neighborhood with a locally owned business, and it only made sense for us to be the first.

"Javits, you say?" asked Mr. Morgan.

"Bed-Stuy Restoration is the Senator's pet project...and it's Bobby Kennedy's legacy," I said.

"If they accept, the state will have to open our centers," said Morgan.

I then admitted I was fully aware that making a commitment of this magnitude without authority could be a cause for dismissal. Morgan smiled broadly. He turned and instructed one of the executives to get Senator Jacob Javits on the phone. Patiently he explained to him the concept of franchising and independent owners and operators—and the enormous investment we were making in the project that both he, along with Senator Robert F. Kennedy, had started so long ago. We only asked the state's indulgence in letting us manage our operators and monitor and train them, weeding out when we had to.

I received a VIP invitation list for the press party, which included Mayor Lindsay, Senator Jacob Javits, Ethel Kennedy, Jacqueline Kennedy, and a virtual *Who's Who* list of others. The state attorney general's office relented, permitted the centers to open again, and confined their grievance to the one single operator. I wrote a speech for Mr. Morgan and enjoyed the press party, seeing the famous people, shaking Mayor Lindsay's hand. The following morning Mr. Morgan walked alone through the warehouse back to my office, stepped in without a word, shook my hand, handed me a copy of that day's *New York Times*, turned, and walked back to his office.

On the front page, a story reported an announcement from Mayor Lindsay: that Mr. Vernon C. Butler had become the first man to receive a business—an AAMCO Automatic Transmission Center—in Bedford Stuyvesant, the first Negro to become a franchisee for AAMCO in the country; and as a result that Ethel Kennedy had said yes to taking Robert F. Kennedy's place on the board.

Chapter 26

The president of Bonanza International Food Franchising, Inc. (BIFFI), called.

"Jerry, consider coming to Dallas for a visit, seeing our headquarters, and meeting some people. I feel certain you won't be disappointed, with Dallas or the opportunity. On the contrary, I believe you will be most impressed."

"I'm flattered, but why me?" I asked.

"Our chairman and his brother have taken a restaurant chain over from a failing Diversa Corporation, Bonanza Sirloin Pits; it was in receivership. We had a public offering and paid the debt, but the struggling steak-house chain needs a turnaround. In return for stock shares, we get to use the Cartwright characters from the television show, *Bonanza*, for up to a week a year—Lorne Greene, who plays Ben Cartwright, Dan Blocker, who plays Hoss, and Michael Landon, who plays Little Joe. None of them have any management interest in the company; we just get to use their television characters. That week gives us time to shoot commercials, do billboards, whatever we need them for. Cash flow is tight. We need the right people to steer us, to develop our franchise. I know your brother Fred from my Washington DC days, when he was VP of training for Marriott Corporation. He said you're just what we need—experienced in franchising, with an entrepreneurial spirit. He highly recommended you. Jerry, you're with the fastest growing franchise in the country. I think you could show us the way."

"I don't know what I know about the restaurant business. I've written training films and commercials for food franchises, though. Pretty detail-intensive business—pennies, pounds, and percentages count," I said.

"What did you know about transmissions?" he asked.

"You have a point. I still couldn't point one out if asked. What's your franchise sales ad budget and how many salespeople do you have in that department?" I asked.

"Maybe five, ten thousand a year, in trade pubs; we have

two full-time franchise sales directors," he said.

"A year? Did you say a year?" I asked.

"In that ballpark, yes," he said.

"We spend ten thousand a month and have twelve full-time franchise salespeople," I said.

"You'll have a free hand—all marketing," he said.

"I don't know. I can't see myself running around in a Jeep, sporting guns, shooting rattlesnakes," I said.

"What car do you see yourself in, Jerry? What would impress you?" he asked.

I turned my chair around and peered over the window air conditioner. An ops manager had just driven in and parked a Mercedes 230.

"A Mercedes 230, four-door," I said.

"I'm running into a meeting now, Jerry. Let me call you this afternoon if it's all right with you," he said.

"Call any time."

I went over to Chet's drawing board and asked him to lunch. I told him about the calls from Texas and asked his opinion. AAMCO was steaming right along; my only problem was not having more participation or influence in the operations portion of the business. I never felt my job was secure at AAMCO— they seemed to have a history of 'changing hats' frequently as John Bannon, who I replaced told me. I knew, from the offers I was getting literally each week, we were the new benchmark on the franchising industry—an industry that was about to bootstrap America into the land of opportunity we believed it was. Franchising was going to add a new word to the vocabulary of Middle America—entrepreneurism. Companies like AAMCO were legitimatizing the franchise industry with strong leveraged growth, strong consumer awareness, and solid operations. The failure rate for an individual going into business alone, on his own, was 70 to 80 percent within the first five years of operation. Under the guidance of a solid franchising brand, concept, and operations, failure of established franchised brick-and-mortar retail operations or locations was a few percentage points. Even if they weren't able to make a go of the business, the business could be sold to someone who might—a resale. Business opportunities dependent on "outside" sales were more vulnerable to the talents and drives of owners and sales teams. Professional, disciplined sales people had a better chance of doing well than people not sales experienced or disciplined—those who opted to sleep in or do their own thing.

The president of Bonanza International called again.

"Jerry, American Airlines has a first-class ticket in your name at the Philadelphia Airport. It is a round-trip ticket leaving Philadelphia Friday evening and returning Sunday afternoon. The plane lands at Love Field, in Dallas. Have a pencil to make some notes?"

"Shoot," I said.

"Love Field is on Mockingbird Lane, in the heart of the city. When we confirm the plane has landed, a new Mercedes 230, four-door, gray-beige, will be parked in front of the main entrance to the terminal. It's yours when you land. Your name will be on a card lying on its dashboard. The key will be resting on top of the driver's-side front tire," he said.

"Mine? Just for coming?"

"It's yours just to come and talk."

"You've got to be kidding," I said.

"Jerry, I lived most of my life and career in Washington, DC—a town known for its bullshit. Wasn't long after I moved to Texas I learned quickly, Texans rarely kid about three things— money, religion, or football—in about any order you name them. When you come out the airport drive, turn left on Mockingbird and drive all the way through Park Cities, you'll go past Southern Methodist University until you come to a tall Hilton Inn at the corner of Central and Mockingbird; it'll be on your right. A suite is paid for, waiting for your arrival, in your name. Will I see you Saturday? If so, I'll meet you in the hotel's restaurant for breakfast, let's say nine a.m.—let you sleep in," he said.

"Gray-beige?" I asked.

"Gray-beige," he affirmed.

"See you Saturday," I said and hung up.

"Jetsetter" was a term bandied about, but I wasn't to learn, until years later, its meaning. It was William F. Buckley, Jr. who explained what it was—that before the airline deregulation in the later 1970s, air travel was so expensive it was only affordable to a few. The fact was anyone who flew before deregulation was generally considered a jetsetter. It was nice, boarding a plane and the stewardess calling you by your name, pampering you all the way, seeing passengers in airports around the country you had seen in other airports or on other flights.

The first thing that sold me on Dallas was flying in under a full moon— coming into Texas at about thirty thousand feet. From as far as a half hour away the city glowed like a mass of sparkling green emerald and pearl necklace from the sky. It stretched on with the flatness of an ironing board, but with its own style and character that was legend. Dallas had everything but oil wells. When I asked a pilot walking through the terminal where all the cowboy hats were, he said, "If you see someone in Dallas wearing a cowboy hat, they're most likely from Milwaukee. Fort Worth is where you'll see the hats and boots."

The gray-beige Mercedes-Benz 230 four-door sedan was sitting dead center in front of the main entrance to the airport, safely in a "No Parking and No Standing" zone. It was obvious someone had arranged what's called in Texas a "whoa-pass" under the wiper blade and parked it there safe and secure. A "whoa-pass," I learned later, was an affectionate, tongue-in-cheek name for a small tablet-like folder you would carry. If a police officer walked up and asked why you were parked or standing illegally, you would simply hand the tablet to him. When he opened and read it, he'd say, "Whoa!" hand it back, and go on about his business. That was power. That was when I learned the difference between money and power. As huge as money, football, and religion were in Texas, power was bigger and usually controlled a little of all three.

The drive across Mockingbird Lane was the second reason I got sold on Dallas. It cut through Highland and University Park—second only to maybe Beverly Hills or Greenwich, Connecticut. Its rich, deep rose-red velvety azaleas and lines of yellow tulips and homes that looked like better parts of Westchester made the decision easy. The company had ample cash in the bank and stock value to pay the existing bills that caused the receivership in the first place and make some acquisitions. Until the restaurant chain could be expanded, however, there wouldn't be enough cash flow from existing daily sales to cover expenses. Seventeen million dollars in annual chain sales only meant half a million dollars in annual royalties coming in—not enough.

To add to the problem, in most instances royalties were split with area developers, the people who bought area territories and developed franchisees under them. It had an operations department that seemed knowledgeable, a likeable training team, and a floundering network of area developers who had invested in large territories—sometimes whole states—and split royalties for the restaurants they developed within their territories with the parent company. As a whole, they were not impressed at what they had seen to date at the national headquarters. The company had a large local advertising agency, Tracey Locke, handling advertising for subsidiaries. By noon on Sunday I was made an offer. A two-year option on twelve thousand shares of Bonanza International stock at two dollars a share. It was selling at forty-nine dollars as of that Friday. Double my salary from AAMCO, plus an added incentive of the Mercedes-Benz I was driving.

The president stood at his desk and extended his hand. "Do we have a deal, Jerry?"

I shook his hand. "We have a deal."

"Congratulations, Mr. Vice President of Marketing. You're now an officer of a NYSE publicly traded company."

I grinned.

"Not a bad accomplishment for a young man in his twenties," he said. "Welcome aboard."

The transition out of AAMCO was friendly. The "marketing lady" just changed hats again; turnover was part of the routine in a highly intense sales and marketing environment. I caught a train into Manhattan and a cab to Brooks Brothers on Madison Avenue, where I bought ten dress shirts, two tailored suits with vests, one double-breasted blazer, gray slacks, two pairs of Italian loafers, and a trench coat. I asked them to ship it to me at the Hilton Inn in Dallas, Texas.

Bonanza International's headquarters was at 6116 N. Central Expressway in Dallas. It was the original Dallas Cowboy building. I would catch elevators daily with the likes of Coach Tom Landry, Roger Staubach, Craig Morton, Walt Garrison, Mel Renfro, Too Tall Jones and sportscaster Verne Lundquist. There was a time Mickey Mantle had an office in the Cowboy building— Expressway Tower, probably one of the more famous addresses in Dallas in the 1960s.

By my second day at Bonanza, I was given the tour of the parent company's "corporate" suite of offices on the tenth floor. The suite was designed by world-famous set designer and builder Peter Wolf. Rumor was it cost the company about a hundred thousand dollars per office, of which there were three or four, as well as a reception area. Hand-hewn, carved, dark oak beams, plush red carpeting, and faux skylights lighting gardens of cactus and synthetic foliage; drapes that would make two trips along an entire wall at the push of a button—the first to cut out the sun, the second to make the room soundproof. Bulky, dark stained heavy oak Texas custom furniture filled the offices out.

If it wasn't for the fact there was no waitress standing in the front lobby without a stain on her uniform, and the fact I couldn't smell Ivory soap, I would have likened this visit to the tenth floor to my trip down to Newport, Kentucky, in my Caddy some years back. I went down to the real world, the simple Bonanza Sirloin Pit digs on the third floor.

"I want to schedule a fifteen-day partial tour of the system," I said. "I want to go see the problem areas first; plenty of time to see the good operators later."

The operations vice president looked at his secretary. "Let's select some units and markets and schedule three weeks of travel and itinerary for him."

"What? Why three weeks?" I asked.

"A fifteen-day tour in three five-day weeks," he said.

"A fifteen-day tour is fifteen days," I said.

"But you'll be traveling on weekends," he said.

"Are the restaurants open seven days a week?"

"Yes."

"Well, so is marketing ... and I don't want any unit owner or manager to know I'm coming. I'll walk in as a customer, go through their line and eat, and then I'll introduce myself," I insisted.

"Some cities have four or five restaurants."

"Then I'll eat four or five times a day."

I left the conference room, went back to my office, picked up the phone, and dialed Peter Sealey in New York.

"Peter, have you heard?"

"Heard what, big guy?"

"I'm the vice president of marketing at Bonanza International Food Franchising, in Dallas."

"What happened to AAMCO? Don't tell me you got fired, again."

"Can you believe that National Distiller asshole firing me like that?"

"Sounds like you've found your niche, big guy— franchising. Go for it. How did you wind up way the hell out in Texas?"

"What can I say, Pete, Bonanza made me an offer I couldn't refuse."

"What do they do?"

"The parent company is like a conglomerate thing, experimenting with a few businesses, but their main grunt— the one I'm with is a steak-house chain, a franchise, kind of like a Tad's—you know, the $1.19 steak served cafeteria-style?"

"I know Tad's well," said Peter. "Here in Manhattan. That type of restaurant is a growing trend in America these days, known as a 'family' restaurant. Not quite a full-service restaurant, making it more affordable, and not fast food, giving it a true sit-down dining experience. I'm proud of you, big guy. Let me know if I can do anything for you. I have a bit of news too."

"What's your news?" I asked.

"I'm moving to Atlanta—the New York of the South—working on Sprite."

"Are you flying Bonanza three-three-two-five-Charlie to Atlanta?"

"I just sold the plane," he said

"You sold the plane? You sold the plane?" I whimpered. "We were going to start the 'Mile High' club in that plane. Girls love that plane."

"Jerry, the expense of keeping it at Newark was too much, impossible, didn't make sense. I bit the bullet and sold it. I know, big guy—many fond memories. Hated to lose it just like when I gave up my first convertible, had to move on."

"Remember our flight to Greenbrier?" I asked.

"I do indeed," said Peter.

"I'm going on a tour of our restaurants, out to meet the franchisees and our area developers. Thought I would get your advice before I headed off," I said.

"Common denominators," said Peter.

"Common denominators?" I asked.

"Look for common denominators. There's quantitative research, tabulated from large numbers of people and there's qualitative research, a theory advanced by a Robert Merton of Columbia. It's about taking an educated gut feel of what's going on in a few samples. Roughly translated, it may mean if a restaurant's windows aren't clean, and there's no window-cleaning policy or procedure, there's a strong likelihood the floors, bathrooms, and kitchen will be dirty as well. But if the windows are dirty and there is a window-cleaning policy, chances are money is being taken from the till and not accurately accounted for, or food is going out the back door. Think tanks I've been in were strong advocates of focus group interviews, from my P&G experience right on up.

As Peter spoke I remembered that common denominators

on the front pages of New York Times newspapers made me a hero at AAMCO.

"Let the training disciplines you've written guide you. Watch for tiny signals in the restaurants, the small cracks that may be pervasive throughout the system, the chain. People are creatures of habit. Bad habits become the rule. Jerry, Coca-Cola practically invented franchising before most American companies existed. Store it up, what you observe, and wait and act on it after you get back to Dallas. Let the dust settle. You'll know when."

"So Pete, what I'm hearing is that thinking for the entire restaurant chain can cause the creation of monitorable solutions? Don't fix one at a time, fix them all at once?"

"Exactly."

"Bringing up issues one restaurant at a time would be yelling, 'The sky is falling, the sky is falling,' having little or no impact systemwide," I said.

"Knock 'em dead, big guy."

"Thanks Pete."

"Stay in touch," said Pete as we hung up.

I stepped on the first flight of the first leg of my fifteen-day trip in total confidence. I had grown up riding with my dad throughout upstate central New York as he went from grocery store to grocery store to see how nicely, straight and warm, his bakery's loaves of bread appeared on the store shelves, and making the owners and employees smile, no matter how small or large the store was. Peter was saying the same thing—almost as if marketing began with the first customer experience.

My first stop was Lubbock, Texas. After the plane touched down and pulled to the gate, I went into the men's room, opened my briefcase, and lifted out a legal pad filled with a week's worth of notes and questions about things to ask franchisees about advertising practices, point-of-purchase promotions, and public relations. Thinking of my talk with Pete, I didn't want to be distracted so I pitched the pad into the waste can and walked to the car rentals. I didn't need questions answered—I knew advertising—I needed to see if parking lots were clean and picked up, if restaurant windows were spotless, if smiles were on faces, if experiences were at top performances. I didn't give a rat's ass about whose toes I would be stepping on back in corporate operations—I had twelve thousand shares of stock selling at forty-nine dollars a share to protect, and a restaurant chain to turn around.

It wasn't long after seeing the fortieth restaurant that I realized the need for a term I coined and planned to sell to the president, *operational marketing*. My experience had been that franchising was a two-sided coin, a marketing side and an operations side, each side minding their own business. Thanks to Peter, I threw that theory out the window. I knew the power of creating awareness and I knew how to achieve it. The formula was Peter's bible. I knew it worked. But I also knew it came with a heady responsibility. Advertising could attract customers, but it would be operations—the customers' experience—that would bring them back again and again. Who in their right mind would try to attract customers for a bad customer experience, especially if they were dependent on repeat business— customers returning? It was settled in my mind: if marketing couldn't influence operations, advertising these steakhouses would be like painting a sinking ship. Marketing had to become paired with operations to save Bonanza.

The trip was exhilarating. I learned that most franchisees felt headquarters didn't know a flip about food service. I learned that many store owners were under the wrong impression that people didn't eat in Syracuse, or Dayton, or Hartford, like people ate in Dallas. Some franchisees thought they had bad locations. I learned that Tuesday was considered the worst day of the week for restaurant sales. I learned that many franchise owners had pride in ownership of a national brand but a tendency to "mom and pop" things with handwritten, homey—comfortable to them—signs and messages throughout their restaurants. They were friendly but unprofessional. I learned that the large menu boards with twelve eight-by-ten full color transparencies of steak and baked potato entrée plates in were turning blue— fading from the bright light bulbs behind them.

All I knew from my writing restaurant training film days was that the overwhelming value of the McDonald's Hamburger system was the public's perception of their continuity. The McDonald's customer in Syracuse, New York, knew exactly what to expect when visiting a McDonald's in Baltimore or Tulsa or Kansas City.

We weren't quite there yet.

I learned that I had a new secretary waiting for me on my return.

Jerome Mark Antil

Chapter 27

"Mr. Antil, I have a carton of mail. What would you like me to do with it?" she asked.

I pointed to the left of my desktop. "Internal mail and memos go here." I pointed to the right of my desktop. "External mail that needs signing goes over here. And call me Jerry; Mr. Antil is my father. Well, actually he's Big Mike. Just call me Jerry, call him Big Mike."

"Yes, sir."

I picked up an internal memo, a paper-clipped set of papers requiring my immediate attention. It was a monthly statement from the company's advertising agency, Tracey Locke. The invoice was for agency services for the previous month for all entities, in excess of $15,000. That would be the equivalent to $115,000 in 2020 money. One entity was Hickory Fare, the beginnings of a barbeque chain franchise with several "prototype" operations throughout the Dallas-Fort Worth area. The third was the "1849 Village," a test of an entertainment complex in Fort Worth that consisted of a movie theatre, a Bonanza Sirloin Pit, and a Hickory Fare barbeque restaurant all together in a park-like setting.

The invoice talked creation of table tents, handouts, newsletter designs—large expenses that wouldn't help clean the windows of the Bonanza Sirloin Pit in Memphis, or any of the ones in Louisiana or Ohio. Most of the agency expenses were my division's expenses—for worthless stuff, in my opinion. I picked up the phone and dialed Chet Zisk's home number in Philadelphia. My art director at AAMCO. I left a message with his wife, Lil, to have him call me when he got home.

"Tell Chet I need him here. You'll love Dallas, Lil," I said.

I needed to convert these agency expenses into something

useful. I walked into the president's office to share thoughts of my first voyage out.

"Thirty percent of our royalty income is going to pay an advertising agency."

"I'm not certain I understand," he said.

"Thirty percent of this huge bill is for hourly fees, not for things we can use. Fees to an agency that I don't think has a clue of the business we're in. We're not even at critical mass. (Enough cash flow to pay the bills.) We can't afford them," I said.

"Jerry, I wouldn't be too hasty. They're a highly respected agency. They have lofty credentials, they're sought after, and have a good reputation in the food service industry," he said.

"But what do they know about franchising?" I asked.

He didn't answer. He couldn't.

"We're in franchising first," I said. "We're in food service second."

"Oh, well, ah ..." he said.

"If we don't see to it that every restaurant in the chain is exactly the same in every respect, the way the controls of franchising agreements allow us to do, there won't be a chain of restaurants."

"Tell me what you need," he replied.

"Make it a policy that, until further notice, the advertising agency is only to act as a service agency—they are not to be proactive."

"Explain," he said.

"If they are service only, they only do things we ask for. If I need them, I'll turn the clock on and use them. If I don't, they can't be running up fees. Can we agree to that?" I asked.

"Yes, definitely," he said. "I'll put a memo out that you are now the only contact with the agency. What's next?"

"I'm heading out for another round. I'll start in Connecticut— to get there I have to fly to LaGuardia and drive up; then to Indiana, Minnesota, Kansas, and back here. I'll have a good fix on needs and a plan of attack shortly after that."

"Sounds good," he said. "Anything you need, ask."

"Tonight, I'm thinking of going over to the Loser's Club up on Mockingbird. Ever been there?" I asked.

"I never have; it's a popular club. Best known for having great music. Big stars go there after hours, sometimes they'll get on stage and jam. I understand it can get wild—lots of local musicians and other artists get on stage and perform. It may be fun. Are you going alone?" he asked.

"Yeah. A guy I met in the music business here, Euel Box, told me to check it out. He says what you said, that sometimes celebrities from the audience climb on stage and perform."

I stood and walked to his door.

"Until I get back from this round of trips, as to what we're talking, let's sit tight and I'll let the dust settle, I'll let it sink in," I said.

"I have to tell you, Jerry, I'm impressed with your approach, and I've passed it along upstairs that you run right at a problem and aren't afraid to dive in," said the president.

"My dad taught me, when a big dog runs at you, whistle for it," I said and left.

Dallas was a music capital, responsible for a preponderance of radio music jingles and stations' musical IDs. The Loser's Club was jam-packed—and in layers of tables reaching down past smoke-filled tiers of drink glass filled tabletops on different levels to a stage, with a sea of head-bouncing and arm-waving like a tide going out. Little Richard, carrot red died hair and dressed in bright colors, was pounding away on the piano, the crowd going Tutti-Frutti wild with him. Dallas was a dry county, alcohol sales prohibited— but for a buck at the door you became a member of their private club and could order drinks. I sat at a table on the top level with a couple next to a wall and ordered Cutty and water. On the wall I noticed a colorful sign for Budweiser Beer. Lighted from behind it had a full-color transparency of the Budweiser team of horses and a Dalmatian sitting on the wagon bench. Unlike our menu board's color shots of steak plates fading and turning blue, the Budweiser picture was bright and crystal clear. I stepped up and stood on my chair, trying to look at it, but couldn't quite reach it. I slipped my loafers off, stood on the tabletop, and reached the sign, lifting it and taking it from the wall and bringing it down to the tabletop. I got a casual glance from the couple sitting at my table, but they were enjoying the noise and the show and turned away.

"Hey, mister, what are you doing with the sign? You can't take that sign. Put it back!" the waiter demanded.

It was then a bouncer appeared on the scene.

"What seems to be the problem?" he asked, blocking out the light behind him.

"I'm not stealing the sign."

I reached in my pocket, pulled out a bill, and handed it to him. As he took it I saw it was a fifty, but it was too late to switch it for a ten.

"I'm trying to see how this sign is made; I'm in advertising is all. I'll put it back," I said.

The monster looked at the fifty. "Well, okay bud, but put it back on the wall and don't break it."

"I won't. Can you get me a screwdriver?"

"What!?" he snorted.

I handed him a twenty. He reached in his pocket and pulled out a jackknife and handed it to me. Within ten minutes I learned that the transparency of the picture in the sign wasn't a film transparency at all. It was printer's ink on a piece of clear plastic. Printer's ink wouldn't turn blue or fade like photo film or transparencies. I put the sign back together and hung it on the wall where it belonged. I finished my scotch, got up, walked toward the front door, and turned back.

"Where you going, mister?"

"Back to my table," I said.

"You've lost your seat walking away from it like that," said the bouncer. "Somebody's already in it."

"My shoes," I said. "I forgot my shoes."

The monster scratched his brow. "You from out of town?" he asked as I returned with them.

"I'm a Yankee," I admitted, leaning on him and slipping

my shoes back on. "A goddamned Yankee."

"S'all right, I'm from Erie, Pee A," he said.

"Oh, you poor bastard," I said.

"You got that right," he said.

"How'd you wind up in Dallas?" I asked.

"I play back up sax at some of the jingle houses," he said. "I tried to get a sax gig here for nights; they made me bouncer."

I leaned into his ear. "I got a speeding ticket in Erie once; I was on my way to Syracuse from Cincinnati, had to leave the justice of the peace my movie projector so he wouldn't lock me up—and give me time to come back with money and pay the fine."

I pushed the door open.

He smiled. "Come back anytime, friend. I'll get you closer to the stage."

I went back to Expressway Tower, had after hour security let me into my office, and wrote a note to my secretary that read:

"You won't see me this Monday, I have an 8 a.m. flight to LaGuardia. I'll be back on Saturday. Meantime I need you to go through the Yellow Pages and get sample books for each of five commercial photographers in Dallas. Tell them I'm looking for food photography. Also, find a sign-maker— one who does big signs and billboards for companies like McDonald's or Budweiser. Do your own homework, check the Yellow Pages, and make some calls on your own. Repeat— DO NOT go through the agency. I'll be back next week. Have photographers and sign people in my office Monday. I'll call you during my trip."

At six-thirty AM Monday morning I was leaning back in a lounge chair at Gate 14, Love Field Airport, a Styrofoam cup of coffee in my left hand, a three-inch thick bound research study of the barbeque business in my right hand, reading it like it was a bible. I had slipped my Italian loafers off for comfort. The study the company spent $50,000 on had me mesmerized. Not only was I learning that in manufacturing, if you had a ten-percent structural failure on, say, a pot you were making to pressure-cook chicken for barbequing, any piece attached to the main piece of equipment would likely have a ten-percent failure also; four connections, forty-percent failure chances.

They called the flight, I stood up reading, walked into the plane, sat in row one, by the window, and absorbed myself in reading about barbeque. It was fascinating. It was a front-page given—virtually everyone loved barbeque. It seemed to me that on that knowledge alone, the company jumped into the barbeque business. In the air, and deeper into the study, I learned more. I learned that barbeque was expensive to produce. Food cost was so much higher than conventional cooking processes because the smoking process shrunk meat. Every pound of meat shrank to maybe three quarters or half a pound of meat. Then I came upon one more statistic. People loved barbeque, but they only loved it maybe once a month, maybe once every two months. Fact was, to survive, a family restaurant needed a family to want to return weekly at the very minimum. High cost of food, low customer-return frequency—exactly why most famous barbeque shacks were just that, shacks. They needed a low overhead to be able to compete in food service.

I fell asleep and was eventually awakened by a stewardess tapping my shoulder, smiling, cheerfully announcing our landing in LaGuardia. After the bump down, I rubbed my eyes to wake up, looked out at the world I was about to conquer, and felt around with my stocking feet for my loafers. I circled my feet around and around, in wider and wider paths of the plane's carpeting. I leaned down and looked. I had a stewardess look. It was then I realized—that when I stood up in Dallas, I must have left my loafers at Gate 14 … in Love Field, Dallas, Texas. The entire first-class cabin broke into cheers and applause on my behalf. I did what any boy from Delphi Falls would do. I took off my socks, walked barefoot in my three-piece suit through the entire LaGuardia terminal—eyes forward, avoiding the stares and glances and comments—flagged a cab an hour out of my way into the city—to Brooks Brothers on Madison Avenue in Manhattan, to be exact. I walked in the store and up the steps barefoot, up to the shoe department, where a crowd was gathering to stare.

"Sir, may I use your phone?" I asked.

A gentleman in a nattily crisp bow tie, staring down at my bare feet, handed me a phone. I called my offices collect and asked my secretary to call Connecticut and tell them I was delayed a few hours but would be there later today. I hung up the phone, bought some shoes and socks, put them on, and left the shoe department of Brooks Brothers to thunderous applause, honoring the spirit of a tall Texan. I wasn't about to remind them I was a New Yorker.

On Monday there were several gentlemen waiting for me in the lobby back in Dallas. I brought them to my office at the same time for a stand-up meeting.

"Gentlemen, tell me who you are and why you're here; should be a couple of categories. Photographers, step over there by the window," I said.

Three stepped over to the window, leaving two men standing in front of my desk.

"Are you the sign people?" I asked.

"Yes. Both with the same company," they answered.

"Good. You can help me," I said.

I had each of the photographers spread out their portfolios for us to look at. Any picture that wasn't of food was dismissed and not considered. One of the photographer's food work stood head and shoulders above the rest. The sign guys agreed. I pointed to him.

"You stay; the others are excused but thank you all so much for coming by. Leave your business cards with my secretary; we will consider you for other assignments that match your portfolios," I said.

They left cordially; the photographer remaining thanked me for selecting him.

"The menu board at each of our restaurants is our customers' first impression of our product when they walk in. They have a wooden box hung high on the wall with a lot of eight-by-ten film transparencies of our menu items. The lights behind them have faded the transparencies, turning them blue. I want you to go to the Bonanza on Inwood Road, close to Lemmon Ave," I said.

"I know that one," he said.

"Good. That's our best store in town. I will arrange with the area distributor who owns it to prepare anything you need. These large eight-by-ten transparencies of our food items comprise our visual menu—a first impression. They should be colorful and inviting. Set up some kind of portable studio—a set, maybe—and reshoot every food item that appears on the big menu board. There are nine separate items. Can you do that without direction?" I asked.

"Do you want me to copy them, shoot them just like they're staged now?" he asked.

"No. Put your soul into it. You're a talented photographer. Make them tasty, western, and wrangling. Hell, use spurs, saddles, anything you want. I trust your work. Just make certain the products and portions are correct in each. If you're not sure, ask a manager to verify that you're shooting exact menu items as they appear. Can you shoot two-and-a-quarter by two-and-a-quarter?"

"Yes."

"That's what we want, then. Better to enlarge from, right, sign guys?"

"Yes," a sign guy said.

"Mine will fade just like the others?" said the photographer.

"No they won't, because we're going to print them on a clear plastic, just like the Budweiser guys do. Printer's ink won't fade and they will look fresh and colorful always, just like original film transparencies," I said.

"When do you want these by?" asked the photographer.

"When you're personally satisfied with them—so proud you want to show them to me and your kids, and get paid, too, of course," I said.

We shook and he left my office. The sign guy told me he could have the film duplicated onto clear plastic through a printing process in eight-by-tens that would always be bright in color when backlit and never fade or turn blue. I told the sign guy and his partner to plan on arranging it, 350 sets of the twelve pictures about to be taken.

"You ready to talk store signs?" he asked.

"Give me a couple of weeks," I said. "I need Chet Zisk for that. Meantime, what we talk about in this office goes nowhere, we agree?"

"Yes," said the sign guys.

They left my office. I thanked my secretary for having it set up, just as I had asked. I walked to the president's office, stepped in at his wave, and closed the door behind me.

"You play chess?" I asked.

"I don't. Why do you ask?"

"Chess is about tactics and strategy," I said.

"I've heard that," he said.

"Tactics means you make every move in such a manner that you put your opponent on the defensive, so he has to back up or hide or protect. Strategy means you look ahead for a checkmate in every move, even if it's several moves away—you move toward it," I said.

"Somehow I think you're saying something," he said.

"We need to checkmate them in my first move," I said.

"Go on," he said.

"There's not a unit out there I couldn't double or triple their sales, if money were no object—but it would ruin them and kill us. They're not ready. We're too sloppy—we're not ready. Christ, I saw a grill man shooting peanut oil on the steaks in Arkansas with a water pistol because he liked seeing the flames jump in the air— thought he was putting on a circus show for customers," I said.

The president started to make notes.

"No notes," I said.

"Ops needs to hear about that, the water pistol thing," he said.

"Let's fix this on the bigger scale."

He pushed his pad away. "What do you have in mind?"

"We need to hit them between the eyes first—get their attention. Then and only then will they listen. Once we are over that hurdle, and they know we know what the hell we are talking about, we can start to move this dinosaur around and herd them.

But I need to buy some time. Will you help?" I asked.

"Give me your plan," he said. "I'll back you."

"Number one, you ran an expensive steak restaurant in Washington, DC—but other than that, they're pretty much under the impression we don't have a clue about the business we're in. Number two, they have a superstition that Tuesday is the worst restaurant day of the week. Most even said if we knew what we were doing, we would know that. Number three, worst thing we could tell them to do would be to discount. Discounts only create bad customer patterns and bad customer habits. Hell, we don't even know who our customer is. So, number four, I need to do a quick study to make a profile," I said.

"Did you ask Franchise Sales if they got any of that from Tracey Locke?" he asked.

"I did. I asked the director if he knew who our customer was. Know what he said?"

"I'm afraid you're going to tell me," he said.

"He said, and I quote, 'Shoot, baby—it's anybody who likes steak!'"

"What's the game plan?" he asked.

"If you get with Operations and the agency, sign them to secrecy, and come up with a character special—one or all of the Cartwrights from *Bonanza*—for Tuesday only," I started.

"A sale," he said.

"Not a sale, no discounts," I said. "A 'Tuesday' special — even have the word Tuesday in the name of it, but make it profitable, no bad examples from corporate—if you do that, I'll pop it out there with a bang between their eyes. It won't turn the system around, but it will turn the attitudes around. I need newspaper slicks—photocopies of our advertisements the newspapers can copy from, several sizes. That will give me time to take care of the other things, so we can present them at a convention of some kind."

"Will do," he said.

"Top secret," I said. "Oh, and new rule. Line art or pen-sketched illustrations on any food going into newsprint from now on. Photographs of plate food look like crap on newsprint. A steak looks like a cow patty, a potato like a ball of horse manure in an eighty-line screen."

The president grimaced. "I get your point," he said. "I'll be in touch."

For the balance of the week, he went behind closed doors like a kid in a candy store, and I closed my door. He worked in secrecy with Operations and the agency to come up with a special that would adjust the chain's attitude. I closed my door to do what I knew best—to write. I wrote the first ever marketing manual for this steak-house chain, including the ABCs of advertising, everything from how to get a stoplight put in front of your store to slow traffic down to having umbrellas near the front door so you can help people in and out in the rain. This manual would be a first.

The president came back with flying colors. They created the "Little Joe Tuesday Special"—a six-ounce rib eye steak, baked potato, Texas toast, garden salad, and drink, for $1.19 (as opposed to the normal 9 ounce at $1.49) and only available on Tuesdays. It rocked. Tuesday became a serious day for sales chain-wide and my phone started ringing off the hook with believers willing to listen.

I hired college students to stand in front of our restaurants and conduct customer surveys in ten cities for three weeks straight, from eleven in the morning until two and then in the evenings between five and eight, seven days and nights a week. It would bring me the treasures of the makeup of our customer, lunch and dinner, weekday and weeknight and weekend. Peter Sealey's rule number one: seek out, identify, and define your universe.

I kept writing. For several weeks I wrote. I had to train a complicated subject in the easiest of terms. I was writing a marketing manual that would read like a children's book. If someone opened the door, I would yell to close the goddamn door. I had lunches sent in.

Chapter 28

It was about this time the tenth-floor corporate staff was cleared out and moved from the company, out from the hundred-thousand-dollar an office digs that reminded me of the brothel in Newport, Kentucky. The company apparently started looking more seriously at the family steak-house business, settled it in on the third floor and hired a new president, Webster (Webb) Lowe, a mid to late thirty-year-old food expert, fresh from the top rung of the ladder at McDonald's corporate headquarters in Chicago, their now former executive vice president. His next post at McDonald's would have been president. Word came down; he wanted to see me in his office on the tenth floor at five that afternoon. The offices were now vacant and dark, with the exception of him.

"Jerry Antil, my name's Webb Lowe. Come in, have a seat, and tell me about you and what you're up to."

Tall, good-looking, already silver-haired at 35, impeccably dressed in an ivory white suit, probably a Pierre Cardin, a silk tie, and Bali loafers. He walked over to a Silex pot of coffee rigged on a temporary table just outside his door, poured two Styrofoam cups full of black coffee, handed me one, and sat down.

"I think I know you," I said. "Webb Lowe. We've never met, but I know the name."

He grinned. "Well, I'm not wanted in any states that I know of, at least I don't think I am."

"Didn't I speak with you a couple of times when I was producing training movies. You were at McDonald's, headed up operations, training, field activities, I think."

"That I was," he said.

"You turned me on to Gee Gee Foods—your area franchise in Washington, DC," I said.

"Oh yes," he said. "My, that was some time ago—maybe a few years? Good memory."

"Mr. Lowe, there's a lot of work to be done. Does your being here mean we're going to get serious about the food business?" I asked.

"It's Webb for starters, and yes, we are—operative word, we. First we're going to lease out this tenth-floor cathouse to cut expenses, and I'll be moving down on the third with Bonanza Food Franchising. The president on three will concentrate on his specialty—meat. He's the best in the country on meat. From this moment on, you'll report directly to me. If we're going to become the nation's largest purveyor of steaks, second only to the army, we had better start lining up supply. Now bring me up to speed on your end."

"Average unit sales are annualized at $125,000; only a handful do $500,000, but they all could. It's embarrassing," I said.

I told him about the research I had going on, that I was using college students and conducting awareness surveys in ten markets, that I had gone through the line and eaten in fifty of the restaurants within the past two months. I told him about the mess with the photos fading in the restaurants' menu transparency boards and what I was doing about correcting them, permanently, by printing them on plastic. I told him I was writing a complete marketing manual, the first of its kind for Bonanza, and that I wanted to create a term and a sense of purpose—*operational marketing.*

"Operational marketing," Webb said. "Interesting."

"It'll be a first for Bonanza," I said.

"It'd be a first at McDonalds," Webb said.

"You're kidding. It would?" I asked.

"Training is key," said Webb. "Happy to see you're focused on it."

"We have to get ready first; that takes training. Then we can advertise," I said.

"Give a man a fish and you feed him for a day," said Webb. "Teach him how to fish and you feed him for a lifetime."

I told him about the Little Joe Special we had created and why, how it had made Tuesday one of the restaurants' best days of the week, how it had gotten the chain to stand up and begin to listen—but there was a whole bunch more to do.

"I saw that special; it was good thinking. Never discount;

discounting sells your product short, cheapens it. Give free samples first—romance it, celebrate it, offer branded specials—but never discount the value of your product. The 'Little Joe Tuesday Special' is a branded special, not a discount. Good job," he said. "I look forward to working with you, Jerry. My heart is seeing us as a world-class operation, and I promise you we will get that operational performance up to world class and quickly."

"I know marketing and I'm an excellent trainer. I know how and when to advertise effectively—like at AAMCO," I said.

"I'm familiar with your successes there," he said.

"We're not ready to advertise yet. We need an operations sweep, an overhaul," I said.

"Meet with me once a week, just walk in. Call me if you're on the road, keep me filled in on what's going on—and try to remember, no surprises," he said.

"Surprises?" I asked.

"Results, not effort, is my style, Jerry. I give my team a free hand. If you make a promise and can't keep it, tell me when you learn you can't keep it, don't make me wait to find out when it's due. Have a great evening, Jerry. It'll be fun."

Webb stood up, shook my hand, and I left. It was now after eight. From that day forward, Webb would meet the key management players weekly, in an informal setting. A movie projector would start every gathering with a showing of the film *Second Effort*, starring Vince Lombardi and Ron Masak. It was our pump, our juice. I loved it—I always loved playing on winning teams—and I had played on a few, on the court and in business.

Every time I watched this motivational film about winning, I would remember learning from my dad, Big Mike, a winner; from Mr. V, a winner; and from Peter Sealey, a winner.

Now I meet Webb Lowe, a guy who, while in his early thirties and with four children, was flipping hamburgers at a McDonald's in Chicago. He wasn't on a fast track, he wasn't on a management team. He was flipping hamburgers. Webb read *The Power of Positive Thinking*, by Dr. Norman Vincent Peale, twice. He then took it upon himself to edit the McDonald's bible, their operations and procedures manual, and he edited words. Webb changed words like "grease" to "shortening." He changed the word "rag" to "washcloth." He combed every word, every sentence, every page, and raised the bar through edits. By his mid-thirties Webb was reporting directly to Ray Kroc, founder and owner of McDonald's worldwide. Now Bonanza was fortunate to have his drive and inspiration leading our team.

He would walk back and forth in front of the projector lights before the film, and reflect:

"If we're going to turn this chain around, folks we need Triage— from here on out we're about triage. Napoleon invented it. In the heat of battle, if a man was mortally wounded, Napoleon's generals would prop him up against a tree, give him a cigarette, a salute, and leave him. If a man's wounds could be repaired, he would be patched up, given a shot of Cognac, and sent back into battle. We are limited in resources and our only intention is to grow beginning now. From this moment on, folks, it's triage. This is war. We need to turn this system around. If they're bucking the system, leave them. If they're bleeding and want help, save them."

In the months ahead things happened.

I shipped the new printed transparencies of the menu items to the entire chain, at corporate expense. The lobby menu-board in every restaurant now glowed.

I bought a few hundred toy wood-burning kits and sent them along with a box of blank wooden ranch-like signs of various sizes, so the store owners could burn or brand their own small counter signs now—"Desserts," "Salad Bar," and so on—while making them look bunkhouse professional and uniform system-wide until our store build out team got their act together.

The barbeque chain eventually went by the wayside just as the research said it should. Webb invented the salad bar simply by moving the salad portion of the Bonanza cafeteria-style line out to the middle of the restaurant—and speeding the cafeteria line.

I hired Chet Zisk, phased out the agency, and drew for him on a bar napkin what I wanted to present Webb for a new sign. The name BONANZA floating over a smaller Sirloin Pit, with red and yellow glowing over black charcoals.

I paid Peter Sealey and some of his cohorts from McCann ten thousand dollars to come up with a series of newspaper ads for Bonanza. I edited out their spoof ad that read, *"Portnoy's Complaint*—I'm tired of eating bad stuff!"* I tacked that one on my wall.

I went down the hall and peered into Webb's office.

"Webb, got a minute?"

"A minute with you? Are you in town or a mirage?"

"I've got something to show you from Sealey, want to see?"

"Of course."

I opened a folder and held up a sketch.

"Bonanza—steak, at hamburger prices."

"It shows value. I like it," said Webb.

I started to step out of his office.

"Jerry, are you a camper? Ever camped out?"

"I grew up camping," I said.

"In the woods?" he asked. "Or did you pitch a blanket tent in your living room?"

"I camped out practically every night when we moved to Delphi Falls," I said. "We had eighty-four acres, mostly woods. Why?" I asked.

"I have to go to a scout-leader training camp this weekend at Possum Kingdom, it's past Fort Worth, I think. I'm a city boy from Chicago. I'm going to head up a scout troop so I can be with my two boys more. How would you like to have our weekly meeting this week in front of a campfire? A bunch of grown dads trying to learn scouting. I'll need some pointers."

"Count me in—pick me up at the house," I said.

On that, what went on to become a few years of camping out began. The scout leader's first test was to build a campfire. Second was to cook our own dinner. On the first night we looked from our campfire out under a moonless night at twenty more campfires with grown men standing with twigs— some with wire hangers in their hands roasting their hotdogs. Webb asked me to find a hand sized, smooth round rock he could smash the anchovies and egg yolks for our Caesar salad—oh, and that the round canteen on that limb was a Chianti red wine and the oval one sitting on the ice chest was the Chardonnay white. Either of which could have got us drummed out of scouting. Webb and I went on to have our regular meetings in the woods and on beaches with a scout troop we watched grow up. We would be on a fifty-mile canoe trip down the Pedernales River with a bunch of boys and be talking about how we might turn around the St. Louis group of franchisees. We would be building a campfire in an Arkansas wooded park or on the beaches at Port Aransas and catch up on how the Bonanza system was developing and maybe I should look at the stores in California.

I was traveling a hundred thousand miles a year, had been to virtually every city in the US several times, and had walked through the lines as a customer in every one of our restaurants. One was on the Minnesota State Fairgrounds, open four weeks a year and profitable. The first time I walked into his restaurant and someone went back to the kitchen to announce me, he came out wielding a meat cleaver over his head— a disgruntled franchisee from the early days—paid his money and never saw anyone since, he ranted. We soon bonded.

St. Louis was a stubborn market. I needed help. I called Sealey.

"Pete?"

"Hey, big guy, what's up?"

"I want you to come talk with Webb about becoming our executive vice president—take over Operation and Marketing. I can set it up."

"You have to be the first man in history to recruit his own boss," he said.

"Actually I learned it from Jim Heekin; Ogilvy made him president but he took it only if Ogilvy stayed on as creative director," I said.

"Way to go, big guy."

"Would you do it?" I asked.

"Set it up," said Peter.

"Pete, eight to ten impressions on television—tell me how to measure it."

"What's on your mind?"

"All through AAMCO I shot from the hip, told them to own the air, or to blitz. Can you show me quantitative numbers, something I can be precise about, pinpoint?"

"Jerry, two-fifty to three hundred gross rating points in a week to your defined audience should keep the seats filled," he said.

"Thanks, Peter," I said.

I hung up and dialed Don Gaffney, my old boss from Cincinnati. I explained that I had a project for his agency if he was interested, a project in St. Louis.

"It's an experiment, Don, a test. I don't want anyone in St. Louis to know who the client is or what we're doing. Got it? You'll be paid by Bonanza, my office, not the local franchisees."

"Got it," he said.

"I'll call you back," I said.

I dialed Webb's office.

"Jerry, I'm reading your memo. I've always been impressed with Sealey—top-drawer guy. Arrange for him to come in."

"Done."

"I need you in Maitland, Florida. Need your feedback," said Webb.

"Will do Webb, but I need to talk St. Louis for a second."

"I'm all ears," he said.

"Electronic—radio and television—buys are worthless with less than two hundred and fifty gross rating points in a week. Spending a nickel that doesn't reach that minimum goal in a week is a complete waste of money and time," I said. "At our average sales it would take eleven restaurants to pay for it at 3% of sales. We only have six restaurants there."

"Go on," said Webb.

"But electronic is still the pick of the litter—more bang for the buck if done right, if you know my meaning," I said.

"Jerry, kids know Ronald McDonald more months of the year than they know Santa Claus—Ronald had them every Saturday morning. I know your meaning. Where are you taking me? And I feel I'm about to be taken," he quipped.

"On that note, Webb, I want to test a theory. If it works, it will be revolutionary in the chain-restaurant industry; it'll be the first marketing formula of its kind. Can I make the buy on our nickel?"

"Make the buy. Give me a full report. Get Sealey in here, go to Maitland."

"I'll head there today."

"We have a camping thing in Oklahoma weekend from next; will you be here?"

"I will. Oh, I just remembered the other thing. There's a chain called LUMS—a hotdog kind of a place," I said.

"I know it well," said Webb.

"They're dropping like flies. I saw them in St. Louis boarded up. I went into a bank and asked if they would be interested in financing and converting them into Bonanza restaurants. Banker said hell yes."

"I can see it now, Jere ... a mini-Bonanza as a low-cost conversion test, building it out full size if it flies," said Webb.

From the airport I called Don Gaffney and told him to call the general managers of the stations personally and buy television, two hundred and fifty gross rating points:

"I want every spot to be run between Thursday late afternoon and Saturday late afternoon in the same one week," I said.

"You're kidding, right? Bonanza will own television for that twenty-four hours. Are you sure?"

"Every spot between late Thursday afternoon to Saturday late afternoon."

"You got it," said Don.

The Sealey-inspired theory worked like a charm in St.

Louis. Sales jumped twenty-eight percent in a week, turning the restaurants' sales and spirits around and pointing them toward becoming half-million-dollar stores. Webb went to St. Louis, invented the Bonanza conversion from empty LUMS restaurants, and opened another five restaurants in the St. Louis market in one day, bringing the restaurant count there to eleven, the number needed to support an adequate television advertising campaign. The advertising committees for other franchisees and markets followed suit, listening to the magic media buy formula and adopting it.

The test was a major discovery. It was the first time a precise actual formula for effective television buying was tested and written into procedures manuals for independent restaurant operators.

Peter flew in for his interview to be my boss. He totally impressed Webb and the other executives and was offered the number-two slot. Both operations and marketing would be reporting to him. He picked out a house in fashionable University Park and planned his move. Seems Coca-Cola got smart. Pete was with McCann and Coca-Cola had an agreement with McCann that they wouldn't steal executives. When Peter resigned McCann for Bonanza, all bets were off and Coca-Cola made him an offer he couldn't refuse and he didn't. The history of Peter S. Sealey at various milestones, at different helms in Coca-Cola, nationally, internationally, and with their acquisition, at Columbia Pictures, is what marketing textbooks are written from.

In Maitland, Florida I cabbed it from the airport right to a television station before I even checked into my hotel. Without asking the franchisee or anyone else I committed to a heavy television buy. I advanced the money from my national budget. The amount I spent would amount to an entire year's budget for the franchisee if it failed. The advertising flight would run its course in four days. When I got to the restaurant, I warned them be ready for the onslaught of business that would result.

"You may have to add a room to the place," I bragged.

I headed back to the airport and flew to Dallas.

"Webb, I made a television buy in Maitland. It should do the trick."

"How big a buy?"

"I advanced them what amounts to be their annual budget at their
sales volume."

"What's the message? The audience?"

"What do you mean?"

"Jere, you're the grand master who taught us. Identify your market etc…"

"You know, Webb, the Bonanza customer."

"Which is typically a family of four, between twenty-five and forty-nine, middle income, right?" Webb asked.

"Pretty much," I said.

"Jere, I have friends in Maitland…not a one of them is under sixty."

"What are you saying, Webb?"

"It's not like you not to do a quick look around, ask a few questions."

"Fuck," I said.

"If it doesn't work, Jere, there's no way we can expect them to pay for our mistake."

"What do I do" Any ideas?"

"I'd do some praying and I'd get back on a plane to Maitland," Webb said.

My spots ran— sales didn't go up a plug nickel. I called Webb and told him the bad news that I chewed up a big amount of cash and fell flat on my face.

"I fucked up, Webb. Big time."

"You're in a hole, Jere. Stop digging and call me when it's fixed."

"They bought and were counting on my hype bullshit. What do I tell them?"

"Your budget is getting thin, Jere. I suggest you follow your own rules and do some research."

"Stay here?

"I'd pitch a tent."

I stayed.

"Jere, a miscalculation like this on a bigger scale, like a regional buy could do us in financially," said Webb.

I let my ego make decisions when my good sense and training should have led me.

For two weeks I stood with four college students in front of the Bonanza interviewing everyone coming in and leaving the restaurant. I drove into neighborhoods, knocked on doors and asked people their feelings or knowledge of the Bonanza steakhouse. Worked out the restaurant was built next to a large, several-acre pond, and the rumor amongst many of the retirees was that there were alligators in the pond and no fence to keep them in. It was the thought of alligators attacking them that kept retirees who made up most of the town from coming to the Bonanza. I called Webb.

"I'm such an asshole," I said. I told him about the alligators and the need for a chain link fence.

"Build one and try again," said Webb.

"For real?" I asked. "Build a fence?"

"Check with the city, check with whoever owns the lake or pond and get a fence up, have a ribbon cutting, try to make the news and this time buy newspaper and get word to their breakfast tables. They won't get attacked by gators at Bonanza."

A new chain-link fence built the length of the property, was properly advertised, and business climbed to record levels and held.

The Bonanza nationwide system of franchised restaurants was now ready. Thanks to Maitland, I was learning how not to lead marketing with my chin. The food operations were up to snuff. It was time for the big bang, the roll out. If I could motivate every franchisee to advertise with a disciplined per cent of sales, there would be no looking over our shoulder again. I told Webb my idea for motivating the entire chain to step up their advertising and asked him for thirty thousand dollars to seed it.

"Jere, if we blow this one, it could bust us," he said. "Sell me."

My chess tactic of market by market turnaround seemed to be working—now my strategy. I had to motivate the entire chain to advertise regularly. Their contracts required them to spend three percent of sales on advertising. I bought an ad in LIFE magazine—for thirty thousand dollars—a full-page ad to run ninety days out. I asked the franchisees to let the customers know Bonanza was "As advertised in *LIFE*." In 1972, being able to use "As Advertised in LIFE" in all our advertising was a nationally credible and trusted endorsement. We could begin to look 'national' like McDonalds.

Virtually every restaurant in the chain jumped on board and advertised heavily the three months before the actual placement of the LIFE magazine ad with the slogan— *Great Steak at Hamburger Prices, as advertised in LIFE.*

Two months later Webb walked me to a sales graph chart he kept on the back door of his office.

"I have to get a new chart," said Webb.

He held one finger at the top of the chart.

"Here's where the chain sales were two months ago."

He held his hand about six inches over the top of the chart pointing a finger to the space off the charts.

"We're up here as of Monday," he said.

There's no stopping us now.

Chapter 29

I wasn't worn out; I wasn't tired; I was bored. The Bonanza steak-house chain was turned around and growing stronger every day, well on its way to $300 million in sales—a quarter billion—not bad—up from the $17 million it was when I arrived and Webb joined the company. I now had nearly a million miles under my belt in a few years, in the US; I had eaten in the finest restaurants in the country, seen the sights in nearly every city in America, had job offers stacked up and created a lifetime friendship, like a closest brother, with my friend and scouting partner, Webb Lowe. He understood when and why I resigned. Said my desk would always be there for me. We talked for an hour. He had the system on a course to an inevitable $30 million a month in sales and six hundred units with average sales volumes pushing half a million each – heading toward the billion a year mark in sales. That was a lot of $1.29 steaks.

My world, that is my first love, was the ground war, the fight, the skirmish, the battle, the tie game with four seconds to go, the come from behind. I loved the memory of being chased out of one of the first restaurants I went to visit in the early days and being chased by a franchisee wielding a meat cleaver, pissed off that he'd never heard from corporate. I was a Patton, a ground-war general. Bonanza had arrived; now they needed an Eisenhower. We brought in a talented guy, Mike Roth—I helped bring him in—who would see to it the restaurant system would grow. Webb's photo image was on the front cover of every important food, restaurant, or financial magazine or periodical there was. Bonanza had become the eighteenth largest food server in the nation. It was time for me to leave. Webb was a star, a food legend, and I, a barefoot boy from Delphi Falls, New York, was listed in *Marquis Who's Who of the South and Southwest*, thanks in large part to my dad, Big Mike, Mr. V, and none other than Peter S. Sealey.

I drove up to Lake Texoma, took my thirty-foot Owens cruiser out to the middle, and dropped anchor, just to fish and think. I sat in the galley, pulled my typewriter to me and typed a letter to my mom and dad telling them I had left Bonanza and was thinking about what's next—not sure what next was going to be. I stayed in the middle of the lake three days contemplating my next move. I was considering a consulting career. Jerry Antil & Associates, marketing consultants. When I headed in and pulled into the slip, I plugged my telephone into the connection I had for it at the slip.

Early the next morning my boat telephone rang.

"Hello?"

"Well hello, Jerry me boy," said Dad.

"Hey, Dad, what's going on? How's Mom?"

"Your mother is busier than she was when we had eight kids around the house. Now she has hundreds."

"Hundreds?" I asked.

"At seventy-one, your mother heads up child counseling for the Catholic Diocese in Fort Wayne. Isn't she something?"

"That sounds great," I said. "How you doing, Dad?" I asked.

"Jerry me boy, what do you say about my coming down for your birthday in a couple of months and taking care of you a spell, cook some spaghetti, we'll catch some fish—you know, catch up? How about it?"

"Sounds perfect, Dad. Let me have a few months to get my act together and a plan going forward. I'll fly you in and we'll play. How does that sound?" I asked.

"I look forward to it, son. We'll empty that big lake down there. What's that fish, like a sunfish, do you remember, son?" he asked.

"Bluegill," I said.

"That's it. We'll catch a ton. Call me, son."

"I will, Dad."

Shortly after that call, my dad took a train trip to my sister Dorothy and her husband, Norman's place in Washington, DC, for a week. Dorothy was a cofounder and now working for AFSCME and Norman was still with the government. The story was that while Dad was in DC, he suffered stomach cramps and was taken to Bethesda Hospital, where they gave him an enema and sent him home. He boarded a train back to Fort Wayne. Mom was at a teacher's meeting when he arrived. When Mom came home, she found a business card with a note on its back from Dad.

"Mom, I went to the hospital," signed, Mike.

He died that night of peritonitis—a ruptured scar in his stomach lining.

I don't remember who called to tell me he had died. I flew to Fort Wayne and sat outside the funeral home. I wouldn't go in and see my dad laid out. When the casket was closed I helped carry it to the church. Before they opened it for viewing, I stepped out of the church and waited for it to be closed and the services to begin.

I didn't cry. My mind was a blank. I only thought of how light he felt when I lifted his casket. I remembered our drives when I was a kid. I remembered being fitted for shirts and suits while he told stories that kept everyone in stitches. I remembered his handing me a hundred dollars so I could buy my first car for fifty. I remembered the long stems in the lobby. I remembered his call when I was on my boat making my plans, his wanting to come down and take care of me.

Mom was taking the body to Cortland, New York, for burial at St. Mary's Cathedral beside my Aunt Kate, my mother's mom.

I touched the casket, said goodbye to my dad, Big Mike and flew back to Dallas and mailed engraved invitations to company presidents and owners in North Texas telling of my consulting availability.

Eventually I was distracted from losing my dad when my phone started to ring. A small Dallas advertising agency, Rosenberg and Honeycutt, was making a pitch for a new restaurant chain, Red Lobster Inns, and asked how much I would charge just to look at what they were going to present and comment on it. I got a call from the president of a company in Fort Worth, Scott Mooring. He and his partner, Floppy Blackman, were starting a franchise called Steamatic Carpet Cleaning and asked if I would come over and chat with them about marketing.

I met with Rosenberg and Honeycutt for five thousand dollars. That was my fee to sit through their entire creative presentation.

"Why do you have creative?" I asked, totally deflating their creative team.

"We're an advertising agency, Jerry. It's what we do," said the creative director. He was being sarcastic.

"Who's your profile, age, when do they eat out, how often, what are their habits? First things first, can't advertise a message if you can't identify and define your target," I said.

"This damn good creative," said a voice in the back. "I think he's wrong."

"What's your agency's objective with this client?" I asked.

"To raise sales," the voice said emphatically.

"Wrong!" I snorted. "Anyone else want to try?"

"Tell us," said Allen Rosenberg. "Everyone, listen up!"

I stood up and turned to the group.

"Marketing has a single objective. To create and maintain a high level of unaided top-of-mind awareness for your name and concept. You have to raise the bar," I said.

"We're saying the same thing," said the voice. "We're saying create awareness by advertising."

"Lone Star Donuts advertises; ever heard of them?" I asked.

"Of course I have, we all have. You're making my point," the voice said.

"No value whatsoever," I said. "I mentioned Lone Star Donuts and you said you heard of them. That's 'aided' awareness. I gave you the name. 'Aided' awareness does not get us there," I said. "If that's all you can deliver, absolutely no value, in my book, at least not enough to justify paying you." Then I continued:

"Name a tissue!"

Everyone said, "Kleenex."

"What are most kitchen countertops made of?"

"Formica," they all said.

"Name a cheese."

"Kraft," they said.

"You named products that were unaided and top of your mind.

Allen applauded. "What do you suggest?" he asked.

"Submit a written marketing plan, on one page. Nothing else," I said. "Let all the other agencies make fools of themselves presenting creative."

"How much to write the plan for us?" asked Allen.

"You owe me five thousand for being here. I'll make a deal. I'll forget the five and write it for seven thousand, five hundred, paid tonight. Or I'll do it on spec, you pay me only if your agency gets the account, but it's fifteen thousand then."

"A marketing man puts his money where his mouth is," Allen said. "I love it."

"You don't know my friend Sealey. He'd bet his plane," I quipped.

"Who?" asked Allen.

"Never mind. What's your poison?" I asked.

"We'll go the fifteen," he said.

"Done." We shook.

The next day I handed him a one-page marketing plan. Objective, strategy, execution, implementation, and cost—I could do it in my sleep. They got the account, which grew to $29 million in annual billings. I got paid my $15,000.

The City of Ogdensburg Chamber of Commerce invited me to come up to give me an *adopted son* award and asked me to talk about my fondness for their town, and about my adventures that had happened with the city's beautification program six years earlier. They just plumb wanted to see me again, have a lunch. My dad would have done it; he would have gone. I went.

Steamatic Carpet Cleaning, a franchise out of Fort Worth, paid me ten thousand in advance to visit them for ten Saturday mornings a couple hours each Saturday.

I taught them everything I knew—it could fit on one page.

Chapter 30

The phone rang at about eight in the evening. It was Mr. V—Mr. VonderHaar, much to my happy surprise.

"Mr. V, how are you, my friend? My God, how long has it been? I've been so bad about keeping in touch," I said.

"It's been a while, Jerry. You started working in my office dropping and picking up paperclips fourteen years ago. Time certainly flies. Your friends at Bonanza gave me your phone number."

"It's great hearing from you Mr. V, how are you?"

"I'm coming to Dallas and I wanted to see if you and I could visit, maybe have dinner while I'm there," he said.

"You bet we can. I so look forward to seeing you and catching up. Did you hear my dad died, Mr. V?"

"Oh, Jerry, I hadn't. He was such a good man—Big Mike. It was a pleasure knowing him. I was honored. When did he pass, Jerry?"

"In March."

"Such a talented man and great father. I'm so sorry. Will late in September be convenient with your schedule? I'll have to look at my calendar, but I'm thinking the last week in September will be best for me. I have a staff presentation the first week in October and will have to be back that Monday," he said.

"That will be perfect," I said. "It's my treat, at the Pyramid Room. Best restaurant in town. You will love this place. It's in the Fairmont hotel, the best of the best—my treat. Let me know when you're coming," I said.

"Mrs. Burke will be in touch," he said.

"Is Mrs. Burke still with you?" I asked.

"I don't know what I would do without her. She's still here and runs the show. She remembers you fondly."

That night I drove home, pulled into my driveway, opened my car door, lifted my left leg out, and set it on the ground. I glanced over at the radio dials on the dashboard and thought of my dad in this same position, adjusting the radio dials while he drove from town to town when I was a kid—I remembered his watching me patiently while I walked out by a fence somewhere to pet a donkey we saw, or a buffalo someone owned. We would drive all over central New York, visiting grocers, finding adventures. I began to weep. Tears streamed down my cheeks as I sobbed, thinking of my dad. I could smell him in the car. I touched my head down on the steering wheel, crying and remembering. I remembered us fishing, driving. I remembered his spaghetti dinners, lifting me when I was young so I could touch the ceiling like he could. I remembered his lining up chairs around the dining-room table so I could walk on top of them around the room and know what it was going to be like when I was as tall as he was.

I went into the house and wrote a letter to my mom, just to say hello. Letters meant so much to my mom.

Chapter 31

I met Mr. V in the lobby of the Fairmont. He was staying at the hotel. We shook hands, stared and caught up with each other instantly, remembering the great old times we'd had together back now nearly fifteen years — practically half my life ago. We walked into the Pyramid Room—reportedly one of the finest restaurants in America, certainly one of the most expensive. The room sat maybe fifty people and had beige suede walls that went up forty or more feet. A wine rack climbed a wall, accessible by a stainless-steel ladder, and the wine steward, Sommelier Sylvano, would climb to the top and ring a bell. Everyone was amused, knowing the higher Sylvano climbed, the loftier the wine and the pricier the bottles.

Maître d' Alberto Lombardi welcomed me by name, shook Mr. V's hand, introducing himself, welcoming him to Dallas and to the Pyramid Room. He led us past a corner table where singer/actress Shirley Jones and her husband, Jack Cassidy, were having a quiet dinner. They were a couple of hours before headlining— starring in the Venetian Room in the same hotel. Stanley Marcus, the genius of the world-famous Neiman Marcus, was with a guest at a table in the back. Comedian Milton Berle and his cigar and family were at a round corner table.

"Sylvano, please meet one of my dearest friends, my mentor, like a father to me, Mr. Edward P. VonderHaar, just in from Cincinnati for the evening," I said.

"It is most certainly my pleasure, Mr. VonderHaar. It's always a pleasure to meet anyone close to our dear friend, Mr. Antil. May I offer you gentlemen a fine wine?"

"Sylvano, this is a special evening, how about uncorking two bottles of Chateau Laffite Rothschild—sixty-six—and letting them breathe?"

"Most excellent choice; I will go ring the bell, gentlemen. If I don't return, it will only mean I have fallen from excitement, with such a fine wine," he said.

"My, how you've grown, young man," Mr. V said. "When

did you pick up such a wonderful sense of fine wines?"

"One of my best friends, Greg Shaban—he's a big deal with Revlon—I'm godfather to his son, Christopher. He taught me. I was always impressed with his ease ordering in expensive restaurants. One time I asked him to teach me about wines, as he was always entertaining bigwigs, he certainly knew the ropes. He told me to get a pen and write down Chateau Laffite Rothschild, sixty-six, and he said that was all I would need to know. I ordered two bottles because I plan to keep you talking until at least eleven, when they close," I said.

"Perfect," said Mr. V.

Sylvano poured the wine and we raised our glasses, first in toast to my dad Big Mike, whose birthday would be coming up next week, October third, and then to our friendship since 1958—a genuine, sincere friendship that had begun fourteen years earlier, when a hapless young boy dropped a box of paperclips and ranted on about the girlfriend he was about to lose to the Lord.

"Jerry, have you heard anything from your girlfriend, the girl in the convent?"

"I haven't, Mr. V. Do you remember the limo ride to fishing in the Ohio River and the charter private plane ride to Columbus and the dozens of roses?" I asked.

"I tell the story often—such a love story, it was," he said.

"Do you remember the time you hadn't heard from me and Mrs. Burke found out I was sick in bed and you put bags of groceries in front of my rooming-house door? I went to pay you back and you told me to pass it on. Do you remember?"

"I do," he smiled. "You were a sick, young man."

"Well, I have friends here, Steven Holley and his wife; when I met them, when I first got to Dallas, they were both in college and she was working and about to have a baby. One day after work I went over to their apartment to say hello. It was unlocked and they weren't there. The cupboards and refrigerator were bare. I was going to raid the kitchen and make a sandwich. I ran to the store and returned and left them seven, eight bags of groceries and told them to 'pass it on, in the name of Mr. Edward

P. VonderHaar.' Steven told me he's done it several times since—in your name."

"How wonderful—thank you. It's a nice feeling knowing it's staying alive and well, a gesture from the heart being passed down."

We talked late into the evening, ate escargot and fine entrees, sipped the finest of wine, which tasted like a mellow cotton in our mouths, and each had a dessert soufflé. We enjoyed cigars Sylvano carefully dipped in brandy and lighted over a candle for us to enjoy with more reminiscences and happy stories of our travels and adventures and our friendship.

"Mr. V, how's your garage looking? I remember painting the four large cement squares on the floor like a big checkerboard—two red and two a buff. You still have that great house with the turret?"

"I do, and the garage floor looks just as it did when you gave it those three coats of red and the buff-yellow paint. Everyone still comments on my stylish, multicolored floor. I let them know you were the artist."

"I remember painting at your place kept me eating for a month or two. I sure remember that—painting your fence, too," I said.

Mr. V slowly looked around the room, taking it in. Mr. V seldom got treated. As the number-one public relations man in the country, he was always the host, the behind-the-scenes organizer. His eyes smiled at the rich suede walls, the unique wine cellar, at one of the most famous retailers in the world, Stanley Marcus, walking by and nodding hello.

"Mr. V, why didn't you ever get married?" I asked.

"I was in love once," he said. "We were close to marriage in my late twenties. An army physical found a heart ailment—not a good one—and I elected not to burden a wife and children in my absence if something were to happen to me."

"You've been a wonderful inspiration to everyone—the students, the university, and the public relations industry," I assured him. "You have a family of thousands who look up to you, who you have inspired. A lot of people think of you as an important part of their lives."

"I've had great satisfaction watching many fine young men develop, grow, and enter the world from Xavier."

As the evening wore on, we stood, walked into the lobby, shook hands, and parted—he toward the Fairmont elevators, I to the doorman for my car and my trip home.

It was the following week, on what would have been Big Mike's birthday, October third, when I called Mr. V to tell him what a fabulous time I'd had seeing him and reconnecting and catching up.

"Mr. VonderHaar's office, Mrs. Burke speaking."

"Hi, Mrs. Burke, this is Jerry Antil, how are you? Mr. V and I had the greatest dinner in Dallas last week and talked together late into the night. I just wanted to call him to tell him thanks, and that next time I'll let him treat in Cincinnati—maybe at the Gourmet Room. I'll come up, for sure," I said.

"Oh Jerry, Mr. VonderHaar died. I'm sorry."

"What?"

"He stepped off a podium yesterday after giving a report. He just dropped over dead. I'm so sorry. I was just about to call you."

"Oh, no," I said. "He was my best friend. Oh, no."

"Jerry, you need to know. Mr. V knew he wasn't well. He had a list of four people he wanted to see and say goodbye to. You were one of them. Jerry, he always considered you one of his best friends, like a son. He would tell stories about you often."

Try as I might, this writer has never been able to find the words to express this one moment of this one day in a year in my life—the day I learned of the loss of my friend Mr. V on what would have been my Big Mike's birthday. Until this memoir, I still couldn't.

(30)